WHAT READERS ARE SAYING
ABOUT *VISIONS OF GLORY*

"If you want greater light and knowledge then read this book. If you want to feel more hope for the future of this world, read this book. I can't recommend this book enough to all who want to draw closer to Jesus Christ."

"What an eye opener. . . . I found a better view of myself and my place in this world. . . . What a wonderful book. Loved it!"

"I could not stop reading, and when I did, I couldn't stop thinking about it."

"This book has profoundly impacted my life. I came away with a deep impression that I need to trust God completely and yield my heart to Him completely. . . . I am truly grateful that I found this book. I have purchased additional copies and given them to friends. They too have been profoundly impacted by its message."

"I could not put this down. One of the most interesting books I have ever read. John Pontius opened my mind to what is possible."

"Whenever I'd lend the book out, the recipient wanted to keep it, so I had to keep ordering more as gifts. . . . It's a "page turner"—one that takes multiple readings to assimilate."

"This book is an important contribution to the literature of near-death experiences. . . . The visionary scenario that plays out is instructive and compelling. . . . This book will motivate you to cultivate your spiritual gifts."

"Totally changed my perspective on what is important in life and where my priorities need to be! I loved it!"

"This is a book all human beings MUST read. . . . It has changed my life for good, and I will never look back."

"Dear Reader, if you truly want to get a bigger picture of what this life is about and how each decision you make ripples out into eternity, this is the book for you. If you have ever wondered . . . what events surrounding the last days before the Second Coming of Jesus Christ might look like, this a fascinating book for you to ponder. I came away with sharpened sensitivity to spiritual matters and hope. A great deal of hope!"

"Just plain awesome. . . . Having read his experiences has made me a better, more faithful man."

"This book forever changed my life. . . . Loved this book."

"I had already read this book on my Nook. . . . I wanted a hard copy so I could re-read it and underline and mark it up and be able to flip back and forth easily. . . . This is a book that will stay with you for a long, long time after you read it."

"I literally could not put it down once I began reading it! . . . This is an IMPORTANT book."

"I have read this book twice and have given away more than 20 copies of it so far. It is the most exciting book I have ever read. . . . Detail, love, and hope abound in this great book! . . . I really can't recommend it highly enough! In so many ways it feels as though it was written for me. It has given me an energy and renewed passion for things to come."

"I would like all of my children to read this book. . . . This has truly opened my eyes. I will read this book many times."

"This book gave me hope and desire to do better, be better, and love more."

"The experiences in this book are amazing. . . . Men and women of all faiths will draw insight and comfort from the remarkable events in this book."

"I've read . . . everything that's been written about near-death experiences. For me, *Visions of Glory* is the glorious capstone. . . . My mind is still reeling and my soul is still vibrating from the experience."

VISIONS *of* GLORY

AS TOLD TO JOHN PONTIUS

CFI
AN IMPRINT OF CEDAR FORT, INC.
SPRINGVILLE, UTAH

ISBN 13: 978-1-4621-1118-3

Published by CFI, an imprint of Cedar Fort, Inc., 2373 W. 700 S., Springville, UT 84663
Distributed by Cedar Fort, Inc., www.cedarfort.com

LIBRARY OF CONGRESS CATALOGING-IN-PUBLICATION DATA

Pontius, John M., author.
 Visions of glory : one man's astonishing account of the last days / John M. Pontius.
   pages cm
 Includes bibliographical references and index.
 Summary: An account of a man named Spencer's out-of-body experiences and visions of the last days.
 ISBN 978-1-4621-1118-3 (alk. paper)
 1. Astral projection--Case studies. 2. Visions--Case studies. 3. Eschatology. 4. Church of Jesus Christ of Latter-day Saints--Doctrines. 5. Mormon Church--Doctrines. I. Title.

 BX8643.E83P66 2012
 236'.2--dc23

                      2012033241

Cover design by Rebecca J. Greenwood
Cover design © 2012 Lyle Mortimer
Edited and typeset by Emily S. Chambers

Printed in the United States of America

10 9 8

To Jesus Christ, for every good thing.

To Terri, my best friend and fellow pilgrim,
who taught me the most important thing I know.

To Spencer, for a lifetime of holding to the rod.

Also by John M. Pontius

Following the Light of Christ into His Presence

Millennial Quest Series:
Spirit of Fire (Formerly *Angels in Coveralls*)
Angels Among Us
Angles Forged in Fire
Angels and a Flaming Sword, Part 1
Angels and a Flaming Sword Part 2

We Three Kings
The Triumph of Zion

Additional books, essays, and
fireside soundtracks are available at:
www.followingthelight.org
and on the UnBlog
http://UnBlogmysoul.wordpress.com

Contents

FOREWORD

V*isions of Glory: One Man's Astonishing Account of the Last Days* is an account of Spencer's three near-death experiences and years of subsequent visions of his yet-future journey through the latter days. All of them are related here as Spencer told them to me in over fifty hours of interviews. Every vision and experience recorded herein is Spencer's, but most of the language is a result of my effort to put into words what Spencer was describing for me in narrative form. I tried to preserve his choice of words and manner of speaking throughout.

Spencer has never spoken most of these visions out loud and has kept them to himself and treasured them up in his heart, which meant he had to dig deeply to find words to describe things which have no analog in common mortal experience.

I have never met anyone like Spencer. He is loving and kind, and his face literally glows with the Spirit as he describes his experiences. He tears up when he uses the name of the Savior, and he is deeply interested in everything spiritual. His demeanor is that of a true Saint, one whose life is fully dedicated to Christ. I did not find any conceit or arrogance in him—just the opposite; he seemed to be unaware of how precious he is, how profoundly revealing his visions are, and how far he has seen beyond the limits of human sight.

Spencer is a lifelong member of the Church of Jesus Christ of Latter-day Saints. He presently serves as an ordinance worker in the temple and has served in bishoprics, high councils, stake positions, and many other callings. He presently serves on a general advisory board for the Church and holds three advanced degrees.

Spencer has died four times, including being stillborn. Spencer once told me, "I don't know why the Lord has blessed me with these visions, it just seems as if the angels that brought me back to life each time left the door into heaven ajar, and the angels have continued to pass through and into my life ever since."

Three of Spencer's visions were classic near-death experiences. The first one took him back to his premortal past. The next took him to the present and near future. The third showed him what would happen in the Millennium and distant future. Many more have been visions that occurred during waking hours, late at night, and during sleep. There is no real pattern in the timing of his experiences, but there is a rich pattern in the content. Each succeeding vision built upon the previous one, continuing the unfolding of his life's story as well as providing the necessary insight and education required to prepare him to meet the challenges he would face, long in advance of his living it.

Much of the information in his visions has been difficult for him to interpret until recently, which was another reason for his saying very little about his experiences over the years.

Because of the personal nature of each of these visions, and the fact that they dealt with his own journey, this has limited his views of things to come to only those places and events in which he would participate. He did not see what will happen in Europe, South America, or Asia. He does not know the outcome of wars or the result of world events. He did not see all of the great destructions of land and sea prophesied by the book of Revelation because they apparently did not impact Spencer's future.

But he did see sweeping visions about the future of North America and the overwhelming events and devastations that would cleanse and reshape this country and parts of Canada. These include foreign invasion, a devastating plague, floods, earthquakes, continental fracture, the dividing of America by a new canyon, the filling of the Gulf of Mexico by a new landmass, changes in weather and the constellations of heaven, the return of the ten tribes, the miraculous return of the Saints to build the New Jerusalem and temple, the gathering of the elect, the miracles of the Millennium, the mission and mighty powers of the 144,000, and the final celestialization of the earth at the end of the Millennium. He saw these things as well as many other astonishing events long prophesied in scripture but never described in such vivid detail as this.

Spencer began to have visions in his early twenties and has consistently been admonished by the Holy Spirit to keep most of these experiences sacred and even secret. The few times he tried to relate his visions to others, it cost him friends and has brought ridicule and rejection in some cases.

Spencer has asked that I not use his real name for several reasons. First, he sustains the living prophet and his preeminent calling in revealing the word of God to the Church. These visions were given to Spencer to prepare him personally for what lay ahead in his own life.

He has never considered that these visions of the future were for or about the latter-day Church. He is therefore reluctant to release these visions in such a way that they may appear to be an attempt to influence the Church in any way. This is simply not the case. Withholding his identity is an effective way of keeping these issues in their proper order.

The second reason Spencer has asked that I not use his name is that he does not want to become the focal point of people's questions or hope for answers. He doesn't want to become anyone's guru. He doesn't want to give firesides or do public speaking about his experiences. As a matter of fact, he has obediently kept his experiences to himself for most of forty years in part to avoid this very possible outcome of letting these visions be published.

He has tried in this book to speak everything the Holy Spirit would give him words to describe. Visions and events that were only personal or too sacred to share have been withheld.

I have asked him thousands of questions to search out details on those events he has shared. By the time this book is in print, Spencer will have emptied his treasure box of visionary experiences he is able to share at this time, and he does not wish to be asked for further information he does not have or is not able to share.

Another reason for his reticence is that Spencer is a professional counselor of children and holds all the degrees necessary to work in this field. He rightly considers his work with troubled children to be his life's calling, and he does not want any form of recognition or curiosity to disrupt this most important work.

I met Spencer through a series of improbable circumstances—so much so that the possibility of it being coincidental is inconceivable.

A dear friend of Spencer's, who knew small snippets of his experiences, moved into a ward with my sweet and very spiritual daughter, and over time they became close friends. In talking of the spiritual influences in their lives, my daughter spoke of me, and this friend of Spencer's spoke of him. They decided, "We should introduce John to Spencer!"

After a period of time my daughter sent me a text with Spencer's name and a suggestion that I call him. She thought we would "Hit it off," as she put it. I'm usually not responsive to suggestions like that because they make for awkward moments of struggling to find common ground from which to "hit it off."

Spencer's friend did the same with him, and he was reluctant to call me for the same reasons.

One afternoon I was walking through the house, and the Spirit whispered, "Call Spencer—now." I knew it was the Holy Spirit, so I went to my study and pulled out my phone not knowing what to expect, but I knew I needed to call right then.

Spencer answered, and I introduced myself. Spencer replied in a most joyful tone, "Yes, I have been most anxious to meet with you! When would be your earliest convenience?" His words struck me as puzzling because I didn't know until later that he also had my contact information. I thought I was cold-calling him. As an additional note of interest, during the many months of interviews and writing, I have tried to call Spencer dozens of times, and have never gotten through. The only time he has actually answered the phone was that first call. In all other cases, I left a message, and he returned my call.

We met the following week, and without resorting to hyperbole, it was the most spiritual two hours of my life. He began to tell me a few of his experiences, and I was thunderstruck. The reason was simply this: I have studied, sought, prayed, and obtained glimpses of my own journey through the latter days, but I had never heard another living person speak of these exact things. In those first few minutes he spoke of those very things in matter-of-fact terms. I could hardly contain my curiosity and my anxiousness to hear more—where I had "learned" of these things, he had "seen" them, and I was intrigued to hear everything he had seen because he appeared to be describing parts of my own journey I had never told anyone except my wife.

I understood most everything he was speaking about. After a while, I felt the Spirit strongly say that he was describing things that he had seen but not fully understood. I asked finally, "Do you know what these things mean?"

He looked innocent as he replied, "No, not really. Not all of it."

I explained what little I understood of the vision under consideration, and he wept joyously, confessing without any evident pride or self-consciousness that he had been searching most of his life for the meaning to the vision that I had just suggested to him. We spoke for the remainder of our first couple hours together of these things. My understanding and his visions fit hand-in-glove, giving both of us a far broader understanding. We were both filled with the Holy Ghost in great degree, even while we received it with wonder and astonishment. As I said earlier, it was the most spiritual two hours of my life—it was also the most revealing.

As our time drew to a close, he simply stated, "I still don't know how to get from where I am today, to what I now understand the meaning of my vision to be."

The Holy Spirit had prompted me just as I walked out of my house to pick up a copy of one of my books, *The Triumph of Zion*. I pulled it from my briefcase and handed it to him, saying, "I felt prompted to bring this book for you. It may be that you will find some of your answers in here."

For Spencer, this initial meeting was like tipping over the first domino. My role of providing insight diminished with time, as the Holy Spirit quickly filled in the blanks his visions had failed to fully reveal at that time of his youth, and they were now becoming clearer to him.

We embraced and then made plans to meet again next week.

Sometime during our second meeting, I had the strongest urge to take notes, but he had said several times that he was telling me things he had never told anyone else. I was hearing things so vast and significant that I didn't dare forget any of it. Spencer's descriptions were detailed about everything. When he "saw" visions, he wasn't looking at them as one might a motion picture; he was in them—a player in the vision with all of his senses engaged. He touched and smelled things, felt the triumph and tragedy of those around him, and experienced the danger and fear exactly as if he were there. He remembered it all in deep detail because he experienced it as if in his own flesh.

Finally, I was overcome with the potential tragedy of all this knowledge being in one person's head alone and then ultimately lost. It was like listening to John the Beloved or Moses describe events the world has pondered for all time, and I was hearing in wonderful detail the dates and times, the places, even the city and street names where things would happen. His words transported me to places I could see in my soul as he described them. I yearned and ached and inwardly felt tragic that these things were never going to be written down to bless others as they were even then blessing me.

As we stood to leave that second time, I said something like, "Spencer, it can't be a coincidence that we met. The sequence of events that brought us together included me moving from Alaska, your friend and my daughter both moving to the same ward, and a thousand other aligning events."

"I know it was not a coincidence," he said softly. "It was a miracle."

"I must say then that the fact that I am an LDS author can't be coincidental either. I want to propose that you ask Father if I might record these visions you are telling me. At least they should be written down and not lost forever, even if you only kept them and handed them down through your family. But I'm hoping Heavenly Father will eventually let us publish them for the benefit of the whole world. These things just seem too precious to be hidden in one person's memories. I think the whole Christian world would rejoice to know these things."

Spencer considered this with a questioning expression. He had told me that he had repeatedly been told to tell no one of these sacred things until the Lord told him it was time. He finally smiled and said, "I will ask Father most earnestly, and I will be very interested in His response."

I left without knowing what to think, wondering if I had over-stepped some sacred line but still believing what I had said to be true, that none of this should be lost. I was also touched by his faith-filled response.

My Apostolic Friend

We met in his office a week later, and he told me this story: "All of these years I have felt painfully alone because of not being able to speak of the things I have seen in vision. They have become a big part of me, who I am, and what I am doing in my life, and I am constrained to silence.

"Until speaking to you I didn't even realize how they could come to full accomplishment in my life—especially knowing my personal circumstances, poor health, and weaknesses. I have always known they were true, but only until recently did I even suspect how they could come to pass. I have been persecuted and rejected the few times I opened up even a little. I have been very alone in this for a long time. It has been one of the hardest parts of this journey.

"One of my assignments for the Church for many years has taken me to the Church Office Building in Salt Lake City once a month. I meet with various general authorities and had come to know and love them personally. Over the years I had become good friends with one of the members of the Quorum of the Twelve. We became personal friends, and we had, as he was inclined to say, 'broken bread' together and spent wonderful times visiting on numerous occasions.

"One evening while alone with him, I was prompted to tell him one of my visions. He listened with great interest and then concluded by telling me it was from God and that I should treasure it up in my heart, write it down, and not speak of it until the Lord told me to. He also counseled me to not try to interpret the meaning of it. He said, 'When the Lord wants you to understand it, He will send someone or give you the meaning, but until then, it is God's will that you keep these things to yourself and don't try to interpret them without further revelation.'

"My apostle friend became a staying power and source of much comfort for me. He became a source of security in this veil of tears and my source of peace that what I was seeing was of God and not something of which I should be ashamed or fearful."

Spencer looked down for a few moments before he continued. When he looked up he was almost in tears. "When my dear friend died, I mourned his loss as deeply as if he were my own father or my child. I could not rise above the grief for a long period of time. I felt that not only had I lost a dear friend, an apostle of the Lord, but also the only person on earth to whom I had been given permission by the Lord to share my experiences.

"I mourned his death for months. At times I had no desire to eat or sleep. I found it hard to function properly. I was sinking into depression. Then one night I was awakened by someone standing beside my bed. It was about two o'clock in the morning, and I was just suddenly awake. I sat up and realized a heavenly messenger was standing beside my bed. This same messenger had conducted me through many visionary experiences, and yet I never knew his name, nor was I allowed to ask it. I moved as if to get out of bed, and instead of stepping back to allow me to do so, He just smiled at me.

"He didn't move his lips, but he spoke to me in the way that I had become familiar with while in vision, where the information just flows into my mind and heart in my visitor's voice. I am able to answer back the same way, but most often I forget and ask my questions out loud.

"He said, 'Spencer', and I knew why he had come this time: because my dear friend, the Apostle, had asked him to. He radiated love and concern as he continued, 'You should not mourn your friend's passing so deeply. He is troubled by your sorrow for him and knows that you realize that he is very happy, finally at peace and free of pain and is going forward with his work. He loves you and therefore asks that you cease to mourn for him so.'

"I felt willing to do anything the angel asked me to do, and I felt the sense of deep loss and grief quickly melt away. A quiet peace replaced the loss in my heart. But I had one more question for him. I said, 'I no longer have someone the Lord has given me permission to talk to about my experiences. I guess I was mourning that loss as well.'

"The angel smiled and replied, 'I understand, but only for a little while longer. The Lord will send John into your life. He will understand you and your visions. You can tell him all you have experienced. He will help you understand them as well. Just be patient until then.'"

Spencer told me that the angel gathered the light back around himself and vanished. Spencer laid back down and, after a long time, fell back asleep.

Spencer looked at me in a penetrating way and added, "When you first called me and asked for an appointment, it was then that I realized your first name is John. I began from that day to ask Father most earnestly if you were that John to whom the angel had referred."

I replied, "Surely he was speaking of someone more important than myself—like John the Beloved, or John the Baptist, or maybe someone from Enoch's city!"

Spencer smiled and said, "No, he was speaking of you. You are the John the angel promised me was coming. I have waited eight years for that promise to be fulfilled. I have petitioned the Lord and He has given me permission to tell you my whole experience and to allow you to write certain parts of it down to be published."

Spencer said he believed this was one of the reasons we had been brought together at this time. "I hope that something we might say in this book will bless some soul and may give hope and clarity in preparing for what lies ahead."

The Spirit burned a fire in my soul, which witnessed then, and still tells me today, that it is true. We made another appointment, and since that day we have met at least once a week for over six months. Together we produced a volume of notes and over fifty hours of recorded interviews.

What you are about to read is, to my thinking, the most comprehensive and powerful insight into the latter days that has come to an average person.

It is not scripture and should not be considered such. It is not prophetic for anyone but Spencer himself. It is simply an account of how the Lord has prepared one humble man, my friend Spencer, for his latter-day mission. You and I are just blessed to be the fly on the wall, so to speak.

As I mentioned earlier, none of this is fiction; all of it is as told to me by Spencer, who takes responsibility for its content.

It is something you may never forget.

AUTHOR'S NOTE

Spencer's story came to my ears as a narrative, which I have prayerfully condensed into an account of Spencer's journeys beyond the veil. Since those first days of interviews and questions, Spencer has read and reread what I have written, and he has declared that this book is a true and accurate account of his visionary experiences.

I have chosen to write in Spencer's voice because all of these things came from him. Nowhere have I invented people or events to flesh out his account—though I have interpreted much of his narrative to make it clear, sequential, and understandable. I have also tried to preserve his distinctive manner of speech and personality.

Spencer and I have changed all names to protect identities and deleted the exact location of some events. In some cases we have understated some horrific events to keep this book readable by general audiences. We have removed anything that we deemed could incite fear or panic if it were read by someone not able to understand by the Holy Ghost the greater story of hope and deliverance.

The appendix at the end of this book contains notable visionary experiences that parallel Spencer's account. They have been reproduced here without modification and may be more graphic than suitable for younger readers.

The scriptures tell us that the times of tribulation are coming and that those who are upon the path of righteousness—who have taken the Holy Spirit to be their guide, who have aligned their hearts and wills with Christ—will rejoice in the changes. Those who righteously take part in the latter-day scene will grow in strength until there is no fear, walking in great power and revelation to accomplish their labors.

Latter-day scriptures also teach us that as the time approaches for the return of Christ, those who abide the day will rise to the full glory of Zion. Translation will be common among us, and we will learn to live without disease or death. We will learn to operate in the fulness of the priesthood, and we will gather in the elect from the world into Zion. There we will teach them, administer the saving ordinances, and protect them as they complete their own journey to Christ's latter-day Zion. There will be angels among us, heavenly messengers, and miracles even greater than those that delivered the children of Israel from Egypt. And, in due time, we will have the Lord Himself among us. The Church will rise to the full glory of its calling and will be the prophetic voice of guidance we all follow as we close this great dispensation of the fulness of times.

These will be glorious times—times never to be forgotten—that will be canonized in scripture and stories and songs that will be sung for as long as descendants of Adam exist in the long eternities that await us.

—John M. Pontius

Chapter One

AWAKENED BY DEATH

My First Experience with Death

I was born dead. When I entered this world, my skin was dark blue and black. The doctor took one look at me and handed me to one of the four nurses in the operating room. I was tiny and premature, and the nurse could find no pulse or respiration. She wrapped my lifeless body in a newspaper and laid me in a stainless steel sink. My mother was bleeding badly, and the nurse hurried back to assist the doctor. They told her that I was stillborn and continued the surgery to save her life. She never told me this herself, but I learned later that she had been relieved that I didn't make it because she had not wanted this pregnancy.

According to my mother, when the nurse returned to dispose of my lifeless little body wrapped in newspaper, she found me struggling to breathe. They immediately took me to Primary Children's Hospital to see if I might survive the ordeal at last.

Later, after my mother had recovered somewhat from the surgery and there was a tiny hope I might survive, they informed her that her stillborn child had "pinked up a bit."

When my dad was eighteen, he and some friends had gone for a joy ride. They were drinking and driving, and they struck an old man on the side of the road and killed him. My father was found guilty

1

of vehicular homicide. But the Second World War had just broken out, so the judge "sentenced" him to join the Navy. He was in the Navy until the war ended. The guilt, shame, and remorse due to the tragic death of this elderly man tormented my father for the rest of his life and contributed to the end of his affiliation and interest in religion, even though his parents remained ever faithful and continued to reach out to, pray for, and worry about him.

He and Mother married, much to the dismay of both of their parents, and endured a rocky and abusive relationship. After their divorce, my mother refused to discuss my father with anyone for the rest of her life. I never met him or knew much more about him than angry references and disparaging comments from other family members.

At the time of my birth, my parents were recently separated but not yet divorced. Mother had gotten pregnant just prior to the separation in a last-ditch attempt to save their marriage. The divorce had turned nasty and verbally abusive. My father left and refused to support her or my older siblings. When she realized she was pregnant, she was at first angry, then furious, then depressed and resentful of her circumstances and of the little life inside her. My mother went back to work as a nurse.

My mother's father was a Methodist lay-minister. When Mother had married my dad, who was a "Mormon," her father had disowned her and told her that she was no longer a Christian and that she and her children were all going to hell. When she realized she could not provide for her family, Mother contacted her parents to ask for help. He reconfirmed that she was not welcome in their home. She had never felt more rejected, alone, and abandoned. This felt like yet another rejection and abandonment in a string of rejections she had experienced from her youth to the present time.

My father's mother, my grandmother, easily convinced my grandfather that they needed to take my mother in and support her until she could get back on her feet. So when this time of great need came, my mother and we children were lovingly welcomed into their home. My grandfather was a bishop at the time, and my grandmother was a worker in the local temple. They were stalwarts in the Church and were loving people. As I grew up, my grandmother became the dearest person in my life.

My grandparents were such a loving and faith-filled influence upon my mother that she joined the Church five years after my birth. They were the solidity in her life, and in mine. They never failed us. We lived a blessed life, and because of my grandparents' steady and sincere influence, affection, and generosity, my mother was able to take care of our financial needs. I often went without things I wanted as a child, but I never felt that we were poor. I felt safe and loved.

In the course of my profession as a child and family therapist, I have seen many other children whose lives and very souls were torn apart by mothers, who did not realize they were harming their unborn child, as they lived lives of anger and resentment because of the circumstances of their child's conception.

I have struggled with these issues all my life and probably chose the profession I am in now to try to heal from those prenatal wounds. It wasn't until 1983, almost thirty-three years later, that I finally understood what had really happened and was able to forgive her and my father.

That understanding came most painfully, and unexpectedly, the second time I died.

My First Post-Death Experience

It was September of 1983, and I was having health problems from chronic internal infections, especially in my kidneys, with several bouts of kidney stones. The doctors wanted to know if my kidneys had been damaged from the ongoing kidney problems. My doctor recommended an x-ray with iodine contrast dye to highlight any damage that may have occurred. It was supposed to be a routine procedure.

I was thirty-three by then, and I had completed a double master's degree and was going to school to complete a doctorate program. Each time I had this kidney disorder, I had to stay home, lose time at work, and get behind in my studies. The doctor finally mentioned that I should just stop drinking soda pop, saying that if it weren't for soda pop, he would be out of a job. I was amazed at how simple the solution was and amazed that he had not mentioned it years earlier. I quit drinking soda, and I have never had kidney problems since.

I was happily married to Lyn (not her real name, of course) by this time. We had five children and thought we were done having children. We were still struggling students, even though I was working full time in a hospital. We were anxious to complete my doctorate program so I could become a tenured professor and begin my own private practice. I was already on several faculties as an associate professor and instructor.

We arrived at the clinic a little early to fill out paperwork. I had to come fasting. We sat in the waiting room, listening for my name to be called. Before the procedure began, I changed into a hospital gown. I was escorted to a narrow metal table and told to lie face up. There were tubes and bottles of liquid dangling above my head.

The room was painted hospital green. A big, black x-ray machine dominated the far wall. The floor was green concrete with a black border. The walls were painted matching colors. It was a typical 1970s hospital procedure room.

I was feeling fearful of the procedure but thought it necessary, so I submitted as the nurse started the IV. She was young, blonde, and attractive. I assumed she was in her mid-thirties. I liked her friendliness, cheerfulness, and confidence. We spoke about the procedure and possible complications. She explained some of the possible symptoms of an allergic reaction to the dye as she carefully injected the dye into my arm.

She said, "If you feel flush . . ." and that very second I began to feel flush.

She continued, "If you feel your skin itching . . ." as I began to itch severely all over my body.

She said, "If you feel pressure in your chest or feel like you can't breathe . . ." just as I felt a horrible crushing feeling in my chest as if an elephant had sat on me. I tried to say, "I can't breathe!" but I couldn't get the words out. I raised my free arm and hand to my neck and quickly drew them across my throat, trying to get the nurse to realize that I was in trouble. I grabbed my throat in what I knew was the universal sign of choking.

It was at that moment that the nurse comprehended my cues and realized something was seriously wrong. She ran to the near wall and pushed a large, red button. A buzzer went off loudly, and a recorded voice from the clinic's PA began repeating "Code blue, room twenty-four! Code blue, room twenty-four!" Having worked in the hospital for many years, I had responded to such a call many times, never anticipating someday I would be the subject of such an announcement.

The next thing I knew, my spirit was sinking down through the table. I had my eyes wide open, not wanting to miss any part of this experience, and I just felt my spirit sink until I could see the underside of the table. I didn't want to be under the table, and in an instant I found myself standing beside the procedure table looking at my lifeless body stretched out before me.

The large black and white clock on the wall right before me read 9:20 a.m.

The nurse tried to find a pulse and couldn't. She swore and shouted back at the control room, "I'm losing him! I'm losing him!" A male technician rushed into the room.

Immediately people assembled to try to revive me. A doctor I had not seen before ran into the room, and for some reason, I immediately knew that he was having an affair with the nurse who started the IV. It came as a complete surprise to me that I knew this. I found my mind full of new information that was coming at me more from my heart than from my usual senses. I also knew that this nurse was recently divorced. I knew how much she valued and also feared this relationship with the doctor who was now working beside her to save me. I knew how hard she struggled to be good at her profession and still be a good mom to her two sons at home. I knew she had terrible financial problems. I knew everything about her, actually every detail of her life, and every decision, fear, hope, and action that had created her life. I could hear her mind screaming in fear. She was praying for help, trying to take control of her fear and remember her training. She desperately did not want me to die.

I looked at the other people in the room and was astonished that I could hear their thoughts and know the details about their lives just as vividly as the nurse.

There is a heightened spiritual sensitivity that comes from being dead that I had never anticipated or heard of before. I knew what everyone was thinking. Actually, it was greater than just knowing what they were thinking. I also knew every detail of their lives. I knew if they were good people or bad, if they were honest or corrupt, and I knew every act that had brought them to that state. It wasn't something I felt or could see, it was just knowledge that was in me.

What was even more interesting to me was that I felt no judgment of them. I simply knew these things. It was like knowing a rose is red; it isn't something to judge, it is just the way that flower is.

What I did feel, which was totally new to me, was a rich compassion for them and their circumstances. Since I knew so much about them, I also knew their pains and their motivation for everything they had done that had taken them to this moment in time. I also felt their fear of losing me.

Their actions and reactions were calculated, forcing them to remain calm. Only the doctor working on me felt a sort of detachment that allowed him to act with less emotion. Feeling their fear and the full impact of their lives caused me to experience their pain almost as keenly as they felt it, and I had total compassion for them. I did not feel fear for myself up to then. I was too busy coming to terms with all of these new sensations.

I found myself standing a little farther away. I think I had stepped back a little to give them room to work on my body, because they were walking or running through the same space where I had been standing.

"I must be dead," I remember thinking. I had to think this process over a few times before it really sunk in. *I am dead!* It finally hit me as I saw my body on the table, me in a new body form standing above it in complete comfort and with no pain. Just moments ago, I was in the greatest pain I had ever before felt, and now I was completely free from all pain and the cares of that tabernacle of flesh. They were now gone. It was such a relief that discovering I was dead didn't cause any great distress. I just accepted that I was dead because I was looking at my body there on the table. I was standing there watching all of these people trying to revive me. They were shouting commands and demands and injecting me with many life-restoring substances.

The next awareness I had was that I was able to comprehend many things simultaneously. I didn't need to focus on any one thing, because they were all clear to my understanding. I felt like I could understand limitless amounts of knowledge and focus upon an infinite number of matters, giving each my absolute attention. This was amazing to me and so different from my experience as a struggling graduate student, trying to memorize volumes of information.

My Life Rehearsal

At this moment, I began to see a vision of my whole life. Because I had this new ability to comprehend so many things at once, the vision was all absorbing and important and curious to me, but I still had a full comprehension of each doctor and nurse around me and what was happening to my body.

The first thing I saw was my mother carrying me in her womb. I didn't just see her, I completely comprehended her, her whole life, her pain and sorrows, every thought she had had, every decision she had made, every emotion she had felt. I realized that in all my life, I actually did not know my mother at all. I had always looked at her from a child's perspective, and I had never been able to excuse her entirely for not wanting me. She had told me the story of how my biological father had left her pregnant, penniless, and homeless. She had never spoken unkindly of the fact that I had been born. However, she had made it clear throughout my life that we children were a great burden to her, and that she was left to do it all alone with no help.

I now saw her completely differently. I watched my own conception, and all of the emotion of that moment. As with all of this, there was no judgment from me or from God. I felt no emotion about it except increased compassion for my mother.

I saw that she had two other children, I being the third. I watched her every breath, every decision, every fear and tear she shed. I saw many people, mostly her professional friends, trying to convince her to either abort me or give me up for adoption. They told her I would be a constant reminder of my incompetent father and what he had done to her. I also saw others, her friends and church leaders, even my grandparents, trying to convince her to keep me and raise me.

I saw and felt my mother's decision process in concluding to keep me. It was as if she had gone through this process so many times that she could see the outcomes from this choice and how it would impact her and me for the rest of our lives. She felt so alone and rejected. She felt like a failure, and that she simply was not able to raise another child. Yet, she was also a nurse who had worked with women in settings similar to her own, and she felt that she could not subject her own child to the adoption process. She decided that sending me off to live with another family would not do anything good for her baby or for herself. She had an extremely difficult time with love, trust, and relationships. She was going through her own depression and sense of loss, so love was not a big part of her decision. She was thinking things like, "Two wrongs are not going to make a right" and "I need to clean up my own mistakes." Her decision was not based upon love. It was based upon rationalization. She kept me out of duty and responsibility.

She had not been raised by loving parents. Her father was stern and physically abusive. Her mother was an invalid who was in her bed for the majority of the day. As I noted, she had been disowned by her parents, and she knew how awful that felt to a child. So, here she was choosing to do what was right, not what was convenient. Her depression and loss drove motherly love far from her.

I realized also that I had been involved in my mother's life before I was born. I had, in a sense, been a ministering angel to her, watching and protecting her through the hard times leading up to my birth. It was a validating and peaceful insight for me. I wanted to be born to her, even in these trying circumstances, and she had made the difficult decision to keep me. I experienced the love I had had for her before I was born, and it has remained with me ever since. It has been a Balm of Gilead to my soul and has allowed me to not only forgive her but to fully understand her as a completely different person, one who really did love me, long before she or I had been born.

I saw all of the events of her life leading up to her going to the hospital to deliver me. I felt her fear and anger every step of the way. She was not healthy either physically or emotionally. The dark emotion of those days had sapped her life and robbed my unborn body of the vitality it needed to survive.

I watched my mother in labor and was amazed to see many angels attending my birth. Two of the nurses in the delivery room were not mortals but were angels. They were either translated persons or resurrected, because they had bodies. They acted like the other nurses, showing emotion and taking orders. But they were only there to help this woman and her child who was dying at birth.

My mother felt so alone. Her main emotion was of abandonment and sadness. She didn't know anything about these angels that were there helping her, which seems to be the case in most angelic interventions. We are aware of only little of what the angels do. In her pain of giving birth under these sad circumstances, she didn't realize that all of these spirit people were there, intervening, protecting, and bringing forth life. Even in her despair, divinely commissioned beings were there giving her strength and lovingly helping her so that she and I could have a life together.

Angelic Nurses

As I was watching my own birth, I saw that my little stillborn body was indeed black and dark blue. I watched the nurse check for a heartbeat with a stethoscope. When there was nothing, she wrapped me in newspaper because I was covered with blood and dark fluids. I even smelled bad, and she didn't want to soil hospital towels. She sadly placed me in the sink and returned to the operation.

The two nurses who were assigned to care for my newborn body turned away from my mother and began working with me in spite of the fact that I was dead. I realized that these two were angels, and they were assisted by other unseen angels streaming forth from heaven's portals. I stepped closer to them. They had pulled upon the newspaper to reveal my pinched little face. It was black in color, covered in blood, and had I been in my mortal self, the sight of it surely would have made me ill. In spirit form, I found it curious and sad, and even more interesting that these two nurses were moving their hands into and out of my body. It was almost as if they were giving me CPR, but their hands were actually entering my little body. With each pass my skin grew a little more pink, a little more lifelike.

I could hear them speaking spiritually to one another, coordinating and focusing their rescue efforts. Much of their speech was praise and prayer, praying for God to bless their efforts and praising His mighty will. They were urgent, but not at all fearful or dismayed. I don't believe they could see me, or at least they never acknowledged me as I anxiously watched on.

I saw that little body in the sink, my own body, gasp for breath, struggling to live. The nurse pulled the newspaper a little farther open and turned to the doctor. Her face was serene, but her voice was one of feigned surprised. She cried, "Doctor! I think this baby is still alive! He has pinked up!"

By this time the doctor had saved my mother and stopped the internal bleeding. He turned around, his bloodied hands held up in front of him. His face was incredulous; nevertheless, he walked over to the sink. He glanced at the clock on the wall, preparing to announce the time of death of the infant. When he looked in, he ordered the same nurses who had revived me to get me out of that sink and warm me up. They turned and whisked me away to the understaffed and poorly functioning nursery. I was immediately transferred to Primary Children's Hospital where I struggled to stay alive for weeks. I was placed in an old iron lung until I started breathing on my own.

When someone sees their life rehearsal, as I have come to call it, they see everything through the great objective lens of God's love. I was seeing my whole birth, and my later life, through everyone's eyes—my mother, myself, my siblings, my grandparents, and my friends—even people I had only accidentally interacted with. The thing that was overwhelming to me was that this experience was like attending your own funeral, and seeing your life spoken of by every-one who knew you—in fact, everyone in your world. Each person experienced you uniquely and differently. Not all of it was flattering or accurate, but oh what a treasure chest of information was gleaned from this unique vantage point!

I saw all of the good I did, all of the love I gave, the service and kindness—but I also saw all of the sorrow and pain I had caused. I saw all of my mistakes and how they affected everyone. I saw some mistakes that not only affected one person, but their children, and their children, on and on. I saw every act ripple through time until its power was dissipated. Fortunately, I was young, and I had tried to live a good life even in my youth, so this life review was not unpleasant to watch. Some of the things I saw made me feel pleased with myself. I felt like I was the only person who was being judgmental of my life.

I comprehended it all in perfect detail. In this great, revelatory detail, I saw myself as every person saw me. All of the judgment was correct and in righteousness. The good and the bad were all sifted in the light of Christ, and His judgment was sound, fair, and gracious. There could be no debate, because my life was recorded in perfect detail. I knew it was true, and I knew it was just.

I am still amazed at how objective my life review was. There was no judgment or emotion about my actions either from myself or from God. I saw and understood how my life impacted my schoolmates, my mother, and my siblings, which changed my perspective of almost every person in my life. In the review, I experienced my life through the eyes of others. I understood with perfect clarity how my decisions affected them, what emotions they experienced because of me, and the impact my words and acts had upon them throughout the remainder of their lives. I saw what their lives were before, during, and after I intersected with them. I also saw the true outcome of their acts upon me, which was at times much different than I had perceived it at the time.

When I saw my biological father's perspective on these events, and his leaving and divorcing my mother, I learned that it was not all selfishness, not all narcissism, as I had supposed all of my life. When he realized my mom was pregnant, he knew, or thought he knew, that I would be better off without him. That may not have been true, but that was his perception. He knew his life choices would only damage me. He did not leave me because of selfishness or because of alcoholism alone, as I had been taught. He truly thought that I would be better off without him.

I understood his pain, his childhood, his conflicts with his parents, and his relationship with his father. I understood those things perfectly, which no mortal can understand while yet mortal; not even my father understood it this way. I understood for the first time that my father actually loved my mother very much. His weakness and history handicapped his ability to let love triumph in his decisions. I also saw Christ's love and Heavenly Father's love for him, no matter what mistakes he had made.

This served to completely change my judgment of my mother and father and my assumptions of why they had done what they had done. This new perspective created great conflict in me because it changed almost every judgment and conclusion I had made during my life. It was all swept away a split second in this non-mortal time frame. I had seen things which now forced me to abandon my anger and resentment. It has literally taken me decades since then to reconcile what I was taught as a child with what I had seen really happen. At times my emotions and old thinking have taken up a bitter conflict within my mind and soul. This is the conflict that took so long to resolve because I knew the truth now, but my natural man fought against the spiritual insights gained through this non-earthly experience.

I don't know, of course, if this conflict would have continued had I actually died. Maybe it would have all been resolved in the love of God, because all of this came to me without judgment or opposition.

When I returned to my body instead of dying and resumed my life, however, it was hard to reconcile my former beliefs with all that I had seen in vision. I was in the habit of thinking and believing one way, yet I spiritually knew a greater truth, one that my emotions had a difficult time yielding to, like a snowflake that remains on a leaf all summer, refusing to yield to the warmth of the sun. I can't even say today that I am done with that work.

One of the obstacles to reconciliation of these conflicting emotions was that my father was already dead by this time, and I couldn't resolve all this with him. My mother had not allowed me to even meet my father while he was still alive. Her strong-held belief and her conclusions and anger would push to the forefront of every conversation we had regarding my father. She refused to disrupt the position of justified resentment she had created for herself, which protected her from the rawness of her pain surfacing again and becoming exposed. I never succeeded in speaking the kindly words I had stored up in my mind regarding him in her presence. I finally had to conclude that I would leave these conversations and insights in the loving hands of our Savior for when He knows my mother is finally able to receive them in His impeccable timing and through the grace of His loving kindness. It wasn't until after my mother's death that I was able to start reconciling with her during several special spiritual experiences with her beyond the veil.

I have had spiritual experiences, not dreams or visions, but visitations from both my father and mother since that time that have assisted me in bringing peace to my soul and I think to theirs.

On one occasion, I heard the waiting room door in my outer office open and close. Someone came through the door and into the waiting room. I was in my office writing patient notes following my previous session. I said without looking up, "Please sit down. I'll be right with you." I heard whoever it was sit down. When I finished writing and opened the door, no human was there. I had this strong impression that my father was in my office. Through that same inner voice I had experienced during my near-death experience, he gave me a specific date, which was the anniversary of his death. I understood that he was asking me to go to the temple on that date. I happily did so, thinking I would see my father. But I went through the session without seeing him or even feeling his presence.

As I was dressing, I again felt his presence, and the message, given in the same powerful way, was that he was now worthy to enter the temple, and he wanted me to be there with him. It was a sweet message. It spoke volumes to me that he had prepared, repented, and was now worthy to be in the temple. As a result I knew that he had embraced and benefitted from our ministry in his behalf. It was and is a comfort to me.

One of the wonderful insights I gained from this first near-death experience was regarding my older sister who became pregnant at age sixteen. I had never understood the powerful effect this had upon her or the rest of my family. While I was living those times, I had my perspective only. I was the third child and my self-assigned role in our family was that of peacemaker. I tried to keep the harmony in our family by inserting myself into everything—including places I didn't belong. I saw that my judgment of her and her circumstances was not correct, even though I was trying to keep the peace.

I saw the impact that her pregnancy had upon my older brother. I watched him take a really long walk for three to four hours. I experienced what he was thinking and feeling and how he felt like he had failed her and the rest of us in some way. I understood for the first time that he decided then and there to make changes in his own life so that he would never let us down again. I was so surprised to see how he worried about his brothers and sisters and took responsibility for us. I was clueless about the intensity of his feelings until I saw him in my life review. It gave me great empathy and respect for him.

I also felt my sister's pain and all of the reasons for her pain. I was not aware, until seeing it in this vision, that my mother and the parents of the baby's father had taken them in a car to Las Vegas to get them married. I saw the pain and tension in the car as they drove there. I lived those events with her in a way that not even those mortals present could have experienced. It was the first time I actually understood my sister and sorrowed with her. I saw my youthful impact on her and how she felt shunned, rejected, and judged by myself and her family. It gave me great empathy for her and brought tenderness into our relationship in the years that followed.

I asked my mother and sister years later to verify what I had seen. My mother and sister both acknowledged that there had actually been a shotgun wedding. This confirmation gave me a rich sense of compassion and closeness to my family. It was a comprehensive illustration of the impact of my life on theirs and why our lives presently are the way they are.

My Friend, the Bully

I was frightened in my young life of the bullies in the school, especially of Jake. He was a year older, bigger, and just plain mean. He seemed to delight in terrifying me. At least once a week, Jake hit me or did something aggressive and mean to me. I went home with many bruises and black eyes because of him. Those were the days when adults figured it was best for boys to work out their problems and learn to stand up for themselves, so my mother and grandparents urged me to learn to defend myself rather than interfering in my life. I finally got up the courage in fifth grade to fight back. In my life rehearsal, I watched that day. I also saw my newfound courage from his perspective, which included the horrible abuse that he was receiving from his father.

When I stood up to Jake and hit him back, it totally changed his thinking about his world. I saw that he felt powerless and victimized himself. My little act of courage showed him that he was not.

He never bullied me or anyone else again. He was changed by that experience. He became my friend because I had unknowingly given him the key to his own freedom from tyranny. Our new friendship allowed Jake to resolve his own relationship struggles with his father. He was emboldened to stand up to his father because of my action. Just as Jake stopped bullying me, his father stopped abusing him when Jake refused to submit, and his dad actually left shortly after that.

Seeing the impact that my friendship had upon him was a revelation to me. I had never suspected that there was any motivation for his bullying except meanness. After the vision, I understood why he had taken his frustration out on me and others.

From my life rehearsal I learned that this was all divinely engineered, that we both needed this close relationship, and it had to start with his bullying me in order to heal him. I saw that I had agreed to all of this prior to our birth. Our divinely ordained friendship had a lasting impact in his healing and his relationship with his family, and upon me. I could not have learned these things without him.

What I learned by seeing all of this was that our relationship was engineered by God and had a significant impact upon both of us. We both changed. I quit being afraid of bullies and of life in general. Not only did my actions begin the healing of his abuse, but his part in my life began my healing as well. I realized that fear was not necessary and that I could stand up for myself and actually make friends because of my courage. That realization still influences me today. Our relationship was ordained and engineered by God to save us both. In my thinking today, it was well worth the few bruises it cost me.

The last thing we did before Jake graduated and moved away was to perform in the musical *Oklahoma!* He played Jud, and I played Curly. In the musical, Jud and Curly are both in love with Laurey. Curly confronts Jud about his bullying and they become friends of sorts. But after Laurey agrees to marry my character, Curly, Jud breaks into the wedding and threatens Curly with a knife. In the ensuing brawl, Jud falls on his knife and dies. Curly, of course, gets the girl. The play was a metaphor of our relationship, which was not lost on either of us.

I have often pondered why God would let me see this life rehearsal, knowing that I was not actually going to die. My assumption prior to this experience was that you see your life rehearsal just one time, when you actually die. I wondered for years why God would give me this powerful insight into my own life and then send me back into mortality.

Relationships Are from God

The truth is that seeing these things changed my life forever and gave me a new perspective on all of my relationships and the purpose of my own life. I do not believe I could have accomplished all I promised to do without these experiences. Actually, I am sure of it.

I now know that relationships are not just serendipitous happenings or coincidences. All of these events happen for divine purposes. It has taught me that God truly blesses the details of our lives. These interactions and relationships, which might seem random in the moment, are ordained to bless and perfect our lives.

Since this intense review of my life, I have looked upon life and relationships as if it were a puzzle, knowing that all things and relationships have divine impact. My question from then on has been where is the divine purpose of this moment, this event, this relationship, or this person coming into my life? What am I to learn from these interactions, from this person's entry or exit on the stage of my experience? I began to pray that God would reveal these things to me and that He would guide me to bless these people, rather than letting me wander unknowing through their lives. My prayer has become, "Let me be your voice, let me be your hands, let me be knowingly involved so that I can be inspired to do thy work in their lives." I have personally failed in this purpose occasionally, but as I have aged my ability has gradually grown stronger and my resolve firmer.

From this vantage point of my life's review, some events of my life that I thought were simple or mundane turned out to be meaningful and purposeful in God's eyes. God really does count every moment of our lives, and if we let Him guide us, those moments become eternally significant.

It is interesting to me though that the negative impact of my actions on people was not the subject of my life review. It was there and I viewed it, but it seemed to matter less than the good I did and how it rippled down through their lives. When I saw the negative parts of my life, the message to me wasn't how bad it was but that if I continued that behavior, it had the potential to take me away from the specific work that the Lord intended for me to accomplish in my lifetime. It wasn't judgmental, just instructive. To achieve my fullest potential I needed to comply with the covenants that I had made premortally or I would not accomplish the purposes of my life. I have to remind myself that God was not showing a life review to a person who was actually leaving mortality, so my experience may have de-emphasized my mistakes to encourage and teach me. I have the sense that if I had actually died, there would have been no purpose in warning me and the weight of my negative acts would have been of greater consequence.

Finding out what we covenanted in premortality to do on earth is a continually unfolding discovery. Sometimes we can only know a tiny next step, and sometimes we are blessed with a sweeping vision of what we will become and do. I was being taught that I had to deliberately choose to be upon the path that God was laying before me, no matter how it came to my understanding, doing everything right that I know to do.

Since I was not going to actually die, the grand effect of my life review was to show me that I had the ultimate choice in my life. I was free to choose what I may; however, my choices would either take me to the light or leave me in darkness.

I also learned that our lives are all recorded somewhere, detail upon flawless detail. Everything we do matters—nothing is just trivial. It is all profoundly significant, and life is meaningful and full of purpose.

Our Lives Matter

I learned to not minimize what is going on in my life. I try to see everything I do as being of eternal worth. I learned, and have trained myself, to believe that I am not just a simple person with little worth or impact upon the world. Everything we do has import, and God is involved in the details of our lives. I believe you can go so far as to say that He is in the minute details of our lives. I used to think God was a stern and divine parent who just sent us to earth and said, "Go to it, and we'll see how you did after you die." But the truth is that for Him, and His angels, we are truly His work and His glory. We are what He is doing. We are what He is about.

I learned that families, brothers and sisters, cousins, and aunts and uncles have divine purpose in those affiliations and connections. Even though it might be easy to criticize or ignore people, in truth, those connections are all-purposeful.

I learned that there truly is a return and report system in our present life, which we don't use properly. I recommend that we get used to doing this in our daily and family prayers and in our relationships, that we practice returning and reporting. "This is what you asked me to do today, this is what I did, and this is what happened"—and then plead for eternal intervention in the details.

I learned that our entire existence is this way. God gives us some element necessary for our journey, even before we were born, then He gives us time to explore and experience life, and then He requires us to report. Now he has given us a body and a mortal experience, and we will all be required to report. The accounting of our lives will be in great detail, for our very bodies tell the story of our lives. Every part of us has written upon it all we do, believe, and are. The Lord can read all this in its entirety. He can and will read us like a book, for it is all within us, written on our very bones, hearts, and sinews.

Dispensational Priority and Purpose

Finally I learned that there is dispensational priority and purpose for why we are here at this time. It is not random. It is not accidental. It is divinely engineered, and when we make our final reporting, we will again see all the reasons why we came to earth now and the interacting purposes and covenants that we made that sent each of us to earth at our specific time and place to do specific things. To us mortals, this is a misty concept, but to God, it is an exact science—divine math, if you will. He records every act of our lives, including his continuing guidance, which most of us ignore.

We spend so much time entertaining and pleasing ourselves that we do not fully realize how important every moment and every interaction truly is to God. Most of us are trapped in our own lives of business and pleasure, so much so that we don't even feel the hand of God directing our lives, nor do we hear His voice, which is constantly directing us.

All of this information came to me very quickly as I stood there watching the doctors trying to resuscitate my body. All of these things were going on simultaneously, and I could focus upon them all.

Visiting My Wife as a Spirit

I became aware of my wife sitting out in the waiting room. She had been reading a magazine at the moment the PA system began blaring "Code Blue! Code Blue!" Lyn began to worry about me, fearing that it was me that was in trouble. I knew she was worried in the same way I knew everything about the nurses and doctors. I wished to be near her, and I was instantly standing beside her. I apparently moved at the speed of thought. I don't recall walking or moving through walls, I was just there.

My complete attention went to her, though doing so did not diminish my understanding or complete attention to what was still happening around my body. I knew I had come through two walls to be in the waiting room with her, but I did not experience passing through them.

I found myself standing right next to her. I could tell everything about her. I knew exactly what she was feeling and thinking. I knew what she had been reading in the magazine she had just placed on her lap. She was concerned and wishing someone would come tell her that I was okay, that I was not the one having the cardiac arrest.

I thought, *Here I am. I'm dead and out of my body, and I can't even communicate with you.* I felt empathetic for her fear and pain, but it struck me as a dilemma, even a bit funny. I could see her and hear her thoughts, but I couldn't talk to her in a way she could understand.

I remember thinking, *How am I going to let you know that I am all right even though I am no longer living?*

I began to wonder if she would be able to sense me, or hear me perhaps, if I moved through her. I asked her in my mind if I could have her permission to move through her. Even though she was not aware of me, her spirit answered, "Yes." I instinctively knew I had to have her permission to do this. I understood this, but I'm not sure why or how. It wasn't until later that I began to understand that entering another person's body is very invasive, and a righteous spirit always seeks permission if it is ever necessary. Evil spirits wait for opportunities when we are spiritually weak or after we have rendered ourselves vulnerable by disobedience to God's laws, and they enter into us in an act of spiritual violence.

After her spirit responded that I could, I moved through her, and I immediately understood the difference between her physical body and her spiritual body. Her physical self had no realization that I was interacting with her. Her spiritual self, however, was fully aware of me and what I was trying to do and say. The problem was that like most mortals, she was only aware of her physical body—captive to it, so to speak—and not in tune with her spirit at that time in her life.

I realized that moving through her was of no advantage to my trying to communicate with her. As I passed through her, I learned many things about what her experience in mortality had been like— what it felt like to be a woman, to be loved, to be protected, and now to be fearful for her protector. I understood her completely, including what it was like to have our sons and daughters, and how hard it was to live with my illnesses and struggles.

Angels among Us

Lyn was sitting in a crowded waiting room. After I passed through her to no effect, I began looking around the room. I could see that there were many spirit persons in the room along with the mortals that were there.

The mortals looked really different from the spirit people. Mortals are solid looking and appear to be completely unaware of anything spiritual going on around them, almost rendering them unintelligent looking.

Spirit people are semi-transparent. I could see through them to some extent, and they seemed to be aware of me and of the other spirits in the room. Some were not happy that I could see them but nonetheless continued interacting with mortals and other spirits as they went about their purposes. All of the spirit people I saw were surrounding mortals, observing them or trying to gain their attention so they could influence them in some way. There were other spirits walking in and out of the waiting room. I could see them, and they could see me. They sometimes acknowledged my presence or walked around me instead of through me.

There were spirits there who did not realize yet that they were dead, or they refused to accept it. These were quite peculiar to me, for they tried their best to act like a mortal even though it was clear to me and every other spirit present that they were dead. I could understand why they didn't know they were dead. Being dead and being a disembodied spirit is a real existence. You still think like you did. You still love and hate just like before your death. You can see people, spirits, and your own body. You can touch spiritual things and spirit beings and feel them. So it is a real and concrete form of existence even though mortal things, like walls and furniture, can be seen and sensed but cannot be manipulated by spirits.

I'm not sure if every spirit has the same spiritual perception I did, but I knew their new lives were real to them, even more real in some ways, because they could come and go to places very quickly and walk through walls and do things mortals can hardly imagine. Being newly disembodied did not feel like the death they had expected to experience, where you just became unaware or nonexistent forever. So to them, they were not dead by their previous understanding of what constitutes death.

These spirits were gathering around mortals, talking to them as if they thought the mortals were listening to them. But the mortals were completely unaware of them just as my wife was unaware of me. These disembodied spirits were trying to get the mortals' attention by various actions, including shouting at them.

These spirits were dressed like normal mortals. They had little glory around them. I began thinking of them as "recently disembodied spirits." Those spirits who had recently died maintained the look, manner of dress, and shape they had while they were mortal because they seemed to still not believe they were dead.

One male spirit was speaking to a young woman who appeared to be his daughter. He was upset about his business, and how she was

21

handling it. He was shouting at her, "You need to listen to me!" but she had no idea that he was even there. He acted like she was just ignoring him, and this seemed to infuriate him even the more. He was demanding that she do certain things with his business and his property, and he was perturbed about whatever it was she was doing wrong by his thinking.

There were other spirits there who had embraced their altered state and had entered into God's employ to do His work according to His will. These angels had been sent back by God to assist their loved ones through this difficult time. These angels had a recognizable glow about them, which told me instantly that they were good and on an errand from God.

These good angels were dressed differently. Some angels wore robes while others wore old-fashioned clothing typical of when they had lived. They were there to assist the mortals with things that were happening. Some were sent to assist and prepare mortals for their own death. They were speaking comforting words, giving instructions, and teaching. Even though the mortals seemed unaware of their helpers, if they were listening with their hearts, they were comforted, and they began to glow the same as the angels who were assisting them.

Some of these good angels were there to minister to the spirits who could not accept their own death. These angels were dressed in white robes and were glorious to look upon. They were following the disembodied and confused spirits, speaking to them when they could get their attention and enfolding them in their glory. They had joy in their labors and purpose in their actions. They were there by commission of Jesus Christ. I understood that all of these angels were family of those to whom they had been sent. Some were recent ancestors, like parents or grandparents. Others were from long ago.

I was just new at observing spirits, and since that time I have learned a great deal more about them and how they work. I know now that there are definite classes of angels and levels of righteousness among the angels. This is visible to the eye when one is familiar with spirit beings. Just as I could tell everything about the doctors and nurses who were working on my body, I could tell everything about each of these spirits. That is how I knew they were family members. I learned that once you are born, your spirit takes the shape of the body it is born into and honors that shape because it was given to them by God. Even though they can change shape or appearance if God desires it, they always return to their natural shape, which is the shape of their former bodies.

I also learned that the greater angels, those with more glory and greater power, can withhold their identity, so that someone like me, with little experience, could not know what their mission was, who they were, or anything about their history. I met a few of these greater angels in the waiting room as they were administering to their charges.

There were also evil spirits in the room. They were there to tempt mortals, disrupt the work of the angels, and to cause any harm they could. They delighted in their mischief. These spirits had no light about them at all but seemed to emanate darkness.

These evil spirits were not readable to me. I knew some things about them, but not their identity or history. They gave me a bad feeling even to look at them.

They seemed to be able to change their shape to morph into some other shape if they desired. I realized that a spirit who has never been mortal has no definite spiritual shape. I saw some of these evil spirits appear as a child, others as a man in a business suit or a beautiful young woman. It became evident to me that the unborn spirits could choose their shape, just as Satan did in the Garden of Eden by appearing in the shape of a snake. This was the first time I realized that spirits who would never receive a physical body had the ability to appear any way they chose. They could take on the appearance of a living individual if it helped them deceive or to fulfill their assignments. They could appear in the image of a grandfather, a dead prophet, or someone's wife if it helped in their deception.

They are out to do great harm, as much as they can, and they did not like it that I could see them. Most of the evil spirits were there on assignment. They were trying to create fear, confusion, and distress, anything that kept the mortal they were assigned to from hearing the messages from the angels of light who were also there. Not only did they speak to the mortals to afflict them, but they laughed and mocked them and delighted in their pain and fear. If they could have convinced another mortal to stand up and torture or torment their assigned target, they would have done so in an instant. They were evil beyond any definition of evil I had before understood.

Most of these evil spirits were there by commission from their master. They were not just out wandering the earth, looking for mischief to do. When they realized that I could see them, they moved away from me, sometimes vanishing and reappearing in a different part of the room. I realized I could communicate with them, but I had little desire to do so, and they refused to do any more than glance at me before they moved away.

The good angels, the ones that glowed with light, acknowledged me with a nod or smile and sometimes allowed me brief glimpses into what they were doing there in that waiting room, but then they quickly returned to their assignment. I knew the evil spirits could see me because they avoided me. But the disembodied spirits, the dead who refused to acknowledge their own death, did not even seem to see me, nor did they attempt to communicate. I believe they could see me, because several of them stepped around me, but they did not talk to me, similar to how people act in this world around one another.

I met spirits in that experience, in the hospital that day, who had not learned this simple lesson of the eternal worth of their own lives; they were still trying to protect their possessions, businesses, and bank accounts, and ensure that their "things" were still theirs. They were hanging around living people, refusing to move on into the next part of their own journey because they had never learned to trust God and sacrifice their worldly possessions in obedience to God's will for them. They would not acknowledge or talk to the angels sent from God to help them move on into their new lives. They didn't even seem to see them, though I could see and hear them plainly.

I could see that before their death, those people had not learned to hear or acknowledge the direction God gave them while they were living, and after their death that deafness to God's guidance persisted. The same blindness and obstinacy and disobedience of mortality simply followed them into the world of spirits.

We should perhaps ask ourselves: Have we accomplished what we came to earth to do? The other side is constantly intervening to help us learn what we need to learn so that we can accomplish our life's mission. We are sent here to accomplish our own work, to heal the wounds of past generations, and to bless those who follow us. The evil spirits are constantly attempting to derail us from our ordained path.

During all of this time of seeing and understanding these various spirits in the waiting room, I remained aware of what was going on with my body in the procedure room. The doctors and nurses were still working feverishly on me. They injected my heart with epinephrine, and my body started to revive. I could feel it calling to me, demanding that I return to it.

I left my wife and walked back down the hallway they had taken me through initially. A voice other than my own informed me that I needed to get back to my body quickly. I said to myself, "I need to get back to my body!" and turned to walk through the wall into the procedure room. They were still working on me, trying to revive me.

I found myself going through a process that felt similar to when I left my body, but it was not ready, and I found the experience excruciating. I tried to remain in it, but it was horrifyingly painful. I exited my body the same way as before, out of the bottom of the table and around to standing beside my body. The doctors were still doing CPR and working on me.

The Ministry of Angels

I looked around and saw three individuals in the room standing opposite to me, across from my body. They were looking at me (not at my body, but directly at me) with expressions of great interest. The two on the left and right were angels who had once been mortal and who were now accompanying the spirit between them who had not yet been born. I knew instantly that they were training him.

The angel on the left was a thin man with a kind of goatee beard about three inches long, as white as snow. I knew that he had lived well into his eighties. Because of the ability I have explained of knowing everything about other spirits and mortals while in that state, I knew who he was.

The angel on the right was a younger man. He had lived on earth later than the first angel. Both of these angels were progenitors of mine. They did not identify themselves, but I knew that they were blood relatives. They were there protecting the life of my body on the operating table. These two older angels did not appear concerned and did not show much emotion. They both had white hair and the aura of wisdom, light, and righteousness.

The young man in the middle was a full head taller than the other two angels. He was slender but strong looking. He had no beard. His hair was dark. He had piercing brown eyes and an aura of gentleness. He had not yet been born, but I felt his profound love for me, which flowed from him into my soul. He was very concerned for me in this emergency situation and did not possess the other two angels' confidence and serenity.

The three angels were speaking to one another nonverbally. I could hear them. The teaching angels were comforting the younger one. "It's fine. Everything's fine. No need to be concerned. We are here to ensure Spencer returns to his body. Have faith." All three of these men manifested love and concern for me. I knew that they were there for me, that I was their concern and their business, and that I was family to them.

When I finally returned to my body, I was not allowed to remember their identity. But I believe I have identified all three individuals through family photos in the genealogy in my possession. The angel on my left was James Henry. He was my great-great grandfather. The angel on the right was his son Harold Henry, my great grandfather. They look exactly like their old photos. The unborn spirit in the center was my unborn son, Spencer Junior. I wasn't able to identify my son Spencer until he grew into his late teens, and I realized one day that he looked exactly like the center angel. Counting myself, there were four generations of family in the room.

As I was looking at them I was given to understand that it is a family responsibility to serve as ministering angels. It is a family responsibility to heal, teach, minister to, protect, and preserve the family connections and covenantal relationships in the spirit realm and in the mortal world. This is their first responsibility as departed spirits. Until that work is done, until the family relationships are preserved and sealed, other things must wait. They were at the hospital to assist me because my mortal work was not finished, and in a way that

I could not understand until much later in my life, my continued life was important to our family and to them personally. My unborn son was particularly invested in my continuing mortality, but there was much more to his concern than his birth. He was acting out of his love of the Savior and under His guidance was there to be with me in my time of need.

In the world of departed spirits, the teaching of the gospel to past generations must come from righteous souls who acquired it during their lives. In other words, you must acquire the gospel here on earth before you can be a missionary and minister to those who departed before you who, for whatever reason, did not embrace the gospel during their mortal lives. This is one of the reasons the righteous departed are welcomed with such joyful reception in heaven, because some of these earlier generations have been waiting a long time for a descendant of theirs to embrace the gospel of Jesus Christ.

Because of this, the spirits of the dead are excited for us to receive the gospel ordinances and authority and then complete our mortal lives and return so we can teach them and bring the gospel blessings to them on that side of the veil.

Even though we are only dimly aware of how the gospel works on that side of the veil, there is almost a mirror image there of everything we do here. Every ordinance we attempt to bestow here has a corresponding ordinance on that side of the veil. We speak of the departed as "accepting or rejecting" our labors in their behalf. Their acceptance constitutes an ordinance in their world. It is one of the great urgencies of that world, to keep up with the work going on here in mortality. The timetable is advancing so quickly that the righteous dead are often in a great hurry to complete their assignments, and they have little time to pay a lot of attention to small matters.

In the great circle of things, most blessings given to mortals also come from their righteous dead. When we pray for a great blessing, need, or healing, Jesus Christ sends our righteous progenitors as ministering angels to deliver the blessing. If we have no righteous forbearers, then the blessings must be attended to by other righteous workers there, of whom there is a short supply. Any angel who is able to deliver these blessings works first with their own families and then goes on assignments to bless others. This means that our blessings may be delayed in coming or seem to arrive just barely in time. They are busy working to establish the relationships and to protect and bless them.

Deceased family are watching and waiting and guiding us into fulfilling our righteous mortal duties so that we can return and teach and bless them. I also learned that it is a great blessing to have been born into a family where those who have died before were righteous, powerful men and women, sealed in the covenant relationships, generation after generation. They have greater power to bless and guide mortals.

I was told to try to go back into my body. I'm not sure if it was the three angels who instructed this or my own thinking, but I rose up and tried and again found myself rejected in a tremendously painful way. I am quite sure that if spirit bodies could be injured, that experience would have done me great harm. As it was, I was unharmed and had no lingering pain except for the memory of it. Again I found myself standing beside the procedure table, looking down at my body.

The Power of the Fall

One of the most profound realizations I had in this experience was to see the difference between my spirit body and that sick body lying there on the table. This was the first time that I had experienced the juxtaposition between my spiritual self and that mortal self. I was aware of the growth that my mortal body was lacking in order to reach the potential of my spirit self. My spirit was eternal, intelligent, perceptive, and powerful. My body was broken, subject to death, mentally slow compared to my spirit, unaware of almost everything spiritual, and weak in every possible way.

It was then that I began to realize how far we as mortals have fallen. I learned that we were different from how we were before the Fall. Looking down on my body, I knew everything about it, how much time it needed and how much growth and exposure to truth it needed in order to be "finished" or completed, to be able to receive all that Father had prepared for it to receive. That was quite clear to me. I understood all the changes my body needed to experience to become fit to return to the presence of the Father, and it seemed almost impossible to accomplish everything in the short duration of mortality.

This first experience out of my body created the recollection and refreshed my memory of who I was and who I might become through obedient choices. I then made a commitment, a covenant you could call it, between myself as a spirit and my body, that I would do everything that I had to do, to allow my body to receive every change and upgrade and sanctification it needed in order to return to Father with me inside it.

While just in my spirit, I was pure, complete, knowledgeable, and I knew exactly who I was and where I came from. My spirit was in the image of God—and I knew this clearly. A spirit does not have a complete veil of forgetfulness when it is liberated from the body. I knew that I came from the Father and had the full potential to become like the Father. When I was in my spirit self, I was all of these things, and there was no question or uncertainty about anything. My spirit self only wanted to do the will of God and nothing else.

But in the body, I was handicapped by spiritual blindness and moral weakness, and I was blinded by the screaming demands of the flesh. I was full of questions, uncertainty, pride, corruption, self-will, and desires for evil. Worst of all, I could remember nothing of my prior life with Father—I didn't even have a clue who I really was. The contradiction between my two identities was overwhelming and paralyzing. I understood that this disparity was all a result of the Fall of man and that I had to overcome those things by obedience to Christ's gospel and laws.

In the next experience out of body, which I will tell about later in this book, I saw all of the sorrows and trials and struggles I needed to go through to refine that mortal body in order to actually arrive at the state I had just promised I would achieve. In all honesty, after seeing all of the trials I would go through, I couldn't see how I would ever make it. My ego was washed away because I immediately knew I couldn't do it in any way except by the full and unending grace of Christ. It had to be a miracle of the Atonement, because I knew my weaknesses too well to think I, or any mortal for that matter, was strong enough to do it alone.

Finally, in my last out-of-body experience, I was shown the end result of that journey, when and how I would eventually triumph over all of these things, keep all of my covenants, obey all of the commandments, and finally bring my body back into the presence of Christ, having overcome the Fall, being redeemed by Christ—then it was ready to fulfill our mission—"our" meaning my spirit and body—in the latter days. Previous to these experiences, I had no idea that there was a distinct preparation for my body. I thought "I" was my body, and I was growing through my experiences. I learned that "I" am in fact my spirit self, who already has a godly nature, and rather than overcoming my body, as in beating it into submission, my struggles were engineered to elevate my body to the stature of my spirit.

I will get back to those other experiences later on. At this point I was still outside of my body in the hospital, waiting for my spirit to reenter my body.

Exploring the Hospital

I decided I had a little time before my body would be revived. I expected it to be revived, mostly because of the confidence and words of the three angels standing there near my body and because I had not been called away from the hospital. I had not seen a tunnel of light or a heavenly messenger as I had actually expected I would. So I just assumed my destiny was to survive somehow and live on. Time for a spirit moves differently than for a mortal, and even if it was just a few mortal minutes, I had time to explore this amazing situation of being out of my body.

I decided to experiment and have a look around. I know that might sound frivolous or that I didn't care about my mortal life. The truth is, I loved my life, my wife and my children—all of it, and I was not hoping to die. But another truth is that I had been sick and in pain for a long time, and being out of my body was a great relief. I felt great peace and a total absence of fear. Each time I had tried to return to my body I found it to be horrifyingly painful. There just aren't words in the English language that would make it possible for me to say how excruciating it was. My body was very, very sick, and as I moved into it, I could feel that sickness and pain beginning to again overwhelm me. But even more than that, it was kind of like being squeezed through a very small opening under high pressure. The process of reentering the body was agonizing all by itself, and the fact that it was sick and in pain made the whole experience the most unpleasant of my whole life so far.

So with this keen ability to perceive everyone's thoughts, even their history and future, and with a naturally curious mind, I thought I might as well enjoy the few minutes I might still have until my body called for me to try again. Until then, I had no plan to attempt it of my own volition.

I had already experienced walking through walls and was curious to experience that again. I felt comfortable doing this because I continued to be completely aware of what my body was experiencing no matter where I was in the hospital.

I turned away and walked to the nearest wall, paused a moment, and then stepped through into the next room. I found myself in a doctor's office, having walked through a wooden desk, a wooden chair, and a leather couch.

Hearing the Wood & Rocks

I paused for a moment to let the flood of information settle into my mind. As I had passed through the desk, I realized that it had been made from three different trees. I saw each tree. I knew them from the moment their seed germinated until they were harvested, milled, and crafted into this desk. There was a living component in the wood. It was intelligent but had little will. It was content to be wood, and it was pleased that someone had chosen it to be shaped into this desk. It was a rolltop desk and quite beautiful. I knew that the desk understood the love the craftsman had put into his work on the desk. The desk also felt pure and worthy because it had never been used in anything that offended God.

I want to say much more about this phenomenon, of understanding physical things, but words fail me. I understood the emotion and motive of the man who cut it down and knew his name and all about his life too, as I did everyone who ever touched or used the desk. I understood everything about the cotton stuffing in the seat and the leather from the sofa. All of it welcomed me and was pleased to communicate to me its life and how it had come to be that couch.

I understood the several cattle whose hides covered the couch and their lives and their sacrifice. They had left all that information with their hides but the spirit of the cow was elsewhere, not in the leather, although still pleased and content with the benefits to mankind that its life and sacrifice had rendered. It was pleased that it was of benefit to the children of Adam.

The Purpose of Things

I might sum it up this way: All things on this earth are placed here for the purpose of bringing to pass the immortality and eternal life of man. Some things are here to feed us, some to comfort us, some to create beauty, shelter, even medicine. Some things are here to bring opposition, pain, and discomfort. But they are all here to create this world that exalts man. All of it is God's plan, and no part of it is dispensable. Even mosquitoes and viruses are part of the plan. My experience with all of these non-human things was that they are pleased that they are fulfilling the measure of their creation, and that the reward for doing so is acceptable and delightful to each of them.

It was stunning to realize that life is so much more intricate than we can imagine or envision while in this mortal body. God has provided a complex and inspired system to exalt us. A big part of it is to give us the opportunity to be in a body, a body that desires almost everything contrary to God's plan. Jesus Christ exposes us via the Holy Spirit to all that is true, speaking to our spirit every time we must choose between good and evil. Then when we sin, we can repent and obey His laws to let the Atonement work for us. All of this process is designed by God to bring our spirit with our body into compliance with the laws of God and to return body and soul, inseparably connected, back to the presence of God to be judged—to report back.

Our Premortal Glory

It was intriguing to me to see that our spirits came to this earth in an almost godlike state. I expect that there are some spirits that came here with impure motives and desires. But I found that my spirit only desired good, only desired to be in harmony with God.

It was my body that was the slave of mortality, desiring things which were contrary to God's plan for me. When my spirit was placed in my body at birth, and it lost all of its memories of my long and good life before birth, it fell, or became subject to the Fall of man when it entered my body. The big part of the purpose of mortality is to be cut off from God, thereby being forced to learn to listen to the voice of Christ and to overcome our body's mortal pull. In the same process, we are also learning to perfect it, to teach it perfect obedience to the will of Christ, and in so doing, to overcome the world—and the Fall.

To me, one so inexperienced in the deep and divine things of the spiritual world, all of this was "delicious" to me. I was thrilled to experience these things and felt love coming from everything I touched—even the rocks, leather, and wood. I delighted in the love I felt flowing from myself back into them. It seemed that everything that had been created by God had its story and was pleased that I had been able to hear them. I only heard contentment and praise of God from these things.

I found that man-made things, like steel and plastic, were harder to walk through, and had no voice. I couldn't discern their story or their history. They were dead to me at that time. I learned later that they were a part of the living earth but did not learn until much later how to experience the earth. I simply was not ready for it at that time—and was hardly prepared when it happened far into the Millennium. Communing with a piece of wood is kind of like having a puppy step on your toe, wagging its tail, welcoming you with its cute little soul and lovable personality. Talking with the earth is like having a planet land on your body, bearing the weight of a great, great intelligence, of a perfect knowledge and flawless memory of all good and evil that has existed on her face, and of the cries of righteous blood sounding up through the centuries for justice, of immense sadness, godlike patience, and the most joyous rejoicing in its final deliverance. It is to stand face-to-face with a living, brilliantly intelligent being the size of a planet, who is both loving and angry, anxious and patient, having been true and faithful in all things. It is not something one can prepare for without great spiritual experience and divine preparation.

I was quite interested in rocks and natural stonework, whose voice was ancient, predating the formation of the earth. It remembered its creation and luxuriated and rejoiced in being beautiful and useful to man. I found that I liked rocks. They all magnified Christ. I liked their company and sense of timeless patience and eternal worship of Christ.

Now consider, if I could enjoy rocks, whose intelligence and agency is so limited and less divine, how much more profound and glorious are human beings, who are so much more than rocks, yet we don't value them except for what they might do for us. Every person you meet has been alive forever! They predate earthly creation and are gods in infancy. Yet we see them as clerks, doctors, friends, family, or even as enemies or a source of our trials. But we seldom see them as they are—potential gods. I saw this as a tremendous impediment to our own growth. It speaks to how far we've fallen because not so long ago in the eternal scope of things, when we understood the plan far more clearly and we understood the worth of every soul, we were becoming gods (with a small "g") ourselves.

In this life, in a mortal body that knows nothing of His plan for us, we resist God. What is His plan? It is to bring to pass the immortality and eternal life of man. So everything we experience is designed to bring us further along that journey.

Through this out-of-body experience, all of this information was infused into my spirit. Since then the veil is thinner for me in some aspects. I can not only remember what God has shown and taught me in vision, but I have His revelatory voice to teach me every moment of my life—just as every mortal does—through the light of Christ and the voice of the Holy Spirit. Having both perspectives on the works of God has thinned the veil in many ways.

While I was walking through the hospital I met other mortals. Some were workers, others were doctors and nurses. I didn't see many patients, as I seemed to be in an administrative section of the hospital. Each of these mortals' lives was completely transparent to me, as if their very being, their every secret and truth and lie was being broadcast by themselves to the whole world. For me, it was all revealed, and all of it was visible to me. I found it oppressive because I could see the trouble they had created for themselves. I could see every mistake, as well as every good act they had done. I felt deep sadness for most of them and could hardly stand to meet another person after a while.

I found that it was much more pleasant to experience wood and rocks than humans. I was intrigued by their intricate history, which each of them showed to me in the instant I touched them. I was drawn to their positive vibe and eternal makeup.

A Cry for Justice

I found a few items in the hospital that were saddened by how they had been used by their owners. A few things had been used in crimes or for violent or immoral purposes, and their voice included a cry for redemption and justice. It was not a shrill or piercing or unpleasant sound—but it was unending, and carried the vivid details of the injustice. I knew that the object itself was not diminished or condemned, but it waited with patient expectation for the day of redemption.

I walked through a wall and into a nice office. It was more nicely furnished than the others, with beautiful pictures on the walls and or-nate wooden furniture. I considered going out the door to see whose office this was, but as I walked through a desk I was stunned by what I felt. It was longing for redemption. I realized that recently a series of love letters had been written at this desk promoting an affair that ultimately would injure many people. I knew the content of every letter and the true emotion and manipulation of the writer as well as the reaction of the reader. I moved away, not wanting to remain in that stream of torrid details. I went through the couch, and it likewise testified of the same affair and unrighteous events that had occurred here, some recently. I could not find any place in that beautiful office that was not saddened or offended or crying for redemption.

Returning to My Body

I was about to leave when I again felt the call of my body. Instantly, I found myself back in the procedure room, looking at my body. In all of my later experiences of leaving my body, I rose up out of it. But for reasons I still don't understand, I left and reentered my body from beneath during this experience.

I suddenly found myself under the table, moving rapidly up through it and into my body from beneath. This time it was more painful than any of the other times. The pain was being experienced by my body, but as I connected with it, I felt it all. I was still aware in my spirit-self—which, as I described, has enhanced sensibilities. For a moment I could feel both my spirit, as it was rocked and pounded by my body's pain, and the pain of my body. The shock of the pain from both sources was overwhelming. Then, an instant later, I was only aware of my body.

I was back inside. I was not just waking up as if from anesthesia but was fully conscious and aware of everything. I was sick—almost as sick as a mortal can be and still be alive. I had no strength to even blink my eyes. I was overwhelmingly nauseated but too weak to vomit. My heartbeat was irregular, and I could feel sickness from all of the medications they had injected into me. I couldn't believe this was actually my body; it felt sicker than I had ever felt it.

I felt "body burdened," as if my spirit wanted to fly out of it again, but my body was holding it down with a tremendous weight. I struggled to breathe. I could hear the nurses and doctors talking anxiously among themselves and then to me.

I opened my eyes. My perception of the passage of time was that I had been out of my body for five or six hours. I had seen and experienced so much and had wandered the halls of the hospital with no sense of needing to hurry, poking my head through closed doors and walking through every wall I could find. Yet when my eyes finally focused upon the clock on the wall of the procedure room, only twenty minutes had expired.

It made no sense to me. I felt confused. They got me up and fed me some orange juice. I felt ill, so they told me to lie back down and rest. A doctor came and told me what had happened. He spoke of it all casually, like this happens all the time. He wanted me to come to his office for a while and rest to make sure I was going to be okay.

I felt too weak, but they enlisted my wife, Lyn, to encourage me. She rolled me in a wheelchair to his office. She did not realize what had just happened. I recognized his office as the ornate office where the love affair had been enacted, but the office furnishings were silent, no longer speaking to my spirit, which was now apparently firmly back in my body.

I told the nurse who stayed with us, "I've been dead."

She shook her head and replied, "No, you just have had a hard time with the contrast, but now you are fine." She was reassuring, but she did not understand what I was trying to say. Everyone who spoke to us tried to minimize what had just happened. They didn't want to hear anything I had to say. In about half an hour, they told us I was fine and sent me home.

Many Different Death Experiences

A major part of this experience was that I began to understand agency and that people are having different experiences after death. This is something I had certainly never supposed.

Some people would not even admit they were dead. Other people, like myself, were just waiting for their bodies to be restored so they could reenter them. These people were having experiences of many different types. Some were given the choice to return to mortality. I didn't seem to have a choice, as I was just called back.

Some of the dead were met by angels of light, who accompanied them away from the hospital in a column of light. At the time, especially after I had tried several times to reenter my body, I considered them to be the more blessed ones.

This out-of-body experience alone has given me decades of information to process and try to understand. Narrating this book is actually the first time in my life that I have tried to put all of these experiences into words. I have wondered, pondered, and prayed about them for most of my life, but this is the first time I have tried to describe them aloud. It is interesting to me to see how difficult it is, how few words there are to describe the true meaning of life and what really happens when one dies.

Back at Home

A few days after we arrived home I began to feel improved. I told Lyn about my out-of-body experience and about my visiting her in the waiting room. I told her that I had actually died. She was skeptical, though she found it inexplicable that I knew what magazine article she had been reading and that I could remember it up to the point that she had stopped reading when the speakers blared, "Code Blue, Code Blue!" I told her everything, how she had looked up and then stood up, how she was dangling the magazine from one hand—all of it. She confirmed to me that everything I said was actually true, though she could not bring herself to believe I had actually been dead for twenty minutes.

She asked for an appointment with my doctor, and we both went. She demanded to know the truth of what had happened that day. The doctor would not admit that I had died. The only thing the doctor would say was that "There were some scary moments when your heart stopped. You were not breathing, but we revived you." He completely minimized the experience and told us not to worry about it any further. I think what he was really saying was, "Please don't sue us."

Chapter Two

PARADISE LOST

Rearranging My Life

I thought about these experiences every day thereafter, pondering them and what they meant. There were so many things that were contrary to my long-held beliefs, especially about my biological father and my birth. I carefully recorded these experiences in my journal. I also pondered daily how to change my life to conform to what God had just shown me.

Before this, my life goal was to advance my career, to become a tenured professor, and to retire by the time I was fifty. My goal was to become rich, to become well known, to write books, and to become famous. I wanted to work in the Church, serving in any capacity, working my way "up through the priesthood" as I thought of it at that time, proving myself faithful and of service to the Latter-day Church.

Following this experience beyond the veil, I spent the next ten years rearranging my life from ego-centric to Christ-centric. It was not an easy transition. I came to realize that almost all of my goals were misaligned with God's plan for me. I had been taught all my life to make money, raise a family, get known by the world, and then the Lord will use you in whatever way, because you will be skilled, rich, and available.

I'm not sure if previous to this experience I had subscribed completely to this goal in life, yet it is what I had been taught all my life by leaders, even by both of my mission presidents. It had never completely rung true to me, and now I knew why. Before this time I had been of the mind-set that I needed to get to a place in my life where God could know me—see my good works and my determination, and then He would know what I could do.

After that experience, I knew that God already knew me—in great detail and far better than I knew myself. What he was teaching me in this experience was, *Spencer, you have it wrong. You need to learn to see yourself as I see you and know yourself as I know you—not the other way around. I already know all about you.*

Being out of my body and knowing without a doubt, with total surety, that there is a grand spiritual work and spiritual world that we can't see, took me out of a circle that circumscribed only Spencer, and expanded that circle of my understanding to include this unseen world of heavenly beings, including family members, angels, and Jesus Christ Himself. It changed me forever.

As I mentioned before, it seemed to me as if the angels had left the door open into heaven. I continued to see people differently than before. I could see them to some extent through God's eyes. I could love them more, and the Lord sometimes sent me to help them in ways that would have been impossible otherwise—miraculous ways, it might seem, if one did not realize that God's hand is always working in our lives.

After this life-altering experience, I began getting information from God to give to my clients. I would upon occasion have to wait for them to stop talking so that I could tell them what I had just learned. Over time, as I became more sensitive to spiritual things and more obedient in my response to them, my discernment improved. My insight into their lives improved. I sometimes saw in vision the things that had happened to these clients, and my compassion and understanding was great for them. I couldn't help but be sympathetic.

We Are Never Alone

Another significant thing I learned was that we are never alone.

Angels are always present—both good and evil. I also realized that by my behavior, mood, or thoughts, I was in control of who was in the room with me. I used to feel negative feelings or emotions and feel overpowered by them. I was startled to realize that I was dealing with dark spirits who overwhelmed me when I gave them permission by my emotions. I realized I was in control, and I worked hard to remain positive and loving, to invite divine beings into my life who uplifted me and those around me. It is a tenet of my faith now that, for good or evil, we are never alone.

I also realized that our agency is always honored, so much so that even though there are good angels around us, we still have to invite their intervention. We invite them to assist us by prayer, by having hope, by feeling faith and belief. Even the words we may think quietly or speak to ourselves, even these matter. "Please show me how!" "Please help me!" "Please, God, help me find my keys." "Please God, save my children!" All of these things trigger powerful things from the other side of the veil. They become even more powerful when we have learned to respond to the promptings of the Holy Spirit because then we can be given the answers to these urgent prayers more quickly and profoundly.

Every time God becomes involved in our lives, He is teaching and bringing to pass our eternal life. When Father answers our prayers, He does so through angels, because the angels grow also. They learn what it is like to be "like" God, to serve and to relay God's answers to His children's prayers. This process is extremely orderly and divinely orchestrated. There is no happenstance or coincidence in their work. The good angels are subject to His command and limited or empowered by our faith. There are no "oops" moments when dealing with God or His messengers. Prayers are never not answered correctly due to an error on the other side. Everything happens as God directs.

Redirecting My Life

So now, all of those worldly pursuits that I thought should define my life were taken away. I was shown that much of what I was trying to do was totally wrong for me. I was shown that it was the wrong pursuit—stop it. I attempted to obey. I did complete my education and established my career because I had seen that it was part of the right path for me.

In my work I often call upon Heavenly Father to let the angels that surround me and my client intervene. I do so with complete assurance that God hears me, and the angels respond. Perhaps I have greater faith in this principle than most mortals because I have seen the angels.

Before this time, I had worked in a large hospital with children suffering from cancer. There were times when I would see with spiritual eyes an angelic intervention to lengthen the child's life and knew it would happen. These times resulted in cures that could only be miracles of God. Upon occasion I also realized that a child's life was at an end, and they had completed their mortal work. The child would pass away shortly thereafter. I would then have a great peace, knowing their lives were short but complete, which comfort I could pass on to their parents and family.

At this time I was home teaching a single sister with three children. This sister had brain cancer, and I wanted to cure her. I wanted to call upon the priesthood to heal her. She asked me to give her a blessing, but when I put my hands on her head, I was shown in vision that she would not live out the year. I didn't want to say so, so I gave her a blessing of comfort, but it was not the blessing I wanted to give her, nor was it the blessing Father had shown me He had in store for her.

She turned to me after the blessing, with tears running down her face, and asked, "Why didn't you tell me what you saw? Why didn't you give me the blessing you saw?"

I asked her what she meant.

She said, "I saw the same vision that you saw. I'm not going to live much longer than a year."

I told her, "I was afraid to say it, afraid that it would discourage you and frighten your children."

She replied, "Since it is God's will, it will help me to accept it. It is what I needed to see, and even though you didn't say it out loud, I saw it with you, and I know it is true. Thank you for this blessing."

She lived about eleven more months and then succumbed, leaving her three young children in the hands of family members. It was just one of many powerful experiences where my spiritual sensibilities and spiritual feelings were greatly enhanced. Unfortunately I wasn't strong enough to speak the words properly, so Father showed this young mother the same vision I saw in her behalf. I learned much about my responsibility to do His work; even though fear tries to stop me from saying what has to be said, it is always the right thing to do. I tried from then on not to fear the emotions and concerns of men more than the will of God.

After this out-of-body experience, my life went through a long and difficult evolution, especially when you consider that such decisions were not entirely mine, because these were my wife's and family's dreams as well. I had instilled my dreams into them for years, and now I was faced with trying to teach them why I had changed my life and my goals.

These changes were not accomplished without resistance. Besides my family, almost all of my colleagues, fellow professors, and peers at the universities, even those who had mentored and advanced me at the universities, all resisted the changes I was making. Some of them viewed me as self-destructive, others viewed me as just stupid. There were even a few who told me that I had suffered a mental or emotional breakdown. I listened to all of these people but decided to move forward with determination to do what I had been shown I must do. I left several of my hospital tenures, retired from several university appointments, and focused on my private practice.

During this time of change my health continued to degrade slowly. My immune system was compromised by surgery and many health problems. I had surgeries on my gallbladder, a burst appendix, and sinus surgery because I had continual sinus infections.

I have had rheumatic fever twice, a heart murmur, and every cold and flu that came to town. It is my present realization that I set myself up for these illnesses by continuing the unhealthy emotional state which I acquired from childhood. I had not yet learned to not let those losses manifest themselves as physical illness. Also, I worked long and hard and didn't eat well. I didn't sleep enough. When I exercised, I worked out too hard or ignored exercise for long periods of time.

The last and greatest reason for all of these health problems was that I was blessed to have health crises in order to experience physical death multiple times and thus to see these visions. I know now that before I was born, I chose this course for myself. I was glad to be able to choose this path for my life, and although it has been hard and painful and always terrifying, I still feel as if my life has been tremendously blessed because of this process in my life. I wouldn't go back and choose a different path even if I could.

By this time, Lyn and I had five children. My wife and children were doing well during these times, though we had the normal challenges of young families.

Tahiti

After all of these medical challenges, career alterations, and family growth, my sweetheart and I decided to take a much-needed break from life and go on vacation to Tahiti in March of 1995. We planned to go with Lyn's parents and her siblings. We all left our children home and were excited to get away. Lyn and I hoped to brighten our relationship, our dreams, and my health by total relaxation and rest in a tropical paradise.

We took a long flight to Los Angeles and then to Honolulu. From there we flew to Tahiti. One of the curses that I have struggled with all of my life is that I cannot fall asleep on an airplane. I arrived in Tahiti sleep-deprived after the twenty-four-hour journey. We arrived on the island of Papeete, where the LDS temple is located.

It was warm and beautiful on the island. A gentle, tropical breeze was blowing. We boarded a boat and traveled to the nearby island of Moorea to the small resort there. We arrived to find that the hotel was a series of charming huts, each consisting of one large room under a palm-thatched roof. The walls were open with insect nets for walls. There was a single bathroom toward the back of the bungalow. The rooms were decorated with island art and paintings. It was completely charming.

It was wintertime back at home, so we went from snow drifts to an island paradise. I remember commenting that this was what Bali Hai in the musical *South Pacific* must have been like. There were towering purple volcanic mountains in the center of the island that sloped downward through lush vegetation to a beautiful park, which ended in perfectly white sand and intense, crystal-clear, blue-green ocean. A coral reef protected the island from waves and from large fish and sharks.

My wife's family and I arrived tired from the long trip. There were about twenty-two of us. Each couple had their own cute bungalow on the beach. We agreed to shower and freshen up after the long journey and then meet at the restaurant that was connected to the resort.

I realized I was too fatigued to go to dinner, and I asked my wife to bring me something back from the restaurant. She was concerned for me, but assuming it was just fatigue, she agreed and left. I turned on the shower and the water came out of the shower the color of mud. I was disgusted and let it run until it became clearer. While I showered, my heart was racing. I suspected it was just a lack of sleep. I dressed, laid down on the bed, and started sweating profusely. I knew something was wrong now, but there was no phone in the bungalow. I felt a crushing pain in my chest, which just kept getting worse. I was having difficulty breathing and did not have the ability to call for help.

The next thing I recall was that I rose up out of my body and to the ceiling. It felt the same as when I had died twelve years earlier while getting the x-ray contrast, except that this time I rose upward out of my body instead of departing down through the bed.

My first thought was, *I'm dying in a foreign land!* I worried about how my wife was going to make the arrangements to transport my body back to America and how the children would be devastated.

I also felt like I wanted to leave the hut and explore around the island, but I had a strong sense that I needed to stay with my body. Right at this moment my wife returned to the room. I willed myself to reenter my body, and I whooshed from the ceiling back into my body. I was able to tell her I was very sick. She sat on the edge of the bed and talked to me for a while. I told her that I suspected I was dying, because I was once again having out-of-body experiences.

She was really concerned and took my pulse, which was racing. She went back to the restaurant to get her father and my brother-in-law. They gave me a priesthood blessing. I tried to stay in my body long enough to receive the blessing but was having trouble doing so. I kept feeling like I was floating away. The priesthood blessing mentioned that I would recover, and that I had further work to do in this life. It also said that if anything needed to be done medically, that I would be blessed to be strong enough to wait until we got back into the United States.

Lyn's sister is a registered nurse, and she spoke to the hotel about other medical options on the island. There was a small clinic on the other side of the island. The clinic only had a couple of nurses and an occasional doctor. We decided I would be better off taking my chances staying where I was rather than trying to make the journey to the clinic.

After the blessing they gave me some aspirin, and I decided I would just stay in bed and try to recover. I told them I was going to sleep and assured everyone that I would be okay, though I strongly suspected that I was going to leave my body again. They were comforted and returned to the restaurant to finish their dinner.

I lay in bed praying, pleading with Father that if He needed me to leave mortality, to please let me wait until I got back into the United States where I could do this without ruining these people's vacation. I also felt like it would be really unfortunate to pass from this life in a foreign land for some reason.

I once again left my body and went to the top of the ceiling. There was a large paddle fan at the ceiling which was running on its highest level. I found myself above my body and to the side of the fan. This time the major difference was that I was totally alone. There were no other spirits to greet me or watch after me. I waited a long time by the fan as I felt increasingly more abandoned and bereft of support. It was disconcerting to me to be in a world I knew was filled with spirit beings and yet to be by myself. I again pleaded with Father to please send a righteous spirit to be with me, so that I would not be dead, lost, and alone in this foreign land.

A voice came into my spirit, as if it entered into my bosom, saying that I needed to go through this darkness to understand that which would be forthcoming in my life. I didn't understand what it meant at that time, but have since been able to understand.

It meant that I needed to understand suffering by viewing evil at its darkest. I was naïve at this time in my life. I wanted to believe in the inherent goodness of people. I was shortly going to see in vision a people whose only purpose in living was to do evil. They preferred evil and debauchery over everything else. They delighted in other people's suffering and were bored and depressed when they were not hurting someone. I did not even know such people existed, let alone constituting a whole society.

I had been shown great light—visions of God and angels—and in order to comprehend greater truth and greater light, now I had to understand its opposite—the pure evil side of the equation. All things in mortality and eternity exist in opposites. To comprehend greater and greater light, I had to also comprehend greater darkness. Even Jesus Christ had to descend below all things before He could rise above all things. The same seemed to be true for me, though in a far lesser degree than our Savior of course. Still, the divine laws that govern these blessings demand the juxtaposition of good and evil, and I had to understand by personal experience.

Therefore, I had to experience feeling this frightening alone-ness—this separation from God. I had never experienced this pre-viously. I apparently also needed to know what it was like to feel completely devoid of the Holy Spirit in order to appreciate and un-derstand the greater blessings I had been shown could be mine.

It was as if God was saying, "This is the time appointed for you, Spencer, to experience these dark things." So, I found myself strug-gling with viewing things I had never, ever imagined could be true. Being on vacation in this faraway place, a place with a dark history, where my work and my children, family, and wife were distracted by other things, became the perfect setting for this dark chapter of my education in heavenly things.

While I was floating near the ceiling, my wife and one of her sisters came into the room. They thought I was sleeping, so they checked on me, touching my shoulder, and then they quietly left the room. They looked at one another and agreed that I was sleep-ing. They left me and sat on the front porch of our bungalow. I was not sleeping but was out of my body watching this happen from the viewpoint of the ceiling. I did not know if I was dead or alive, because this felt much different than my experience twelve years ago. At this point I still did not have the ability to leave the bungalow.

The Diorama of Hell

The rest of what I am now going to relate, I still don't completely understand. It was shown to me as if it were a diorama passing in front of my spiritual body. It was three-dimensional, but I was not in the scene, I was looking at it as a spectator. What I was shown was the history of the spiritual and non-spiritual practices of the ancient Tahitians.

I was shown that initially they were an enlightened and spirit-filled people, even innocent and undefiled. They knew about Jesus Christ, His role, and His mission, which had come to them from holy men and women who had established their cultural heritage. I saw that their understanding deteriorated over the years as their founders died, and those who believed became fewer in number. They sank to the most gross and graphic form of human torture, debauchery, sexual perversions, and spiritual darkness imaginable. Actually none of it was imaginable to me, I just saw it and was sickened. In truth, I'm still haunted by the memory of it. Among many other heinous things, they were sacrificing young virgins and killing infants and children in the most awful manner they could devise. It was horrifying to me then and horrifying to me now, because I saw it as it had happened, in great detail. They were doing this in part because of false religion, and in part to avenge themselves of similar atrocities of their enemies. Their minds and hearts, and everything they did, were saturated by war, revenge, and a lust for everything evil.

I could see and feel each person involved in these atrocities. I could feel the hatred, rage, and resentment of those who were doing these horrifying acts, as well as the fear and anguish of their victims. I was spared actually feeling their pains, but I experienced them on a spiritual level that was not actually pain but an understanding of how horrible it had been for them.

I could also hear the prayers of the few people among them who were still followers of Jesus Christ, who had the Holy Spirit, who were still hanging onto the truth. These faithful few were like scattered little fires of truth all over these islands. They hated what was happening to their people and mourned the generations that were lost. They were also compelled to deep secrecy of their beliefs, for believers were prized as victims.

Not only was I seeing the suffering and horrifying pains of those who were being tortured, but I was seeing evil spirits who were reveling in their pain. These evil spirits were glorying in it and urging the mortals to do worse and worse things, giving them "inspiration" on how to prolong the suffering of their victims.

I don't believe mortals could even think of such evil acts and then forge a society and tradition of such debauchery without the evil spirits urging them and instructing them in not just performing these acts but in how to also "religionize" it over many years to make it become traditional and acceptable to their entire society. The whole scene reached such an insane hyper-frenzy of evil that it was frightening to me beyond anything I have ever experienced, before or since. I tried to turn away, but the vision would not leave my eyes.

I personally felt like I was being exposed to the depths of hell. I was completely repulsed by this vision, although I knew that I was not being punished in any way. But it persisted for some time until I was sick in my soul and begged most earnestly to have it end.

In my first experience in 1983, I experienced nothing like this. There was no dark or horrifying side to that experience. Now all of this was poured out upon me in all of its hellish hue. All this time I was pleading for God to close up this vision and asking Him, "Why must I see this? What does it have to do with me?"

I cried out to see no more of this horror with all the power of my being, and I was finally released from the dark vision in front of me.

The Intercessory Prayer

I next found myself transported to the outside of the Beehive House in Salt Lake City. This struck me as quite odd, to go from viewing the dark history of Tahiti from a distance to actually being there in Salt Lake City. I was no longer looking at a vision but found myself participating in what was happening, actually experiencing it with all of my senses, not just seeing it.

The first thing I saw was television cameras and other media people surrounding the Beehive House. They seemed to be from all around the world. There were news people speaking Japanese, Chinese, French, and many other languages, including English. I recognized local TV stations and crews.

These journalists were standing on the west side of the building mostly and in the corridor between the Church Office Building and the Lion House. They were surrounding that whole group of buildings.

Finding myself delivered from that horrible vision in Tahiti and now standing in and among news crews in Salt Lake City, I thought, *What am I doing here? What are all these people doing around here?* I was asking this question of God.

At this point I remember beginning to accept that I was dead, and that my body was still in Tahiti. I felt sorry for Lyn because she was going to find me dead soon. I knew she loved me and that it was going to be a terrible shock to her.

I began to feel the spiritual powers I had felt before, to go where I desired and to read people's minds and hearts. I no longer felt lost in the circumstances around me. So I asked, "Why am I here?"

There were no other spirits there that I could see. I could only see the mortals around me. I again asked God, "What is going on?" He replied, "You are not going to die in Tahiti. However, I will show you that which will surely come to pass."

I was told that this vision was a metaphor, a "type" of things that would shortly happen, not an actual occurrence that I was viewing, or even that it would happen just this way.

At that moment I could feel the thoughts and the emotion of all these individuals waiting around the buildings. They were excited, in great anticipation of some important event. Among some of them, especially the local news crews, there was fear and sadness. They had long poles with those fuzzy microphones on the end, as if they were expecting an announcement of some type. I discerned that they were waiting for the announcement that the current prophet of the Church had passed away. This caused me to sorrow because the current prophet was my friend. In the course of my service, I had been in meetings with him many times, and I loved him.

I found myself at the back of the Beehive House. I had never been there before. There were metal stairs going one flight up the back with a green door at the top. The stairs looked like an emergency exit rather than a part of the original plan of the building. I climbed the stairs like a normal person, step by step. I could feel and hear my footsteps, and I could feel the handrail with my left hand. It was perfectly vivid and real to me. I arrived at the top and opened the door, which felt hard and cool to the touch. There was a security guard sitting at a raised desk with a video monitor right inside the door. He was watching the screen intently. He did not see me or acknowledge me. I again asked, "What am I doing here?"

The voice I had heard earlier replied, "You have much to learn. Go down the hall."

So I walked down a long hall, and at the other end of the hall there was another security guard facing me. He was sitting outside of a door to my left on a folding chair. He was reading a set of scriptures. It was a triple combination with a name embossed on the cover. I didn't attempt to read the name; I just assumed they were the guard's scriptures.

I moved past him and through the door without opening it. I did this because I knew I was in spirit form and did not need to open the door. I found myself in a square bedroom, about twelve by twelve feet, with a tall, pitched ceiling. There was a large bed to my left with a patchwork quilt that was ornate and beautiful. It looked to be an antique. The furniture was old and beautifully crafted. The room appeared to be a set, like in a museum. There was an antique washing stand with a porcelain pitcher and basin.

After I had taken this all in, I was suddenly aware of an elderly man kneeling on an antique oval rag rug beside the bed. I realized at once that it was my apostolic friend of many years. Initially I could not hear what he was saying, and even so, I felt like I was intruding. I discerned that he could not see or hear me. As I mentioned, this was a vision to teach me, not an actual happening. I asked again, "What am I doing here?" because I felt like I had no right to be here.

I turned to leave the room, and then I started hearing him speak. The voice of the Spirit said to me, "Listen well."

Because he and I had worked together on several church projects, we had become personal friends. I turned back to face him, still feeling that I was intruding upon sacred events I should not be seeing or hearing.

I was shown this great friend and servant of God in an intercessory prayer with Father regarding himself and what he would experience in the future. He was pleading for the will of the Father to take place in his behalf and his family, and that he would be able to endure it well and be empowered to "drink of the bitter cup without becoming bitter myself." These are words I heard him speak as he poured out his heart in prayer.

It was confusing to go from seeing the debauchery of Tahiti's past to this sacred scene of suffering and righteous acceptance of the Lord's will. I now believe the stark contrast was to teach me how suffering could actually sanctify and bring about exaltation when the sufferer submits to Christ and lets that suffering purify and complete their mortal experience. I was watching my friend begin his journey into this suffering. He was not praying for escape, but for strength to endure it well.

I learned by all this that it is through suffering that mortals learn compassion and endurance and faithfulness—but that there has to also be a great willingness to be purified and uplifted in this way. I was seeing my own future in a way too. I understood that I would also be called to suffer so that I too could be purified, completed, and Christ-like when I left mortality, and I had to submit to this process willingly. This is what the angel meant when he told me, "I will show you that which will surely come to pass." He was saying, "You will suffer, and you will successfully submit and thereby be purified." It has taken me many years to arrive at this understanding. I don't believe I was prepared to submit to any more suffering than I was then experiencing at that time, being dead in Tahiti and all that that implied. The Lord has been merciful in allowing me to learn in that moment, and then I could more fully embrace when I was prepared many years later.

My vision changed. I saw that my friend was in the same position, beside the same bed. The only thing that had changed was that the rug under his knees appeared to be a sheepskin rug. This time I was astonished to realize that he was pleading for me, in my behalf, and for what I was going to be going through. He was speaking in the same fashion as before, but pleading this time for me. He was weeping. Both of these prayers were long, protracted, and beautiful pleadings with Father. His words overwhelmed me. I felt deep concern that I was somehow creating this pain and struggle in my friend. It also confused and troubled me that he had seen something of my future struggles, which obviously worried him in my behalf. I had no idea what future struggles he knew awaited me.

I asked Father in mighty prayer, "Please bless this man that if it be possible he might not have to endure these things on my account," and I pled to know, "What have I done? What has happened to me to cause my friend this struggle in my behalf? Why am I seeing this? Please help me to learn what I must learn from this!"

I was frightened that he must have seen in my future that I was going to make some great mistake or walk away from my ordained path, which is something I never hoped to do. It frightened me to ponder these possibilities.

Beloved Prophet

At that exact moment, I turned and looked to the right side of the bed, and I saw the current prophet of the Church. You will recall that I knew this noble servant of God well from my service with him and others of the Twelve. I also remembered the reporters outside the building waiting for the announcement of his death.

He was smiling at me. He said to me without moving his mouth. "Spencer, it will all be all right."

My Apostle friend was still kneeling there, and I still felt like I was intruding in his prayers and supplications. I was confused by seeing the Prophet in this visionary metaphor. Because this was not an actual event, I understood that my friend could not hear or see either myself or the Prophet.

The Prophet then started walking toward me. To my knowledge the Prophet was still alive, yet here I was seeing him as a spirit. I also wondered why I, who was not going to die in Tahiti according to what I had just been told, was here in this room witnessing all of this. The last time I had seen the Prophet was at the dedication of a temple two months earlier. He was in a wheelchair and frail and appeared not to have much time left on the earth.

When I saw him in the room, he was spry with a bounce to his step. His voice was strong and clear. He was buoyant in his spirit and smiling from ear to ear as he walked toward me in this vision. He was, as I re-membered him from long ago, soft as velvet but a true lion of the Lord.

He said to me, "It is time for me to leave." He put his arm through my right arm and escorted me outside the room. We passed through the door without opening it. Yet I could feel his arm on mine as if we were both mortal.

He stopped in the hall and told me he was looking forward to once again seeing my grandfather and grandmother with whom he had served when he had been a stake president and my grandfather was a bishop serving under him. He then let go of my arm and turned to me, looking at me earnestly, and again said, "It will all be all right."

I did not know what he meant. My mind was worried about my body in Tahiti and about my Apostle friend, and about why I was see-ing the Prophet and this whole vision. I did not reply but was taking it all in with considerable amazement and confusion.

The Prophet continued walking away from me, down the hall in the direction I had come in. He turned back to me and exclaimed, "Just like my Savior said, it is finished!" I knew he was speaking of his own life and rejoicing that it was now over and that he had tri-umphed. He nodded to the guard and smiled as he addressed him by name, "Ryan." The guard nodded and respectfully replied, "President."

The Prophet then walked through the closed door by the guard and disappeared from my sight.

I was amazed to see the guard acknowledge him because I had previously thought the guard was a mortal who could not see me, but now I realized that he was an angel with a real body. I couldn't tell if he was resurrected or translated, but he was not a spirit.

I felt it was time for me to leave also, and I proceeded to follow the Prophet through the door. The guard looked at me and called me by name. "Spencer, would you wait a second?"

I paused at the door and turned back. The guard closed the scrip-tures he had been reading, zipped the cover closed, and then handed them to me. I took them and noted that my name was embossed at the bottom of the scriptures. Both the book and the cover were green. I had never before seen the standard works with a green cover. I was pleased to receive them and mystified by the symbolism I sensed but could not understand.

I thanked him warmly, took the scriptures, and left by walking through the door. I never spoke of this experience to my wife, but the following Christmas, she gave me a green copy of the scriptures, embossed exactly as in this vision. I have treasured it all these years.

I have since realized that seeing the green scriptures in vision and then receiving the identical books in the flesh was a witness that what I had seen in the vision would in time manifest in the flesh. It was not a comforting realization, but I also accepted that the suffering I had seen in the vision of Tahiti and heard of in the prayers of the Apostle in my behalf were essential to my growth. I also knew, "It will be all right."

My next recollection was reentering my body in Tahiti. Returning to my body this time was much more painful than in 1983 after the failed medical procedure. After a long while I felt well enough to sit on the edge of my bed, making sure my spirit was once again firmly inside my body. My body felt heavy, so I just sat there. It was now the middle of the night. My wife was asleep behind me in the bed. I sat there a long time, thinking about the vision and what it might mean. There were many things about it that even today are not clear to me.

It took about three days for my body to regain some strength. I joined my wife and family on vacation but moved slowly and rested often for the several weeks of our trip until it was time to return home. I shared some of my experiences in the vision with my wife. She believed what I told her and expressed gratitude that I had not died and had stayed with her. She was sweet about it, and I appreciated her willingness to just believe me without any possibility of proof.

While we were still in Tahiti, we heard word that the Prophet had passed away on the night that I had been out of my body and had seen the vision of him. This caused me to ponder over and over what I had experienced in the vision, if it was really him or just a vision. I rehearsed it again and again in my mind. There was so much of it that I could not understand; first and foremost was why it had happened to me!

My mind went back to the horrible scenes of Tahiti's history. It felt like I had been allowed to see what the human condition can deteriorate to when the light of Christ and truth are extinguished.

It seemed to me that the Spirit of God had withdrawn from all but a few of those people, and this had left them in the grip of Satan's power. I felt like Satan was still laughing and rejoicing in the condition into which they had devolved.

I pondered why I was allowed to interact with the Prophet, who had just died that same night. He was exuberant to be out of his body. I saw what he had gone through in his life and in his own experience with approaching death, and I had never realized any of it. I didn't even realize the experiences our Prophet had endured in his life which created his velvet-and-steel persona and character that was required to fulfill his earthly mission. I saw how he had been forged in the refiner's fire and how he had endured it well unto the end of his life.

It occurred to me then, that you don't have to be an Apostle or prophet for the Lord to search after you, and refine you and purify you into your greatest self.

I have come to believe that what I was being shown was the extremes of human experience—the dark and the pure. The experience is hard for me to talk about even now. It brings back vivid memories I wish I had never seen yet can't seem to forget.

The flight back to Utah was difficult for me. When we got home, I went in to see my cardiologist to see what he thought about my experience and the horrible pains I had experienced in my chest. He did an EKG and a treadmill test. They found that I had a valve that wasn't working well. I believe the cause of my second experience with death was this faulty valve. He wanted to insert a pig valve into my heart to replace the faulty one. I declined surgery to replace it because I felt impressed that it wasn't necessary. Since that time, my heart has completely recovered, and I have not had a similar episode.

CHAPTER THREE

VISION OF THE SAVIOR

I t seemed to me that following these near-death experiences, the angels left the doors to heaven ajar. I began to see many things of the Spirit. I did not think I was anything unique that I should have visions or prophetic dreams, yet they came to me often after these earlier struggles, and they still do. I sometimes feel as if the doorway into heaven is right before me, and with an act of will, I could step through it, but I never have. The temptation to not return to mortality would be too great, I fear, and I would step out of the ordained mortal path I now see before me.

Vision of the Savior

The following vision is the first one I experienced without having to die. I was sleeping, but it was not a dream. I was not "seeing" it, but rather was present in the vision, experiencing it with my five senses. The phrase Paul used to explain such an experience was, "Whether in the body, or out of the body, I know not." It was exactly that real to me, and that difficult to tell if I was once again out of my body or experiencing it in the flesh.

It was about 4:00 a.m. by the time I got to bed that night. I had been completing some important work and had lost track of time. I was exhausted as I lay down after saying my prayers, and I fell into a deep sleep.

My first recollection was that I was hurrying from the parking lot toward a stake center where I had been assigned to speak. It was the same building I attended every Sunday for years. In my mind I was late for a leadership meeting and was therefore rushing into the building. I was halfway up the walk on the backside of the church when I heard, "Spencer."

The voice was familiar to me, and I turned around to see who had spoken my name. I was astonished to see Jesus Christ standing in the parking lot where the sidewalk begins. I knew His face. I had never before seen Him in mortality, yet I knew Him. His face is the most familiar face in the universe. My spirit instantly knew Him, remembered Him, and loved Him. I remembered everything about Him, everything He has done for me.

It felt to my soul as if I was seeing my most beloved friend for the first time after decades of absence. I felt my heart racing in my chest. He did not introduce Himself because I recognized Him immediately. He communicated with me verbally, but every word He spoke was rich with non-verbal truth that entered my soul far faster than words.

He was wearing a vibrant red robe that hung across His right shoulder, and was tied up with a clasp on His left shoulder. He wore a cloth belt of the same color about His waist. The robe hung to His ankles and hands and had long sleeves. He wore old-time sandals on His feet.

He was tall, possibly a little over six feet. His form was masculine. He had a sturdy build with big shoulders and strong limbs. His face was not thin, as is depicted in some paintings, but full with high cheekbones. He had a dark beard that was closely trimmed. His hair was the color of His beard and was long enough to touch His shoulders. His eyes were the most beautiful and clearest blue one can imagine.

He smiled at me, and I dropped my briefcase and ran to Him. His arms engulfed me. I can't find words to explain how it felt to be embraced by Him. A flood of memories returned of being comfortable in His arms long before. I felt His love for me radiating from Him. I knew by instinct that He knew everything about me, yet there was no sense of judgment. I felt from Him a complete sense of His confidence in me and in my capacity. It was amazing to me, because I have never had a lot of confidence in myself.

I did not look for the marks in His hands and feet. I don't know why I didn't look, even today. I remember thinking later that day, why didn't I look? Perhaps it was because I did not need to see His wounds to know it was Him. I was so taken by His love, power, radiance, unlimited capacity, vast knowledge, and perfections that it never entered my mind to look.

His feet were not on the ground. I was surprised how he could hold me with such firmness. He was standing—not floating—but he was not standing upon our mortal world. He was not occupying the same space that I was on this planet. In that space that He was occupying, everything was radiating from Him, as if He were the sun and everything rotated around and came from Him.

His face was welcoming, smiling, pleased to be with me. It felt like we had embraced like this often before, which surprised me. My family is not "huggy," and I had never learned to enjoy long or emotional hugging. Yet in this embrace, I wished it could go on forever. After a long while He put His hands on my shoulders and pushed me gently to arm's length.

He looked me in the eye and told me He was pleased with my life thus far. He thanked me earnestly for my service in His name. He told me that He loved me and that from this time forward I would do much good for the Kingdom. He paused for a second, then added that the righteous desire of my heart would be granted. I knew exactly which desire He meant. It was my great desire that I truly would rise to endure my future trials well and thereby be purified.

Little did I know that there was so much more to righteously desire than I could possibly perceive at that time. As the years passed, I learned many more things I fervently desired to do, and all of them became the richest longings of my heart, all of them falling within the promise I had just heard.

What Is in a Name?

He again said, "Spencer," and for a moment I saw myself as He sees me and knew myself as He knows me. As I mentioned earlier, to God and angels, someone's name is a spiritual container for everything that can be known about a person—past, present, and future.

In that moment He spoke my name, I was given to see and feel the full meaning of my name to Him. It melted my heart and still does to this day every time I think of how He said my name. The love he bestowed upon me in that one word cannot be described in any mortal language.

So when I read Isaiah or Samuel, where the Lord speaks their names, or where the Lord calls Nephi or Moses by their name, I believe I know what they felt. When I read of the first vision and hear, "Joseph, this is my beloved son," I wish everyone could know what young Joseph experienced when he heard the Lord say his name. Because when you hear your name from the lips of our Savior, you never again hear your name the same way—ever.

Since that time, when people say my name who don't really know who I am, it almost feels as if they are treading on sacred things.

It also makes me marvel at the many names Jesus Christ has in the scriptures, because each name and title bears within it some unspeakable language that contains the full and true meaning of that part of the Lord's glory and perfections.

In the few long seconds that He held me, Jesus taught me many things that entered my soul as a burst of pure knowledge. These were precious and spiritually intimate things, all of which thrilled me to the center of my being, but I was not allowed to remember them in detail after the experience ended. I only remember receiving those things and rejoicing, but the details have evaporated. I hope in a future day to hear Him speak them all again.

He nodded toward the stake center and said, "You are needed. You need to go to your assignment." I took a step back, still looking at Him, wishing I did not have to leave, but He had instructed me to go, and I turned and took a few steps away. I stopped and turned back. He again spoke my name, and I was again engulfed in love and tears. As I watched, He began to fade slowly, then He was gone.

I immediately became aware of my bed and bedroom. I was weeping openly, joyfully, in a way I had never before experienced. The joy of this vision was so supernal that I was rejuvenated and sleep left me. I immediately got up and wrote all of this down in my journal. When morning finally came, I dressed and proceeded with my day without any trace of fatigue or sleepiness.

I read my journal from time to time now, and I see the profound incapacity I had at that time to be able to express this experience in words. Even today, it is clear that there may not even be words to express such an experience.

I remember pondering it the next day. I opened a hymnal and read the words to "I know That My Redeemer Lives." The words of that hymn express better what I experienced than my own words could at that time.

To Really Know

To really *know* that He lives, that He is a perfect, benevolent friend who loves me enough to leave the heavens, come to earth and take the time to embrace me, to have a relationship with me, and with all of us who seek Him—this is the sweetest knowledge I have ever known. To know that He knows you far better than you know yourself, and yet He loves you better still and is willing to show you who you are in His sight and what you are capable of—this is why I love Him so, because He first loved me.

How Far Man Is Fallen

One of the things that struck me then, and still does today, is how far we have fallen. I have mentioned this before, but it keeps coming back in these visions. I believed at that time in my life that the Fall was mostly about Adam and Eve and this earth. But I keep being shown that it is even more about mankind and how powerfully the Fall darkened all of our senses. We lost our memory, not only of God, but even more sadly, of ourselves. We don't understand our own worth. The scriptures teach us of God's glory but hardly mention the glory that mankind left when we accepted the mortal challenge.

I have come to realize that the Fall has a profound effect upon us. The fall separated us from the presence of God so thoroughly that we no longer hear the word of the Lord as we could if we schooled ourselves by obedience to Him. Our hearts and our minds are cloud-ed and impaired—handicapped by the Fall. We are spiritual "Special Needs" people, quite literally disabled in every possible way. We are, in God's view, a mortal child who was born blind, mentally impaired, and paralyzed.

This is not an exaggeration. When we fell to mortality, we could no longer see existence as it truly is, full of spiritual beings on un-countable worlds. We fell from being intelligent enough to under-stand vast truths. We participated in the creation of worlds before we were born, but at the moment of birth, our greatest skill is the ability to suck. Before we became mortal we could go to far distant places in the blink of an eye to serve God. Our backyard was the vast creations of God; but after birth, our greatest physical ability was to blink and swallow. We left God able to see distant galaxies and gaze into the past and future, but after birth we could hardly focus upon our mother's face.

This is the glorious, indescribable power of our Lord and Savior, that He offers us a means to bring us back out of this mortal darkness and back into His presence, where all of these divinely engineered flaws are wiped away, and we become far more than what we were before. He wants us to have all that we had before and much more, and He gave His life to not only provide the path to these glorious things, but also to bestow upon us the empowerment of His grace, so that we are sanctified by Christ. Then He changes us to be like Him, not because we deserve it, but because He loves us and has empow-ered us to triumph when we obey Him.

Trying to Make Sense

A difficult outcome of this experience was that I kept asking my-self, "What am I going to do with this information?" I didn't feel like I should go telling everyone I met. I didn't know what to say or how to say it. I didn't have the words to express it. I suddenly felt isolated. One of the hardest aspects of obtaining some vast knowledge, I have found, is having nobody to talk to about it, no way to express it, and no way to rejoice with another mortal.

Another dilemma I encountered was that I didn't know how to reconcile the person I knew myself to be with the profound nature of what I was shown I could be. I knew I hadn't earned it, that I wasn't good enough to deserve it. I didn't even know how to become the person that Christ had shown me I could become. There was a gulf of darkness in my understanding. I could clearly see who I was then, and I could clearly see who I could become—but I could not fathom how to transition between the two. It was like a caterpillar being shown that it would one day become a butterfly. It was glorious, but I just couldn't imagine how it could ever come to pass.

One of the most difficult aspects of this was that I felt compelled to "make sense" of these visions and experiences. I was an educated man with three advanced degrees, and I wanted to create a purpose, maybe a calling or a divine mission for myself from all of these things. I wanted to invent or create a way to arrive at what I had seen I could become. So I went through the process of reasoning, "So this must mean that . . ." and then I would try to make whatever I had concluded happen. This was a terrible mistake. I found that none of my logic could penetrate these mysteries, and no amount of pondering or deduction could show me how to get from where I then was to where Christ had shown me I could go.

About twenty years later, my Apostle friend finally cleared that up for me during a private meeting. He said, "Spencer, do not make the error of trying to read meaning into these experiences. Just accept them as they are. Don't try to put your interpretation on it. Keep your own logic out of it. It is what it is. When you try to interpret it, it will lead you down roads where you should not go. Keep the experience pure. Wait for the Lord to reveal the meaning of it to you. Wait for the Lord to give you the interpretation. Wait for the further light and knowledge the Lord still has to give to you so you can complete your mission."

Healing the Children

In this experience I also learned that I had chosen the right profession. I knew my work with damaged and abused children was my calling at this time. I felt great peace in the knowledge that I would be able, in some small way, to impart safety and peace to these injured children. And because of this, there was a healing of my own abuse when I was a child, because Christ was doing for me what I did professionally for these children. I was bringing them to Christ where all true healing occurs. Only Christ can heal these children, especially when they have been emotionally, sexually, or physically abused.

From that day onward I could go into a room, or sit on the stand in sacrament meeting, and I knew who in the audience had gone through those abusive experiences. This gift of discernment in knowing who I should serve and how to serve them has been the whole reason for any success I have seen in my profession.

Since that time, I have frequently gone to public events, such as a symphony or a civic activity, and while sitting there, the Spirit would say clearly about some stranger in the audience, "You are going to work with that child." In a few weeks, or even a year, that person and often their whole family would enter into therapy with me. It is a wonderful but painful gift of the Spirit.

I say it is painful because of this unusual capacity I gained to go with them to those dark and evil places in their hearts, and to retrieve them—snatch sometimes, or coax them, with the help of Christ—out of that darkness into the light. They experience a type of being born again. When an adult or child will submit to this process and allow me to act as Christ's agent in guiding them through this, they are healed of that abuse completely and permanently—even as I was when I met the Savior that first time.

There is a parallel to this healing I am blessed to undertake from time to time. Christ had to be abused, spat upon, and cruelly treated as an essential part of completing the Atonement. He descended below all things, so that He could overcome all things. And when He overcame all things, then He was prepared to take us by the hand and lift us above all things. In a much smaller way, this is what I attempt to do with the children. I experienced the darkness of childhood abuse both in the womb and in life, and when Christ healed me, then I was enabled in some way I don't fully understand to be a part of healing the children.

In similar ways, we each experience trials and cruel experiences, but if we come unto Christ and let Him heal us, then we can reach out and bring others to Christ for their own healing. It is a gift to do so, but we must pass through our own sorrows so that we can serve Christ in His name.

Layers of Meaning

The last thing I want to mention that I learned from this experience is that anytime Christ descends and speaks to a mortal, it is so weighty with meaning that mere words cannot convey the fulness of the truths given. The message is layered. First are the words He speaks, and then there is a vastly larger body of truth you receive spiritually, layer upon layer, more truth than you can understand for years afterward. One small moment in the presence of the Savior can last for a lifetime.

This is the reason the scriptures are so powerful, because they contain the words spoken by Christ, and this layered truth is still there, spiritually interwoven with those words. It takes a lifetime of spiritual growth and obedience to be able to receive the deeper layers. They are truly there, and they contain the great mysteries and greater truths He desires that we acquire and enjoy in our lifetime. Any circumstance we find ourselves in, the answers are given within the recorded experiences of people who spoke with the Savior.

As life-changing as these early experiences were and as much as I learned by these things, they were but the overture to the grand symphony still awaiting me.

I was shown and learned many things I must yet accomplish in mortality. I was given a great mission to fulfil if I was true and faithful. I will relate much of this future mission in the chapters to come.

CHAPTER FOUR

DEEPENING TRIALS

Following this time, I had four or five major experiences with angelic visitors and visions. These were not near-death experiences but mostly occurred during many sleepless nights. Each of these experiences felt real, with all of my senses fully active.

Waiting to Die

The visions I had seen never departed from my thinking, especially when I grew quite ill. The next few years were full of fear and uncertainty. I completely, powerfully believed the things that I had seen, but I also believed I had to be alive to accomplish them. The fear and uncertainty arose from the growing sense that I was never going to recover and would die having not accomplished my life's work.

I had continual pain with my teeth and sinuses. My health and energy got progressively worse. Everything I had seen in the experience of my Apostle friend and the Prophet came to pass. I now understood why my friend was praying so earnestly for me.

I had chronic sinus infections that would not respond to treatment. My health insurance dropped me, which was a terrible blow because my health was faltering, and I was counting on the insurance to provide for me during this time.

I was continually trying to reconcile what I had seen in these visions with the rather obvious fact that I was dying. I considered it obvious that if I died, I wouldn't be able to do the things I had seen. Dying also seemed to mean that I had failed to complete my life's mission and God had taken me from the earth for that reason. As you can see, I was in survival mode, struggling to move forward but paralyzed by awful health, doubts, and fears.

It was about this time that I was released as a counselor in the bishopric due to my illness. I was simply not able to complete my calling as I wanted and as the Bishop needed. I asked to be released, but it was a difficult and emotionally damaging decision because it seemed to confirm my fears that I was not going to be able to do the things I had seen in vision.

Looking at this time of my life from the perspective of twenty additional years, I can also see that my own fear was adding to my sickness.

My life became a round of trying to rest enough to work a few hours, then going back to bed, then struggling to work a little more. I was pretty sure that my life was about over, and I admit I was scared.

I was convinced my problem was with my heart. But every doctor I went to found something new to diagnose. I became so ill that I really believed this was the end of my life. I was just going to slowly get worse and worse until I passed away.

The experience of hearing my friend pleading for my life became a reality. He was still alive at this time, of course, and came to my home six or seven times to give me blessings and to comfort me.

An Apostle's Advice

One Thursday afternoon, after his meetings with the Quorum of the Twelve in the temple, my Apostolic friend came over while I was too sick to get out of bed. I was pleased he came to visit. I counted him a dear friend and confidant. I had been allowed to relate to him many of my visions and experiences. He helped me greatly to understand some of them. The others he taught me to accept that they were of divine origin and to wait upon the Lord for further light and knowledge. I leaned upon his wisdom and probably could not have endured this time and this suffering without him.

He sat at the end of my bed and literally stayed there for forty-five minutes without speaking. I tried to make conversation, but it failed.

I finally said, "Elder, I know you are very busy. There must be a reason you came over. Do you have something to tell me? I'm going to stop talking and just listen."

He was silent for another few minutes, then said, "Spencer, you need to learn to be content with what the Lord has allotted you."

To be honest, it wasn't what I had hoped to hear. It didn't sound like profound apostolic advice or a promise that I would get well. I felt like he did not understand how sick I was and how horribly this was interfering with the mission I had seen in my visions. But in the days and weeks following, I began to realize that this truly was a message from the Lord. I was consumed with my education and with all of the work and time I had spent preparing to be able to do what I was doing with the children. I wanted things to be the way I wanted them to be. I was not willing, or maybe just not aware, of how to accept that the Lord had a different purpose and resolve for my life.

I felt similar to the little cottage C. S. Lewis describes. I just wanted to be a little cottage, but the Lord wanted to rebuild me into a mansion. I was expecting a remodeling, a little upgrading, and some new carpet. The Lord was knocking my entire house down all around me because it had to go in order to make place for His master plan for my life. He wasn't remodeling me, he was rebuilding me.

I couldn't understand the visions anymore because I had accepted the idea that I was going to die. But all of the other experiences and visions I had had indicated that I was going to live far longer and do much more. I had often discussed the obvious paradox of my life with my apostle friend. I think what he was telling me was to quit plotting a course for my life and just trust the Lord to bring me to those things my faith was telling me I would do. He was trying to assure me that everything I had been promised would come to pass but that I needed to quit fighting against the process that the Lord had engineered to bring me there.

It was difficult for me to see at that time. I was in a condition of having the trees block my view of the forest. I didn't realize I was already in the forest. I saw the forest as far, far away, and I was struggling to survive long enough to fight my way there. I was holding up the process by insisting upon arriving there on my own terms and preferably without suffering and death being a part of the path.

Cancer

A little later I went to an oral surgeon to find out why my face hurt so badly on my left side. It had become unbearable, and no pain killer I possessed would touch it. It felt like my face was on fire. I could not touch any part of my face under my left eye. I couldn't sleep on that side because the pillow hurt my face.

The surgeon did tests and found a darkened area in the x-ray, which led to a diagnosis of osteomyelitis of the jawbone and orbital bones. This was not known to be cancer as of yet, but my infected jawbone and sinus cavity needed to be removed. He said parts of my jaw and facial bone would have to be replaced by titanium plates. He said I would lose all of my teeth in my upper left jaw and that I needed the surgery immediately. It was hard news to hear. My wife and I wept and talked about what to do for many hours.

I got three other opinions, which only confirmed the first doctor's diagnosis. At the same time, my cardiologist and regular physician both believed I would not survive the surgery. My whole team of doctors concluded that I should just go home and prepare to die.

In my short life thus far, I had made many good friends, people whom I loved and who loved me. This included a young lawyer in the area who visited me often and kept track of my life. He had a good friend named Jason who had recovered from cancer similar to mine. Jason was a righteous man who considered that his healing had been an intervention from God, and he had covenanted with God that he would use all of his means to help anyone the Lord showed him, particularly in situations similar to his. Subsequent to his covenant, God had given him considerable wealth to fulfill this promise.

My lawyer friend had introduced Jason to a German physician practicing in Mexico who was having great success with replacing the diseased bone with sea coral instead of titanium. This procedure caused less trauma to the body and facial tissues, and the coral was not attacked by the immune system as a foreign body, so the chances of success were much higher.

Surgery in Mexico

When Jason found out that I didn't have insurance, our merciful Savior moved upon him to fulfill his covenant in my behalf. Through my lawyer friend, Jason offered to pay all of my expenses to go to Mexico to have this surgery.

My wife and I prayed for guidance and the Spirit testified to me that this was what I should do. Ultimately I went to Mexico three times for three surgeries—two major surgeries and one minor one. Jason paid for all of it, including Lyn's travel and expenses. The interesting thing is that Jason hadn't met me at the time. I met him for the first time three or four years after the surgeries. He came into my life in a miracle, and he has never allowed me to even suggest repaying him. He humbly assures me that it is a miracle and a privilege to have been an instrument in the Lord's hands. I continue to praise God for him to this day.

The second surgery was the most complicated and lasted eight hours. They removed my cancerous sinus and upper jaw and placed pulverized sea coral into its place. Even so, I returned home three days after the surgery.

Two days after arriving home, I unwisely agreed to give a lecture at the Justice Center in Salt Lake City. I did this because we were desperate for money, and it was an opportunity to make up some lost income. I didn't feel good enough to go, and I didn't feel I should. I'm quite sure the Holy Spirit even warned me against it, but the mortal world was loud and insistent, and I yielded to the wrong enticement.

Early in my presentation, my heart began to race. I started burning up with fever. I sat down right on the floor in the middle of the lecture. One of my colleagues took me home. My wife quickly took me to my doctor's office. I was diagnosed with an infection in my heart muscle, which can happen as a result of oral surgery. This type of infection is quite often fatal. I should have been on antibiotics before and long after the surgery in Mexico, but for some reason that was not dealt with. My doctor put me on massive oral antibiotics and sent me home. The doctor said he didn't dare send me to the hospital because of the risk of catching an additional infection. I arrived home and deteriorated quite rapidly.

Of all the illnesses I have ever had, this was the worst. Every moment I felt closer to death. Because of the extreme suffering of my body, and because I was still dealing with all of the post-operative recovery from the three surgeries in Mexico, these were dark days of pain and suffering indeed.

I found myself daily and nightly having experiences with "the other side." Spirits came into my home and stood by my bed. I was in and out of consciousness. I was so weak that I didn't try to talk to them. I just watched them. They came two or three times a day and often during the night.

In all candor, my doctor should have put me in the hospital because I was dying. Every moment was agony, and every moment I felt a little worse. My strength was completely gone, and I lost all will to live.

My Beautiful Angel

My deepening health crisis affected my sleep patterns. I often slept during the day and then lay awake at night. It had become my habit to ponder and pray during these long sleepless nights. One evening while my wife slept beside me, I was praying when I saw a young woman coming down the short hallway outside our bedroom. She turned and entered the open door.

I was not asleep, nor had I been, and I was not hallucinating. I have experienced hallucinations and delusions from fever and drugs, and this was neither of those. I was at that moment awake, coherent, and curious. I felt the Holy Ghost warm my soul, and all fear and doubt evaporated.

Her hair was long and dark, almost black. It was thick and slightly wavy. It extended to below her shoulders. It was not tied in any way, but fell freely on her shoulders. She had a beautiful face with high cheekbones. She had the most beautiful, penetrating eyes I have ever seen. They were brown with turquoise streaks in them. I know that sounds unusual, but that's what I saw.

She looked to me as if she had come from a time many thousands of years ago. She was not walking but was floating, moving toward me without moving her feet. She wore a long, cream-colored gown with no seams or visible closures. It appeared to have been woven in a single piece and could only have been put on by pulling it on over her head. It was beautifully made, with a delicate but intricate pattern in the fabric. This beautiful garment covered her from her neck to her wrists and to her ankles.

Her clothing was not glowing white, as I had seen on other angels, but cream colored. Her gown was embroidered in the same cream color around her neck, sleeves, and hem. Her gown seemed to shimmer, as if it were silk in the sunshine, moving gently on a breeze. Her face, bare hands, and bare feet glowed slightly brighter than her gown.

Her face was familiar to me, as if I had seen her all of my life, but I did not know her name, and she never introduced herself to me or even spoke with her voice. I was in my body and did not have the ability to know everything about her as I had while in my spirit. She was a mystery to me. She just moved to the left side of my bed. When she was closer, I could see the complexion of her face and hands. She looked human to me.

Without speaking verbally, I heard her voice in my mind. "Do I have your permission to do what I have been sent here to do?"

She did not explain what she intended to do, nor did I perceive what it was until she was almost done. I had previously learned that angels of God always ask permission, and by her asking and by the burning in the bosom I was experiencing, I knew she was there to bless me in some way.

I knew that she loved me like a brother or son. Her affection felt like warm sunshine upon my face and chest. I felt nothing but joy and peace in her presence. And from the moment she had arrived at the side of my bed I felt no more physical pain, so I was anxious for her to remain as long as possible. My whole being trusted her implicitly, and my heart answered before my mind could form words. "Yes, please!"

When my mind actually caught up with me, I began to wonder, "Why would God send a woman to me this time?" My question wasn't about her ability; it was just that all of my previous angelic visitors and guides had been men. I told myself to shut up. "Quit questioning and just enjoy this experience as long as it lasts."

As soon as I thought this she smiled, as if satisfied finally with my permission for her to proceed. I knew she heard every word I thought because it is the way of all divinely commissioned beings. They know everything that can be known about us.

She rose up into the air and positioned herself horizontally over my body. She never touched me, even though her face was no more than a foot away from mine. She was close enough that I could see the small veins and pores of her skin. Her clothing and hair were not responsive to gravity, but were falling toward her feet, the same as when she was standing.

She had a most pleasant look on her face. I found myself closing my eyes and luxuriating in the absence of pain and sickness. I became aware that she was taking something away from me, probably my physical symptoms of pain, and by doing so, she was clearing my mind for the message she was commissioned to deliver.

I suddenly remembered my visit with Jesus Christ in the parking lot with great clarity. I felt all of those things again. I saw His face and felt His love, and I remembered how I felt when He spoke my name. All of those details came back into my mind.

I suddenly understood the vision I had in Tahiti with a totally new understanding. I saw the experiences in the clinic when I had died from the x-ray contrast, all with a new understanding and a new clarity. What I had remembered most clearly from those experiences was what my five senses had recorded. She was allowing or enabling me to see them again from the eternal perspective I had once had when I first experienced them. I had not forgotten those events, but had shifted my understanding in the last twenty-six years to accommodate what I thought was my impending death. She was not only allowing me to recall the events but to understand once again the deeper meanings within them and that their promises and prophecy were still true.

You Are Not Going to Die

I had been playing this message in my mind, over and over, "I am dying—soon." I was troubled that my life was about over, and my mission, as I had seen it in vision, had not yet happened. I learned from this beautiful, unnamed angel that I still had many things to do, and all that I had seen before was written by God into my mortal journey. All of it would happen. This was her message to me: "You are not going to die at this time." She literally commanded me to stop thinking of myself as if I were dying. She stayed in that position, hovering over me, for an indefinite length of time. It might have been seconds or hours, I just don't know.

It was also the same message my apostle friend had tried to convey a few days before.

Without the pain of my body to interfere, and with the deep peace of her presence, I fell asleep. When I next awoke she was standing beside my bed, looking at me. She instructed me to write all of what I had just learned in my journal and to remember it and never doubt it again. She said that whatever else I needed to learn and see to continue my preparations for my life's work would be coming to me shortly.

She also communicated to me that my life was being preserved, not for my sake alone, but for the sake of others, those whom I was going to serve. I learned many years later that those people I would serve were her people.

She said that I had been prepared from before the foundation of the earth for this mission, and that I should never again doubt that any earthly event, accident, illness, or even death could stop it from occurring.

I'm not proud to admit that I did not have significant faith at that time to believe in the visions God had shown me rather than believing my body, which I thought was quite obviously dying. It is hard, maybe inhumanly hard, to feel your body dying, shutting down, life draining out of you, and still have faith in long-ago promises of a seemingly now-impossible future—but I should have. I should have just believed and rejected my body's attempts to die. Then my faith in God and my Savior would have raised me up. I am certain of that. Still, at that moment in my weakness and deep need, her message was profoundly comforting to me. She had come to arrest my decay, to set my thinking aright, to realign my feet with the true path of my life.

She left the same way she came—out through the open bedroom

door and down the hall. I never saw her again. I have thought about her many times and wondered who she was. My faith told me she was a long-ago progenitor of mine. These people who minister to us from beyond the veil are almost always family. When I see her again I want to thank her and ask her name.

I lay there for a while, totally exhausted and spent. My mind kept rehearsing the experience of her visitation over and over. I finally fell soundly asleep and did not awaken until late morning.

I'm Healed!

I awoke with a bright memory of everything she had done, and my heart cried out, "I'm healed!" But, when I began to move, I realized my body was as sick as before. However, my attitude was no longer sick. I no longer thought like a sick person or contemplated death. I knew I was no longer dying and ceased to lie there just waiting to die, wishing it would hurry up. Her gift to me was that from then on I fully expected to recover, and I began improving immediately.

I was excited when I told my wife about the experiences of the night before. She did not receive it well, neither the message nor how it was delivered. She did not doubt what I told her, she just didn't know how to receive it. What I had forgotten, as deathly ill people do, was that she was suffering right along with me. I wasn't dying alone; I was taking a piece of her heart and her love and her peace with me. She had accepted the inevitability of my death and had actually been expecting it that very night. It was a process of grief that had torn away a piece of her soul, and she didn't know how to get it back just because of words. She didn't know how to go from hopelessness to joy that abruptly. Even when she believed my words and accepted the truth of what had happened, she had to wait a while for her mind and her heart to unknot themselves. I also think that some primal instinct was telling her not to expose herself to such hope only to have it dashed to pieces in short order. When she saw that I was actually recovering, she began to rejoice with me.

CHAPTER FIVE

CAVES, KEYS, AND CALLINGS

Three Visitors

About a week later, I awoke in the morning with the impression that I was going to have three visitors that day. I liked having visitors because I was still recovering from the surgery and infection, and boredom was a problem at times. It also struck me in a comical way because Ebenezer Scrooge had been told that he would have three visitors too, and you know how that worked out.

The first visitor was an older gentleman in our ward. He came and sat with me and read scriptures to me. He was kind to do this, but he stayed two hours, which left me quite tired. I slept for a long time after he left.

The second visitor came at about 5:30 that evening. This was a brother from our ward who just dropped by on his way home from work. He said he felt impressed to come talk with me. He stayed an hour and said that he felt impressed by the Spirit to tell me a few things.

The first was that I could be healed and that I needed to work on obtaining the faith to be healed. The second thing was that I had many things to do before I died. These two things struck me as interesting. I believed he was inspired to tell me those things because I knew that at some point I would be healed. I had seen it in vision several times. I had seen myself in a body free of disease and doing much more, but on a greater scope than he was implying. I felt like I did have the faith to obtain that blessing already and was moving as quickly as I could to obtain it. I didn't tell him that just a week ago an angel came into my bedroom and reminded me of these promises and healed my mind of my "I'm going to die" thinking. I accepted his inspiration in bringing that message to me. It was another witness of what I already knew to be true.

By the time he left I was completely exhausted, and I was not looking forward to a third visitor because the first two had exhausted me without leaving me with something I could truly use to upgrade my endurance or change my circumstances. I wasn't feeling critical or ungrateful for their kindness, just tired.

That same night I couldn't sleep because of the unrelenting pain in my face and chest. I was no longer fearful of dying, but the surgeries in Mexico had left me in a tremendous amount of pain. Because of our financial condition, I could not afford prescription pain medication, and the only things I had were Tylenol and Ibuprofen. They simply were not sufficient.

The Third Visitor

My wife and I were watching the evening news in our bedroom. At about 10:15 p.m., I heard a loud knock at the front door, which was only a few feet from our bedroom door.

I asked Lyn, "Did you hear someone knocking on the door?"

She answered that she had not. She asked if she should go check the door.

I realized in that moment that this was my third visitor and that I would have to go with them. I was actually thinking it was another person from my ward, and I'm not sure why I thought I would have to go anywhere. But I said, "No, don't answer it, please. I will have to go with them, and I'm just too tired."

She gave me a sympathetic look, not because I was tired but because she assumed I was hearing things now. She turned off the lights, kissed me, and rolled over to go to sleep.

I couldn't sleep because my pain and exhaustion were so

overwhelming. I know this sounds odd, but I really was too exhausted to sleep. I heard another series of knocks at the door. Whoever was at the door began knocking every few seconds, over and over. I lay there thinking, "If I get up, I will have to go with them."

I finally began to realize that it might be an angel coming to take me from mortality. This was the ongoing war between my understanding of my physical condition and what the beautiful angel had so powerfully taught me, that I was not going to die. Up until now my faith had been stronger than my thinking, but on this particular night, I found myself once again wavering. I chided myself and anchored my faith once again.

I must have fallen asleep, because I awakened at 12:50 a.m. to someone knocking again on the front door. It was not an impatient knock but just sounded like someone knocking. This time I realized that the knocking was on our bedroom door, not the front door. I knew it was not one of the kids, because the knock was stronger and higher up on the door. The thought came to me again that maybe this was a part of dying, and I would have to go with them.

I realized that I was soaking wet from perspiration from the few hours I had slept. I felt desperately ill, the kind of ill where you are too weak to raise your arm or to cry out for help. I had incredible pain in my chest again. Despite what the beautiful angel had told me, I knew I could not live much longer without a miracle—which I did expect, but had yet to receive. And still the knocking on my bedroom door continued to resound with intermittent and insistent knocking.

I immediately left my body. I think my body was just too ill to keep my spirit within it any more. I moved upward and out of my body to a sitting position on my bed. I looked back to my right and could see my face and shoulders propped up on a pillow. My face was pale with a look of pain, and my body was not breathing. I felt so grateful to be out of it. The pain had stopped, and I felt full of energy and vitality.

You have to remember, I had died twice before, and this time the relief I immediately felt by being out of my body was almost like a drug. It infused me with euphoria and liberation. I was so grateful to be out of that sick, pain-racked body. I was rejoicing, and I felt far more than thrilled. I was jubilant even though I fully expected to return to my body and live on to complete my mission. I could not doubt the angel's words, but for this moment, I was overwhelmed with gratitude to be pain free, even for a while.

I stood effortlessly and walked to the door to answer the knock. I looked back at my body, which was still lying in bed beside my wife. I felt connected to my body, as if a divine rubber band was connecting us. I knew that this was the spiritual assurance that I would be back. This was not death but another chance to learn and see the things of God.

My Angel Guide

I tried to open the door and could not. My hand passed through the doorknob. So I walked through it. I found myself facing a pleasant-looking male angel. He was an angel of light and had the full brightness of the other angels I had seen who had come to minister to the newly dead. But the instant I looked upon him, I knew that he had not come to take me from the earth. He was not the "grim reaper," so to speak. He had been my guide on several other out-of-body experiences, so I recognized him even though I didn't know his name. It was a spiritual recognition. I trusted him and was ready and willing to go with him.

The angel spoke to me verbally, not to my spirit as in other instances. He had a body and was not a spirit. I realized that I, now in my spirit self, was less substantial than he was. He held out his arm and said, "Are you ready to go?"

I replied most gratefully, "Yes!"

Unlike the other angels who had just floated through walls and doors, he opened my front door by turning the knob and walked outside. It was daytime outside. It didn't even seem odd that in my bedroom it was a little before 1:00 a.m. and outside it was midday. What I concluded from this was that I was now in a vision, even though this felt real and tactile.

The angel closed the door to my home. We walked down the front steps and started walking down the sidewalk. He was on my right, with his arm through mine. I could feel him and the warmth of his arm.

It felt so good to walk again. I hadn't been on my feet for weeks and had been ill even longer. It felt marvelous to do all of this without pain or fatigue. I felt as if I could walk without effort for days. I felt exuberant to be with him, like a little child who wanted to express his happiness by running, jumping, and laughing. I didn't, of course. I wanted to remain with him. I understood that he had something to teach me.

We kept walking a long distance. We walked past businesses and houses. Cars passed us on the street, and people walked past us on the sidewalk. I am sure they couldn't see us because we stepped off of the walk to let them pass. It was a visionary experience, but it was realistic. There was a light breeze, and I saw that the breeze was blowing the angel's hair and affecting his clothes. I looked down at myself, and I realized that I was in my pajamas. I didn't feel awkward at all, but I noted that I could not feel the breeze, and it was not affecting me or my clothing.

I thought, *How strange! Here I am in the presence of an angel, and he's the one with the body and I'm the spirit, and we're walking, on foot, up into the mountains!* It was marvelous to me. I wanted to question him, but I felt like I should wait.

I felt no labor or fatigue. I was walking effortlessly, which for a deathly ill person is like unexpectedly winning the lottery.

Then the angel said to me, "The first thing we will see will explain to you why you are experiencing your life as it presently is."

I replied, "Great! I would love to know the answer to that question."

He was friendly and interested in me. My mind was spinning with questions, and I'm sure he was hearing all this. He smiled frequently as we walked in silence.

I felt like he knew me better than I knew myself. He was completely engaged in this event of showing me what I needed to know. Even though we were not chatting as we went, I knew that there was purpose in everything he did.

Caves and Bars

We proceeded up a canyon I had been to many times. We walked a long way to where the paved road gave way to gravel. I could feel the road beneath my feet, but we were moving faster than walking speed, as if walking on a moving sidewalk at the airport. We arrived at the canyon quickly. The scene was familiar to me. I had been there many times on picnics and outings.

As we stepped onto the gravel, the scene changed to a different set of blue-gray mountains with tall cliffs, facing me with three towering mountain peaks jutting into the sky above the cliffs. The sky changed to a more sunset hue even though it was midday. There was a stretch of water between where we stood and the mountain, as if we were on some island out in an inlet looking at the mainland. I could smell the ocean air and heard the waves breaking on the cliff face.

I did not know where the vision was taking me. I was given to understand that I was now looking into the future at what the purpose of my life would be. I concluded that I was seeing a type or a metaphor of the purpose of my life, not actual events that would happen just the way I was seeing them. But I also understood that the mission being suggested by this metaphor would actually happen, if not exactly as I was seeing it now.

I began to see our surroundings through spiritual eyes, as the angel was seeing it.

He asked me, "Do you see this mountain?"

"Yes."

"What do you see?"

I walked closer. There were lights high up on the mountainside. Finally I realized they were coming from the mouths of four big man-made caverns. The caverns were about twelve feet tall, and about one hundred fifty feet wide at their opening. The openings had bars on them, as if they were prisons. The caves extended deep into the mountain, with doors leading beyond what I could see. The four caverns occupied most of the mountainside.

I replied, "I see four large chambers cut into the mountain with bars on them. What does it mean?"

He replied, "We need to come closer."

The view changed instantly. I found myself standing right in front of the bars, on a wide ledge between the bars and the cliff face. We were high up the mountainside. There was a wide but steep road descending down to the valley below.

I looked in and saw thousands of people in the chambers. There were rooms within for large groups, cooking areas, and massive gardens of flowers and vegetables. Deep into the cave I could see closed doors along the back of the chambers. I assumed they were bedrooms, storage rooms, and other necessary accommodations. The people did not seem to see me, even though some of them were quite close, so that I could see them clearly. They were dressed well and going about their lives. They did not seem to consider themselves captives, but were healthy and happy. Children of all ages played and tended to chores. I watched them without understanding. Their whole circumstance seemed so improbable to me.

"Who are these people, and why are they in here?" I asked.

The angel pointed to the locks on the bars. The locks were on the inside. They had locked themselves into the caverns, and the bars were of their own construction.

"What does this mean?" I asked the angel. "Why have they locked themselves in the mountain?"

He smiled and replied, "That is right. These individuals have locked themselves away because of the persecution, abuses, and mistreatment they have endured from religious organizations and from the abuse of governments and the authority of the world."

I perceived that this was both a good and a bad thing. They had isolated themselves from the world, but they had also isolated themselves from further light and truth.

I asked, "Why are you showing me this? What does it have to do with me?"

Then he showed me in vivid detail the pains and sufferings and abuses these people had endured while living on this earth. They had been persecuted and killed for generations before they found a way to separate themselves from the world.

He said, "Only individuals like you, who have been willing to undergo similar pain and abuses as these people have, will they ever listen to and trust. You must continue to drink of this bitter cup and not become bitter yourself. This will give you the experience and knowledge you need so that when you are called to work with these people, they will trust you and recognize in you that you are a fellow sufferer and refugee from persecution. These sufferings and your personal triumph over them will be written on your very soul and into the sinews of your body, and they will recognize it and trust you."

Then he said something that I have pondered for years. He added, "They will see that you also belong to the 'Fellowship of the Suffering of Christ.'"

The Key

While I was trying to understand all this, a young woman came toward us carrying a key in both hands. She did not look like the people within the caverns, but she was an angel of light, like my escort. She wore a long white glowing robe. She was beautiful and quite young.

He took the key from her and handed it to me with both hands, with great reverence and care, as if it were precious and fragile. The young woman angel remained, watching me hold the key with great interest. I studied it for a moment, marveling at the beauty of the craftsmanship. I turned it in my hands several times, admiring it. It was unlike anything I had ever seen.

The key was about a foot long, shaped like a modern key, with a rounded handle and a shank with saw-like ridges on it and grooves along the side. It was heavy, as if made from solid metal, which looked and hefted like solid gold. The feel of the metal was soft, like velvet, not hard like gold. The handle was about six inches across with precious gems infused into the metal. It appeared as if the jewels had been cast into the metal, because I could not feel them on the smooth surface of the key. But each stone was clearly visible and sparkling within the metal as if the metal were transparent over the stones. Each gem seemed to have a tiny light source within it, which made the key sparkle like glitter with light that came from within the key rather than as a reflection of the sun.

The pointed end was emerald green. The shank was blood red, and the handle was a vivid blue. It looked old, perhaps millions of years old, though it was not scratched, worn, or damaged. It was so intricate and beautiful that I thought of the Liahona, which had been crafted by God Himself. I am certain that no human could have made this key.

I noted that there were symbols on the key, which I could not read.

The Meaning of the Symbols

"What do the symbols on the key mean?" my escort asked me. I immediately felt the meaning of the symbols enter my mind. The key itself represented a mission to rescue the people whom I could see on the other side of the bars. The key represented the ability to unlock the bars that kept them in their self-imposed prison. The colors represented the qualifications of whoever God sent to actually accomplish the work of unlocking the bars.

The red stood for sacrifice, but not in the way that I had previously understood sacrifice. The knowledge I received included a full understanding of the condescension and Atonement of Christ, but it also symbolized a willingness to likewise sacrifice as Christ has, to be prepared for this mission. In order to receive the key, and the assignment it represented, one had to be prepared by sacrificing their will, their earthly possessions, their health if called upon, or even their lives if need be, to follow the path God ordained to prepare that person with charity, faith, doctrinal purity, sound understanding, and, most of all, perfect obedience to God's will. This is the course Christ had submitted Himself to, though His suffering was far greater and for all mankind. This lesser suffering we go through is to prepare an individual for their specific mission. It took me years to realize this is the reason the angel called it "The Fellowship of the Suffering of Christ."

I was given to understand that there was no other way, and no other path to this type of service. It was a path that could require the shedding of blood and sacrifices of similar magnitude. When a servant of God followed this path to its end, it left a recognizable mark upon the servant—a glow, if you will, of righteousness. It was a preparation that made it impossible to fail, which those to whom he or she would minister would recognize and then follow.

The blue handle represented the royal bloodline, which I immediately knew was the latter-day priesthood. We also have heard it called "The holy priesthood after the order of the Son of God." The blue represented three things: First, the receipt and righteous magnification of the present priesthood. Second, it represented the receipt of the "fulness" of that same priesthood when worthiness and the timetable of God called it forth. Third, it represented a fore-ordination to this very mission to release these people. Only that specifically ordained officer of the priesthood could manipulate the key. The handle is how it is gripped and operated.

The emerald green tip represented a renewal and re-creation of life. The tip is the "business end" of the key. It enters the lock first, and it must be perfectly aligned with the lock in order for any other part of the key to operate. The green tip signified the full outcome of the red and the blue, sacrifice and priesthood, which, as described in the Oath and Covenant of the Priesthood, brings about a renewal of the body. This is why the green tip was entitled "Renewal and Re-creation of Life." This renewal can represent anything from prolonged mortal life to a healing of all disease to being translated, as was John the Beloved and Enoch's city. It also represented the renewal that these individuals would pass through as they accepted Christ as their Savior and no longer were afraid of Him and those who represented Him. They must accept the ordinances of the gospel, which would allow each of them to be renewed and eventually set free from their present self-imposed imprisonment.

The key in my vision is representative of the key every latter-day builder of Zion will obtain for their specific mission. Each individual will probably not see an actual key being handed to them, but they will go through this same process that was shown to me of sacrifice, priesthood, and renewal. It took me many years, until just recently in fact, to fully identify the meaning of the parts of the key. Even knowing what the angel showed and taught me, it has taken my soul a long time to realize how it could actually come to pass for myself, to make me into a builder of Zion. I have come to understand that in order to complete my life's mission, I had to receive this key in the ordained way, by becoming a member of the "Fellowship of the Suffering of Christ" and by doing it freely, willingly, even joyfully.

I now understand that it is a personal journey of great consequence. It is not a pathway for seekers of comfort and casual service. I did not realize I was even upon this path, or that my suffering was a part of any path other than a process of my life. Nor had I ever considered that I was one of those whose premortal calling included any unique service—until the angel handed me that key.

This key represented the full course and calling of the priesthood. Only with all three of these elements can we claim the blessings and the honor of serving in any great cause. When we do this, we are no longer serving the Church, our families, or even ourselves—we are serving Jesus Christ directly and doing the Father's work of preparing the world for the end of time and the return of Christ.

Along with all of this information came the confirmation that what I was seeing was not real but a metaphor to teach me why I was going through the hardships and suffering that have been such a big part of my mortal journey. I was being taught that all of my life I have been engaged in this process of preparing to meet the qualifications and attributes of one who will be handed a key to a portion of the latter-day work of building Zion. In this mighty work we will free people from their self-imposed prisons, whether real or figurative, and bring them to Zion.

The key did not represent a call to preside or to be a latter-day prophet. It represented the process of acquiring, through the Atonement of Christ, the degree of personal purity and sanctification that qualifies the recipient to serve in this great work. It is a work that, as you'll see in future visions I will describe, is fully organized and carried out by the latter-day Church. This is not a path that leads outside of the Church, or even on a parallel course with the Church, but one that brings you into the heart of the ordained mission of the latter-day Church to prepare the world for the return of Christ.

The only additional meaning I gained was to show me that I actually could accomplish this, that it really was possible, and that I should be seeking to complete my qualifications and then finish the work the Lord was showing me was mine to do. I should continue to accept that the process of my life was not taking me to physical death, but to the possibility of grand service in the latter-day scene.

I felt this admonition enter my soul without words, "Spencer, you are out of your body, but you are not dead. Don't give up, because these things need to be sealed into your heart and mind. These are the things you promised me you would do—so don't give up. I am giving you this information to bolster your courage to go forward and strive to accomplish these things. Don't be discouraged about going back into your body. Your body will not hinder you from your preparations. It was necessary to bring you here to give you a signifi-cant glimpse of the work you will do and to prepare you for what it will cost you to qualify to do it."

This information entered my soul rich with love and empathy but also with deep power. I knew it was not my angel-escort speaking to me. I was just beginning to understand, standing there with this heavy key in my hands, when the angel said, "What do you see now?"

Tunnel of Light

I looked around me and realized we were no longer before the chambers with bars, and I no longer held the key. We were in a tunnel of sorts, and I had the sensation of moving at great speed.

I discerned that the tunnel was "alive." Perhaps it would be more accurate to say, it was a part of my being. It was "mine," and I had created it.

My escort smiled again, "That is right. It is a portal, and you cre-ated it. Only you can use it."

I thought about this, then asked, "So, does each person make their own portal before they come to this earth?" The tunnel felt like it was as much a part of me as my hand or foot. It was my understand-ing that this portal was how I came to this earth to be born and how I would return to God when I was at last finished with mortality. I could "feel" the tunnel, the same as one feels their arm or fingers.

He seemed pleased, "Yes, that is correct. Everyone creates their own portal, which you now perceive as a tunnel of light but which is just the best way for you to understand what is happening to you. It is a divine power you learned long ago, which enabled you to come to earth, and eventually to return to God. Everyone must create their own."

We were moving without walking, but it felt normal and fa-miliar. I knew exactly how to move forward in the tunnel. It was an act of my mind, like wanting your fingers to close around some-thing. I did not need to touch the tunnel because that was just how I perceived this form of travel while still limited by mortal intelligence. I was moving at the speed of thought.

The far end of the tunnel was profoundly bright. The light was not coming from the end of the tunnel but from the tunnel itself, as if it grew more divine the farther from the earth it progressed.

As soon as we entered the tunnel, or the portal, I felt less mortal, more empowered and divine. I could speak to my guide verbally or by thought, and he answered me just by thought. We discussed many things as we proceeded through the tunnel. Every question I thought about, I saw that event or thing in perfect detail, including its creation, existence, and present glory. It was similar to when I walked through the desk and leather couch in my first experience. This information just entered my mind in bursts of understanding. I did not have to ponder or sort it out. I simply received the answers to my questions.

My memory of this experience today is that we spoke of many things and that I learned rapidly. I was not allowed to retain in my mortal mind most of what I learned.

Folding the Universe

I asked, "Does the earth have a tunnel of light?" The scriptures inform us that the earth is an intelligent and living thing.

He answered, "Yes. God provided a similar means for the movement of the earth to where it now is."

I then experienced, as if I were actually there, how the earth "fell" from where it was created and moved to where it is positioned now. I had the impression that it took thousands of years for it to arrive.

The image I saw appeared to me to be a "folding" of the universe. It looked like the universe was folded in on itself, like a sheet of thick paper or fabric so that where the earth was created and where it was to go were on top of one another. The earth was then moved from where it emerged and physically "transitioned" to its new position. This moving of the earth occurred during the entire creative process. By the time it arrived, it was prepared for mortal man.

I also saw that when it is time for it to return to its original location, the universe will again fold and the earth will be moved back to its place of creation.

The image I saw revealed that even though we only perceive one plane of existence, there are an infinite number of planes stacked, or layered, in the same space. These planes are not truly "universes" because they are less about infinite stars and suns and worlds as they are about God's organization and exaltation of all of His creations and His assigning unchanging glory and laws to each plane. Human language does not give us adequate words to describe such things, nor does human intelligence give us the ability to understand such things unless our minds are opened for a moment. While I was with the angel, I could understand all of this clearly. I believe I remember most of what I saw, yet now I have only a fragment of the understanding of what it meant or by what principle it occurred. What I learned then, and what I have been allowed to retain, has taken me many years to acquire the words to describe, even to myself. If you consider that this is the only time I have said many of these things out loud, you will understand why I still struggle for words.

I did understand that the reason the universes were "folded" together was because it was more efficient. The word "easier" doesn't apply because God has all power, and nothing taxes His power or ability—it was just more efficient, and it is the way it has always been done.

There is a celestial arithmetic about this vision that was amazing to behold. I realized that this mighty folding of the universe was not magic to God. It was more like brilliant spiritual technology. I saw that God possesses vast laws, principles, and science—if you will—of how to do these things within His understanding and power. They were beautiful to behold, like a divine dance with stars and planets as the performers. When men do math there is always the infection of error and mistakes. God's arithmetic is always flawless, and I saw that the entirety of His creations were the recipient of His flawless Godly engineering.

All of the glorified universes I perceived were one of three glories—Celestial, Terrestrial, or Telestial. There were other types, which were not types of glory. These were wonderful places without glory where beings who had not qualified for a reward of glory during their lifetimes were ultimately sent. These were of every type, of every description, and were created in response to their desires. They wanted nothing more to do with God or His intervention in their lives, so He gave them what they wanted—whatever it was—and there they would stay throughout eternity, unable to challenge God's authority ever again.

Our earth is presently of the Telestial order, but before the era of man, the earth had come from a Celestial plane. It was not yet celestialized, but it was created there. The transition from a Celestial realm to the mortal realm is what constituted the Fall, and was accomplished by this folding process.

When a person dies or when they have an out-of-body experience, as in my case, their own tunnel brings them back to their original place and to their original structure—which were both spiritual in nature. This power to return to God is only perceived as a tunnel of light. It is not physical and is not actually a tunnel but is the sure way God has provided for our spirits to return to Him.

When we are done with this Telestial experience, we will no longer need this tunnel between earth and God. We will then be able as spirits, and eventually as resurrected beings, to move instantly across vast distances by the power of God that will be inherent within us.

We needed the tunnel of light because a flawed mortal does not have the ability to initiate travel as does a spirit. Similar to leaving a rope dangling over the cliff so we can climb back up, we left the tunnel of light as our sure means of returning home after we have discarded this fleshy tabernacle.

Meadow and Lake

I was pondering these things as we arrived at the end of the tunnel. I found myself standing in a beautiful meadow. There were fully grown trees nearby of many varieties. Some were in blossom, while others were heavy with fruit. A short distance away, a blue lake reflected the beautiful arrangement of trees and bushes beyond. There was no sun in the sky, and I understood that the light by which I perceived these things was from the Son, not the sun.

I was aware that there were several varieties of fish in the lake, as well as many other varieties of plants, but no other animals. The meadow and lake were striking, with magnificent displays of flowers and flowering shrubs of many varieties.

A narrow stream was flowing between myself and the lake, emptying into the lake a short distance away.

Just to my right I saw a decorative fence about three feet tall. It ran along the stream for a little ways, then off to my right. There were beautiful benches built into the wall every few yards. The wall curved in places so that the benches formed an alcove for people to sit facing each other to converse.

Initially I just walked around looking at the wall. I had never seen such a thing before. The wall was made of bricks of white stone about a foot square

I sat along the wall on one of the benches and felt it welcome me, giving me love and praising God. Had I not experienced this aspect of spiritual communication and connectedness with all things in prior visions, I would have been startled. But I felt connected to everything I could see. In previous experiences of walking through desks and walls on earth, I had also understood the history of those things, every event of its existence. With these things, the wall and trees, there was no history, yet I understood that these things were almost eternal in their existence. This was a spiritual world and nothing changed, nothing aged; nothing grew old or died or was harvested and coerced by man into some other shape. So they were just as God had created them—no change, no history.

I was waiting for my guide to catch up with me and show me where to go. He had arrived with me but had not accompanied me to the meadow. I was not certain where to go without him, and I accepted that he was allowing me this interval to experience this place. I didn't know where I was, but I was also not concerned or worried. Everything was as it should be.

I stood and walked to the end of the wall, stepped through the stream, and walked to the lake. The water in the stream and lake was crystal clear. I could easily see to the bottom of the lake, which I had never experienced in mortality because of reflection or impurities in the water. I could see fish swimming as if they were birds in the air. Everything was worshiping God and welcoming me. I walked to the edge of the water and knelt to dip my hands in it. It was cool, but when I withdrew my hand it was not wet. I stood and put my toe on the water, not in, but on. I felt like I had done this before. I just knew I could.

I stepped onto the water and walked out a dozen steps. I could look down all of the way to the bottom. It gave me the feeling of flying, because the water was so clear. When I moved my feet, the water rippled just as water does on earth, but my foot was on a solid surface and was not getting wet. I walked back to the shore and onto the grass, and this time, I decided to walk into the water.

I realized that walking into the water was something I had learned to do before. On earth, the natural response of water is to let you sink. Here, obviously, the natural response was to support you. I decided I would try again.

I stepped into the water, pressing my toe a little deeper. The water came to my ankles, and I walked in a short circle ankle-deep in the water. When I again reached shore, I was still perfectly dry. I tried again, this time up to my knees, then again up to my waist. I realized that I was actually getting into the water as much as my belief allowed me to. I finally decided to just walk into the water until I was fully immersed.

The water did not resist my desire, and I walked waist deep into the water. I could feel it, but I was not getting wet. I splashed a little on my clothing, and it ran off, leaving me dry. I walked deeper. I knew I was in the spirit, and my body was somewhere on earth, so I had no fear of drowning. Still, just as I stepped in over my head, I held my breath. I waited a long time before I realized that I was not experiencing a lack of oxygen. I slowly released my breath—and saw no bubbles come from my mouth. I carefully inhaled and was breathing air, which I realized, or the understanding came to me, that I was remembering my body's need for oxygen. The spirit had no such need, and there was no air going in and out of my spirit, even though I had the sensation of breathing. I walked around the bottom of the lake for a while. There was no resistance to the water. I just walked as freely as on dry ground. The bottom of the lake was like a planted garden, with beautiful floating plants and paths between them made of sand. I touched a few fishes, which did not scurry away but radiated their small love for me.

When I was satisfied, I walked to the shore and emerged dry upon the grass. I looked back at the lake, quite amazed by the experience until I realized that this lake was not filled with H_2O, it was water in a spirit state and had the appearance of mortal water but few of the properties of water.

The most profound aspect of this experience so far was that everything was praising God. It did not have a voice, like a human sound, but it communicated by its spirit, and by its connection with all things, its love of God. I also realized that the instant I arrived in this new place everything knew me. It all knew and reverenced and respected the fact that I was after the image of God and that I had come from a mortal body. It knew that I was a son of Adam, and it loved and respected me. I knew nothing of this place from any memory of mine, but I felt truly connected with it.

All of these things, whether grass or stone or bricks in the wall, were pleased with their existence. They were content to be what they were. But it was also my realization that none of these things had a will. They were not capable of "wanting" to be anything else. This whole place and everything in it was aware, full of praise of God, but it did not have a personality, agency, or will to be anything else.

As I have often noted, this is hard to describe. There are no powerful, passionate, explosively meaningful words to describe such things in any mortal language, so I admit to stumbling a little with this explanation. When you are in the spirit, words are not necessary, and anything can be fully described by a single thought and understood in totality by anyone you address.

I was fully aware that this whole meadow and everything I was experiencing was here because the will of God had organized them into this existence, into this form, into this place. It had been done for God's purposes and had remained unchanged longer than man had been in existence. They had heard the voice of God call to them to assume this shape, and they still listened for His command. Their purpose was as if they were constantly asking, "How can I serve you? How can I be of value to you? This is why I am here." Even the flowers, when I bent to touch them or smell them, were worshiping God and expressing joy in their beauty only because I had thought to myself how glorious and beautiful they were, which expression they heard and understood.

Of course, I did not assume to have any authority to change them and would not have attempted it under any circumstance. How could

I improve upon something that is already perfect? Everything was at its highest level of life and vitality. When I stepped upon the grass, it was not damaged, it just "received me" and felt pleasure in my use of it.

The colors were beautiful, distinct, and more brilliant than earth colors. There were colors which I do not believe the human eye can distinguish, but which, if I had to name, were mauves and pastels in stunning variety.

I don't remember seeing animals other than the fish. This place was like a painting where the artist just wanted fish in the lake and chose to paint nothing else. It was not a reflection of mortality. It was a place God had created to be exactly what it was—to radiate beauty for the senses to behold.

I was still looking at the lake when my guide returned. He asked me if I was ready to go with him now. Through all of my interactions with him and other angels, they always asked my permission to continue. Once I have given it, they often directed my attention, or asked me questions, but it was always my choice to go, stay, or continue.

I said, "Yes, I am ready now to continue."

Spiritual Childhood

Instantly we were in another place. I recognized it immediately. It was my home, where I had spent all of my spiritual childhood.

The building before me was immense, stretching to my right and left as far as I could see. It consisted of many beautiful parts. There were majestic arches, tall walls, windows of every shape, stunning architecture, and glorious ornamentation.

The structure was made of a stone-like material, white in color, but more like pearl, with gold and silver streaks that seemed to be moving slowly around larger emerald veins, as if they had occurred in natural stone. Each block of stone was about as tall as a man.

A long-ago memory arose in my mind of watching Father create it. It had come to its present form over a long period of time—though time was just the limited way my mind understood it. It was just a continuation of the eternal now in my memory. The building had taken shape with purpose. God wanted a room to teach me in, so the building had obeyed His desire. He loved columns, and representations of the beauty of His earthly creations near the tops of the columns along the ceiling and over the doors, and it had all obeyed. I realized that some rooms had been "created" to teach me my first lessons of things I would encounter on earth. Others had been shaped to allow me to see and touch objects to teach me, such as books, art, tools, and many other things needed to prepare me for earth life.

It was less of a building than a divine place that had assumed the shape of an earthly building for my education. It could take any shape God conceived. It did not require work, workmanship, tools, or trades to change it. It simply flowed, in joyful obedience, into any shape He wished.

My guide opened a large door that was made from a single piece of wood. There were no joints or seams, as if God had asked a single tree to assume the shape of this elaborate door. The wood was unpainted and beautifully carved with natural wonders from earth—flowers, animals, children, men, and women in loving moments.

The room beyond was a familiar entryway. The whole of what I saw radiated a sense of vibrant excitement that I was back. The walls and columns were of the same divine stone as outside. The ceiling was vaulted, resting upon four fluted columns with light radiating from everything. The floor was darker, more like a natural marble of a dark emerald green. There was a closed door to my right, a wide hallway directly before me, and another closed door to my left.

My guide led me to the corridor before us. It was about twenty feet long and ended in an arched window that looked like pearl. It appeared to be fluid, with smoky white colors shifting in it. As we approached it, it turned clear so that I could see through it. The large room beyond was again familiar to me.

He looked at me and asked, "Do you know this place?"

I said with tears of joy streaming down my face, "I'm back home!" In my mind I thought, *This is where I used to live before I was born.* I knew I was back in the spirit world, where I grew up as a spirit child. Many sacred memories and scenes flowed through my mind of my spiritual childhood, which I choose not to relate here. I stood there for a long while, never entering but watching and remembering my past.

My Room

When I was satisfied and again ready to move on, my guide took me back to the entry and to the first door I had seen. The door opened for me as I approached. I recognized it as "my room," almost like a bedroom for a mortal child, but there was no bed here. The room was about twenty square feet, with a high, flat ceiling. The walls and floor were of the same material as the foyer, but with slightly different colors, lending more toward blue and mauve. I loved this room, and I felt as if it was all "mine."

The only furniture in the room was a large rounded-top chest sitting in the middle of the floor. It was about three feet by four feet, with an arched lid and rounded corners. The top was a beautiful red with highlights of burnt orange. It was made of the same material as the rest of the home, but it was thinner and brightly colored. The sides of the chest were a vivid canary yellow. I knew that I had picked these colors and changed them often to suit my childhood whims. The lid could be opened, but there were no visible hinges.

I stepped to it, and after walking around it, I glanced at my guide questioningly. He smiled, and I slowly raised the lid. The substance gave my mortal memory the message that it was heavy, but it felt feather-light as I opened it. Within were strange objects I had never seen in mortality. There were utensils of strange shapes and different sizes, white clothing, and tools that I had used. I knew exactly what each tool and object was for as I stood there in the Spirit, but since returning to mortality, that information has not remained with me.

I realized that I "owned" them, but also that such things were common to our premortal experiences. Still, their connection to me had been a part of my early experiences. I picked up each one, looked at it and remembered what it was for. Every object in the chest was an achievement of mine. Each object represented an accomplishment, like a trophy of sorts, of a lesson learned, ordinations I had received, stages of development that I had achieved. These objects signified my worthiness and preparation to participate in the object of the lesson—not just in this world but in the mortal world as well. These things were like certificates, authorizing me to actually do those things. Each ability and authority was gained by a long process of qualifying for and earning that authority.

I had received these objects as tokens of lessons I had learned, and qualifications I had achieved. Some of the objects were actual tools to assist me in that act. To my memory of these things, they seemed to me to be divine technology, objects endowed with power by God to allow and assist me in doing some necessary service or act, like the Liahona that assisted Lehi's family or the Urim and Thummim that enabled seers to see the future. The white clothing was carefully folded and was sacred and ceremonial in nature. It was all a part of my matriculation to spiritual maturity.

As I picked them up, the lesson learned, the process of learning, and the joy I felt in the achievement returned to me. I treasured each object with all my heart and pondered on them and then placed them carefully back in the chest. Nothing in the chest was a toy or whimsical object. Everything had deep, eternal meaning to me. Each object recognized me and was happy to see and interact with me.

I felt no reason to hurry. My guide was watching me, smiling and enjoying my discoveries. It was as if I had an eternity to examine them. After handling them and understanding them, I remembered the nature of the room. I realized that I had possessed the ability to change the room into anything I needed. If I desired to read a book that belonged to mortality, like scripture or a scroll written by a mortal prophet, I simply desired it, and the room would change to provide that thing to me. It came in the setting it had been used, in a palace, a cave, or on a desk; this is how it appeared to me. I could touch it, pick it up, and read it. I could feel and even smell it. It was not the actual object summoned from some eternal storage vault but a flawless spiritual re-creation or representation of it. Each object was perfectly like the original, including all of the memories and history a spirit individual could experience from the original object.

If I wanted to see something large, such as the birth of Christ or the creation of the earth, that event would surround me. I could watch it and learn from it, interact with it, see the angels and divine beings who had enacted the original events. I could move around it and see it from every angle with perfect clarity and experience everything and everyone involved in the initial event. In short, it was magnificent, and it was the most perfect classroom in eternity—and all who desired it had one just like mine.

I recalled as a child spending eternities in this room. Once again, there was no time in that world, and the concept of time, of linear existence, was difficult to comprehend then. The idea of change, aging, decay, and opposition were difficult concepts. It was like a jellyfish trying to understand automobiles. There were no comparable experiences in my childhood thus far, and I remember pondering all of these concepts of mortality.

Saying I spent a lot of "time" in this room would be incorrect. I spent vast portions of eternity here. I never changed. The room never changed except as I desired. I never tired, felt hungry, or grew weary of learning. I was enthralled with all of it and did not desire to do anything else unless Father, or some other need, interrupted me. When I had a question, I didn't need to go to Father for the answer. The question formed in my mind, and the room changed to provide the things I needed to learn.

My education was not random; it was programmed, sequential, and ordained. It was the same sequence of training all of Father's children experienced—though I was aware that not all of Father's children, my siblings, were curious about all things or pursued their education with such devotion and intrigue as some of us did.

Like a boy in a free candy store, I stayed in this room and interacted with these things for a long time (speaking as a mortal) until my heart was content.

My guide waited for me, enjoying my enjoyment. When I was ready to go, I carefully folded everything back up and put it all back exactly where it had been. I slowly and reverently closed the chest and stood there with my hands resting upon its smooth surface. It was a long goodbye for me. I felt both my own joy and the communion of those objects in the chest, all of which praised God, loved me, and longed for my return.

As I walked back into the entryway, I suddenly remembered my eternal siblings, Mother, and Father. I did not remember myself as being one of billions. I remembered uncountable siblings, all loved and loving, but I do not remember sharing Father and Mother with them. I only remember being individually and singularly loved and cherished.

I remember Father well, His power and majesty, His face, His hands, His form, His touch and tender care. Even today I remember playing with Him, running my fingers through the soft hair on His arm, laughing with Him, going to divine destinations, sampling future earthly delights, tasting new things, viewing divine events, watching galaxies and eternities flare into being under His hand. To my memory, I was the only one present at these times, though there may have been multitudes of us, each of us feeling individually shepherded through childhood. Most of my spiritual childhood was spent in His tender care, in His arms, in His lap, in His heart.

I remembered Mother equally well while there in my premortal home. She was present in all of my memories then, but almost nothing of these memories returned to mortality with me. My heart remembers Her equally powerful love and personal attention to me, but I do not remember a single event with Her, nor does Her face remain in my mind today. I do not know why this is, but it seems consistent with Father's reverent protection of Her throughout all of His dealings with mankind. The odd thing is that it feels right to me that I do not remember. As powerful as I remember Her love to be, I am spiritually content to know only what I know. Somehow this is right.

I asked my guide to show me the rest of the house. He agreed happily and took me to the corridor that ended in the smoky window. We walked side-by-side down the wide corridor and approached the glass. It was not transparent, but milky-looking with shifting colors that moved like smoke within the glass. Looking into it gave me the sensation that the glass extended to innumerable, far distant places. He just continued walking, and I followed him right into the glass. I understood as I passed through it that it was a portal that connected distant places. It felt like we were still in my "home" but were now somewhere far distant.

The Library

A second later we stepped out into a room filled with people working at desks. Each desk had a large window before it with the same purpose as my room. They were studying the images and objects on the screen. Like my room, they could handle the objects, turn them, touch them, and experience them in every possible way. Books that they desired to see did not need to be read. Just touching the book and handling it communicated the full burden of information to them. One touch was sufficient, but longer exposure was delightful as it allowed one to experience the book in greater depth, enjoying everything about it, including the life and events of the author's life. If they held it long enough, they could experience every person who had touched it and everything about them. I remembered my own experiences and knew that there was a point where the information was not uplifting and the object was returned to the screen.

I believe these people were like myself, recently departed mortals who were now continuing their search for light and truth. They were dressed in flowing white robes. Their faces were glowing with happiness.

There were people carrying objects through the room, taking them to the people seated at the desks. The people here were all engaged and busy but not hurried. There was a sense of eternity, but also a pleasant desire to learn as quickly as possible. They were all happy. This seemed to be a central library or information hub for people to learn. When they accomplished some level of learning, they received identical tokens of their education, just like those I had found in my chest. These were the objects the instructors were carrying through the room to present to the learners.

As we walked through the room, there was a circle of light that preceded us. The people in each new place knew we were coming, who we were, and what our purpose and needs were—in fact, everything about us. The information about my guide was blocked from me, but not from the others in the room. I was never allowed to know who my guide was nor where he was from.

God, Time, and Law

It was shown to me that God does not dwell in a reality limited by time or distance. He exists outside of time and can move forward or backward through the construct of time. He created what we call "time" for our perception and progression, but He is not Himself subject to it. Anywhere in His creations, and any "when" in His creations, He is there. He can and does act in the past, present, and future, but to Him it is all "now" and "here," before his eyes. He can as easily speed up time for His purposes or stop it from progressing, all without our being aware of it. Since He can also see the end eternal outcome of all things and all people, He can influence or change anything, anywhere, and anytime He desires to bless the eternal outcome of our lives.

All of the things that we accept as mortal laws, like gravity, physics, light, heat, or speed, are all creations of God. We are bound by them unto life or death, but He is not. They are "laws" that belong to the Telestial order. They function by His command and as He decrees, but He is not an inmate of the Telestial order, and therefore He is not subject to these "laws." When I first saw the Savior, He was standing above the earth, but was firmly anchored in His chosen place. These things do not violate the "laws" of nature but operate above them in obedience to Celestial laws. Father has ordained that time as perceived by mortals shall only go "forward," but He Himself is not subject to that edict.

As I relate further in this book, as we grew close to the Second Coming, after we had labored to serve God for a long time and had acquired a greater measure of God's power as it operates in a Millennial world, we began to have the ability to work without limitation by time or distance. It was the only way we actually finished the work assigned to us prior to His coming in glory.

Returning to Visit My Body

The next awareness I had was of being back in my bedroom at the foot of my bed. My body was still in the bed. I looked at the digital clock on my bedroom table. Exactly one hour had elapsed, though I had the sensation that we had been away for days and days.

I knew that my body was dead according to the worldly measurement, but I was so thrilled with what I had just experienced that I wanted to wake up my wife and tell her everything I had just learned.

Without verbal language, my guide told me that if I wanted to talk to my wife, I would need to go back into my body, and this experience would be completed.

I realized there was more he wanted to show me and that it was not time to return to my body, but for some reason we needed to visit it—perhaps to keep the link between my spirit and body strong while he took me on further journeys in the spirit.

I told him, "If you have more to show me, let us go; I'm ready!"

CHAPTER SIX

ANGELS AND DEVILS

Evil Spirits and Temptation

We didn't walk out the door; I just found myself in a different place. We were in a small home office. It was late at night. A young man in his underwear came into the room quietly, looking around him stealthily as he entered. He closed the door softly without turning on the light. He went to a computer and turned it on. As he waited for the computer to warm up, I felt a growing sense of excitement coming from him. I knew that his wife and two sons and baby daughter were asleep elsewhere in the house, and that he intended to view pornography. I understood this just by being in the room with him. As with previous experiences, I understood everything about him—his life, his decisions, his desires, his distress. I perceived that he was a good man, a returned missionary, and presently serving in his quorum presidency.

My guide said to me, "He is here to view pornography."

I saw eight spirits enter the room. Four of these were evil spirits who had once been mortal, the other four were unborn evil spirits—Satan's minions. The disembodied looked human and wore clothing typical of the period in which they had died. The evil spirits were less substantial, generally smaller, with misshapen features, making them look slightly inhuman. They were agitated, active, jumping around in a frenzy, shouting their commands to the young man in excited voices.

The disembodied spirits said little at first. They had little ability to be heard by the young man. They were there trying to satisfy the sexual passion they had developed during their own lives. There were both male and female spirits. Their sexual addiction had followed them into the spirit world. Their addiction was unending, painful, and impossible to satisfy. It haunted them. They were desperate to try to satisfy it endlessly. They were pleased that they were going to shortly experience it through this young man. They were intent, watching him, urging him on though he could not hear them. They were not looking at the porn on the computer screen; they were watching him closely, putting their faces in his face and screaming at him, mocking and taunting him. They didn't care about the images; they cared about sharing the body sensation of sexual gratification.

The unborn evil spirits were there to trap him, to entice him on, to remind him of the upcoming thrill. They cared nothing for experiencing his passion. They had never had a body and were not capable of understanding the thrill—they were there to control him, to make him obey their words, to keep him involved and under their "spell" as long as possible.

They gathered around him, waiting for him to become fully involved in the sexual ecstasy he hoped for by viewing these images. The evil ones were reminding him of certain websites, urging him to go on, whispering to him how thrilling it was going to be. They told him which images to view and how he should feel about them. They argued against his conscience, giving him many reasons to ignore the voice of his conscience and carry on. They placed their hands on him time after time, causing him to feel thrill after thrill. They urged him as he clicked at his computer to seek after the thrill, to remember it, to need it more than anything else. They were most interested in keeping him focused upon his own body, and his own thrills so effectively that he could not feel his relationship to Christ, the Holy Spirit, or remember his family. All he could think of was himself and the guaranteed gratification that was just a click away.

The more excited he grew, the more frenzied the evil spirits became. They became more aggressive, jumping at him, hitting him with their hands and cursing. It was a loathsome thing to see.

I realized even more powerfully from seeing this that all addictions are purely selfish; they guarantee the instant gratification of the flesh. Relationships are not guaranteed, and the gratification, the positive payback of the relationship, must be carefully maintained and worked at. This is the reason that people turn to addictions, because they are instant, require little work, and the results are guaranteed. It is also the reason evil uses them and promotes them so carefully, because they push the user away from all meaningful relationships, especially those with the divine.

I understood that he had been awakened from his sleep by one of these tempters who had been influencing his dreams, urging him to awaken and need a sexual high. As soon as he made the choice to get out of bed and actually partake, the disembodied spirits had joined in. They were drawn to him like a moth to a search light in a dark sky. They came at once. By accepting the temptation, and deciding to do it, he had given them permission to enter him and experience his sexual thrill with him. I saw many disembodied spirits competing to enter the small room with him. The evil spirits remained at just four.

When he made the decision to partake, all of his good intentions and desires were immediately drowned out by the passion and the control of the evil spirits. The good spirits that had been near him as he slept were forced a distance away until he could not hear them. Eventually they left, driven away by his choices.

When he reached a pinnacle of lust in his body, a black tear or rip appeared at the crown of his head. In that instant the disembodied spirits began to attack. They looked like football players tackling the guy with the ball. They were hoping to share just a moment of his physical feelings and excitement. They acted like hungry dogs going after the same carcass. There was fierce competition among them to be in him longer. They fought to be next, screaming and cursing, throwing each other aside to enter. As soon as one or two spirits entered, no more could enter. The evil spirits screamed and dove at him repeatedly until a weaker one inside was expelled and they took its place. It seemed to me that the ones who were expelled were exhausted, jerking on the floor as if they were in a sexual thrall themselves, mimicking the actions of the young man at the computer. I tried to turn my face away in disgust, but I could not. The image was before me no matter which way I turned. The evil ones quickly recovered and rejoined the fight to reenter over and over.

The lust and addiction that these disembodied spirits had built up in themselves while alive as mortals still haunted them. They couldn't get rid of the lust because they did not turn to Jesus Christ, who could have healed them even after their mortal lives ended. Without His grace they couldn't satisfy the powerful need of the addiction. They couldn't escape it. Without any way to satisfy the addiction, it caused them pain, and they hunted across the globe for any opportunity to experience the thrill again, and thus lessen their pain even for a brief moment.

My guide communicated to me that when these spirits entered their victim's body, they could not fully feel what he felt. It was filtered, or buffered, to them. It was only partly satisfying, and they could not remain long because of the competition. So they attacked again and again.

The disembodied spirits were surrounded by darkness, and as they passed through this man, the darkness they possessed went into him. He could feel it as waves of dark longing, and it urged him to seek harder for more thrilling porn, harder and darker images, urging him from soft images to violent—even perverse and vile. He resisted at times, and they screamed at him, throwing themselves at him in a frenzy.

When the young man had entered the room, I knew from the light that came with him that he was a good man. I could see the light that he possessed being dimmed as he sat there. I saw that there was far more glee in Satan's minions that he was breaking his covenants, than that he was viewing pornography. Their glee was greater in the fact that he was a good man, than if he was any off-the-street kind of guy who did this sort of thing without needing much temptation. Their triumph was greater, their conquest was sweeter, and their control over him was more precious, due to the fact that this young man had made covenants to avoid such things. They delighted in the pain that this would cause his wife and family, and they relished the opportunity to eventually afflict his wife with all the dark emotions she would feel that would separate her from the Holy Spirit.

My last view of this guy was of him leaning close to the screen, breathing heavily, while unseen by him, the four dark spirits screamed at him to continue, and another dozen disembodied souls threw themselves through him in a frenzy of unsatisfied lust.

One of the most tragic aspects of this scene was that these spirits from the unseen world were offering him a sense of false relationship, giving him the sense of being fulfilled and satisfied by this experience. He was beginning to accept these unseen visitors as his companions, and he was starting to enjoy having them, welcoming their influence in helping him to decide to partake once again in his secret world of filth.

In the Bar

The tragedy I felt for this young man was quickly driven from my mind as I found myself outside of a nightclub, looking at a line of young people in their twenties standing in line to enter. I could hear their thoughts. They were longing for the thrill that they hoped was inside. There were more disembodied and evil spirits there than humans. They were standing near the mortals, urging them to continue waiting, telling of the thrill awaiting them.

I next found myself inside. There were many people tightly packed on the dance floor, dancing closely, drinking, and smoking. I could hear their thoughts, which were a continual stream of obscenities, rationalizations, and sexual lusts. Much of their thinking was more vile and violent than how they acted. They looked like normal young people on a dance floor. If they could have heard each other's thoughts, there would have been no restraint at all, but an ensuing scene of bestial acts.

I was both intrigued and repelled. I did not want to experience this darkness. I had never been to such a place and found this experience distasteful and disturbing. My spirit guide remained beside me, and I felt comforted by the fact that he did not seem affected by this scene.

As in the line outside, there were more disembodied and evil spirits here than there were mortals. Just as with the young man viewing pornography, the evil spirits were focused on specific people, those who were thinking and feeling the greatest lust and thrall. They grew more aggressive in urging them to think darker thoughts and have stronger lusts.

The disembodied spirits were waiting for specific feelings to arise in the humans. Some were looking for sexual fantasy, some for intoxication, some for drug-induced euphoria, some were seeking violence and domination. When the humans reached a certain state of intoxication, or when they abandoned themselves to the instructions of the evil ones, an opening occurred near the crown of their heads. When it opened, it looked to me like a black tear in their spirit, similar to the young man at the computer. The closest spirit rushed at them and entered like fog being sucked into a vacuum.

The other disembodied spirits rushed forward, pushing and fighting to be next. When an evil spirit entered into a human, they only remained for a few seconds, or a few minutes at most—depending upon the ability of the spirit. When they were finally expelled, they seemed to squirt out of the body at random points. They seemed exhausted but satisfied when they came out. They came out violently, mimicking the actions of the human. When they realized they were expelled, they screamed and immediately jumped back into the spirit battle to be next.

Once they were inside, they not only felt a limited portion of what their host was feeling, but they could be heard. Their dark passion added to the height of the thrall in their host. They urged their hosts to do things, to escalate the situation, to more aggressively seek greater thrills.

I saw other disembodied spirits going around the room. They would pause to listen to conversations, watching people's behavior, trying to find someone most likely to feed their needs. It seemed evident that they could not read people's thoughts, but they were masters at judging and reading people's intent. They also listened to the evil spirits and what they were urging. If someone was successfully resisting the evil suggestions, the disembodied would move on. If someone was about to "open up," many disembodied spirits converged upon them.

The disembodied spirits were waiting for the mortals to be beat down by the evil minions. They were working together. They evil spirits wanted to spiritually destroy their targets so that they could obtain permanent control over them and cared nothing for the experience of the mortals. The disembodied delighted in the physical sensations of the mortals but had no desire to dominate, only to prolong the experience.

From the evil spirits' perspective, having a mortal yield to their temptations gave them power over the mortal. If they suggested an act, and the mortal did exactly that, they set their hooks a little deeper. They were not after the thrill; they were after dominion of the soul, and eventually, lifelong control. They knew that if they could tempt with enough cleverness and deception that the human responded— they would gain a little more control. This was their method, but their real goal was to gain enough control that they could keep the Holy Spirit from having any influence in the person's life at all. They weren't just trying to control behavior; they were trying to ensnare these people in the chains of hell.

I saw that people who had already been entrapped by them could hardly hear their own thoughts. The voice of the evil ones had become even more powerful than their own mind. They would do anything their evil controllers said, even while thinking it was their own idea or their own wishes they were fulfilling. Once these evil spirits had total control, they then desired that the mortal should quickly depart mortality, so that their possession became permanent. They thereafter urged them to risky behavior, acts of violence, and even suicide to hasten the day of their mortal death.

The disembodied spirits were not trying to harm the humans so much as to share in their physical thrills and addictions. I saw spirits who were addicted to smoking try to snatch the cigarette out of the hands of mortals over and over, as if they could not understand why they could not actually grab it.

Through this whole experience, I could not only see what the evil ones and the disembodied ones were doing, but I also knew what they were thinking, both spirits and mortals. It was more than I could stand, and the scene changed.

At the Horse Race

I next found myself at a horse race. Now, I've never been to a horse race, and I had no idea what one was like. As soon as we arrived, all of the thoughts, emotions, and experiences of everyone there entered my mind with perfect clarity. It was a large track with large stands and thousands of people. There was a thrill of excitement in the air, which I quickly realized was being promoted by tens of thousands of evil spirits.

Almost the same thing was happening here as at the bar. The evil spirits were working to enhance their control over the mortals by creating this great distraction. Even though the races were less dark and promoted less lust and sexuality by far, it still created an ideal circumstance for the evil spirits to urge them to high passions, desires and fears, with soaring highs and crushing defeats, which kept them far removed from the Holy Spirit of God. The good angels were few in attendance here, being kept away by the mortals yielding their will to the evil ones.

Many of the people at the track were there for the thrill of gambling, which was being highly promoted by the evil ones. Many of the people had lied or deceived to be at the track and had opened themselves up to the evil ones in so doing. Some were there to drink, to deceive, and to satisfy their addiction to gambling. These were surrounded by evil spirits who encouraged them and told them what to feel, urging them to bet on certain horses, giving them a sure feeling of a win, which also guaranteed a crushing defeat. When they won or lost, the disembodied spirits pounced on them to share in the experience.

Here at the track, there was a greater opportunity for the good angels to intervene. In the two previous experiences, the people were fully sucked into the evil of the moment. Here, some people were praying. Some were praying to win, some to help with their addiction, some were praying for help to know how to explain their losing so much money to their wife or husband. Even a thought of God, a prayer, a request, an intention to do good, an act of regret or kindness, brought the good angels. They could then surround the person, protecting them from the evil ones for as long as that attitude persisted.

There had to be some act of free will to invite the good spirits. Sometimes the bright angels whispered, "Leave this place." Sometimes it was a suggestion like, "You need to call your wife." Sometimes they gave them a memory, perhaps of a promise, or an event from that person's life's experience that encouraged them to make good choices. Then it was up to the mortal. If they followed the prompting, the minions of Satan moved on to someone else. Light began to grow brighter around the person, and the good angels spoke encouragement. They had a chance to think clearly and to escape.

Entertainment

The scene changed again to several rapid views of mortals seeking various entertainments. I saw inside movie theaters and in homes where people were watching TV. I saw glimpses of amusement parks, casinos, and large sports events. I saw people listening to music from stereos and earphones. I saw people laughing at parties and endlessly hanging out with their friends. I thought these were everyday things of no spiritual significance.

"Why are you showing me these things?" I asked. "What is the significance?"

He replied that these were all of the ways that the people unknowingly move themselves away from the Spirit of the Lord. I realized in each of these scenes that the good angels were absent or pushed away some distance. The people in these scenes were so involved in the entertainment that they weren't listening to the Holy Spirit. They weren't doing something evil, but they were not listening to God, which was what the evil spirits labored so hard to accomplish in others, yet these were willingly isolating themselves.

I also saw that evil spirits were urging them to view more and more violent or sexual content. They were urging the people listening to the music to become enthralled, to dance and shake and gyrate, to feel sexual or physical highs, to focus on their bodies and physical beauty—anything except God.

I saw people obsessed with eating, with not eating, with dieting, with acting, with dancing or performing, with fashion or beauty, with sports, with dating, or with school—none of which were inherently evil. They were just so focused upon these things that the voice of the Holy Spirit, as I saw being delivered by the good angels, was pushed far away.

Since we as mortals cannot often see the world of spirits, either good or bad, we are truly ignorant of most that is going on around us. It requires some spiritual insight, usually gained by costly negative experiences, to realize how life works. Mortal life is only a dim reality. The angels live in an eternal realm, which is the brightest and truest reality. Mortal life will end; their lives will not. They know how incredibly important this little time of mortality is, and because they love us and are in the service of their God, they labor to get our attention and lead us into a life that will end in glory.

Spiritual Gifts

I was shown how spiritual gifts work. There are good gifts, and there are evil gifts. We choose good gifts when we obey the Holy Spirit. These are gifts of love, joy, peace, faith, healings, prophecy, and many other gifts. When we repeatedly choose obedience to what is good, we create a spiritual link with Jesus Christ. He changes us into His spiritual likeness, and we grow brighter and brighter in this process until we become children of light, and we receive our wages from our Savior.

We choose evil gifts by obeying the temptations of evil spirits, which is the same thing as saying to yield to a temptation from Satan. We choose evil gifts by obeying a lust to obtain some physical thrill or high. When we give in to any amount of evil, we are creating a spiritual link, like coupling train cars together; and when we allow this to happen over and over, we are changed, darkened, and dragged down, until we become servants of darkness, and we receive our wages from the master of darkness.

I observed that there are many people who are governed by the voice of Jesus Christ, who are like lanterns being carried through darkness. They push the darkness away by their approach, and the dark angels must depart. Evil beings are powerless to penetrate it and are compelled to depart.

The same thing is true of people who are ruled by evil. They become lamps of darkness and push the light away. They become a force of darkness, even while walking in the brightness of spiritual day. Everyone who associates with them is darkened by them, and the good angels are powerless to penetrate it—until that person by an act of free will asks for help or prays for guidance.

The Chains of Hell

I saw that when any person manifests even the smallest particle of faith, even just a thought or an idea—anything that moves them toward hope, obedience to truth, and faith in Jesus Christ—then the darkness is penetrated by a small degree of light, and the angels once again speak the words of Christ as the Still, Small Voice. If people choose to respond correctly to that voice, the darkness will begin to lift. There will still be a long road and many more correct choices to make, but the process is begun.

The "chains of hell" are when a person becomes so enamored with their lives of darkness that they can no longer even hear the Still, Small Voice of the angels shouting truth from the distance to which they have been pushed. When a person yields to this degree, they lose their moral compass and can no longer tell the difference between good and evil, right and wrong, love and lust, and eventually, mercy and murder. The only "good" they acknowledge is whatever brings them the fastest satisfaction of their lusts and addictions, and no price seems too high.

The Ministry of Angels

I saw the angels of light who are assigned to us. They are real. They have direct access to Christ's guidance and are anxiously engaged in our lives. They remain with us throughout our lives unless we choose darkness by our thoughts, acts, or words. Their ability to direct, influence, and guide us is completely controlled by our choices.

There are also more powerful angels of light who are assigned by Christ to bless us in certain times of need, as when I was dying in the hospital. These angels come on assignment, and in harmony with our assigned angels, they deliver the blessings Jesus Christ desires us to have.

Every time I have had my eyes opened to the world of spiritual things, there were more spirit beings in the room than mortals. Most of the godly angels seem to be our ancestors, people from our family who love us and who have been sent to aid us at special times.

We don't have this more powerful type of angel with us

often. They come on special assignment, and when there is a pressing need or greater blessing to bestow. We invite them to help us by rejecting temptation and by calling upon the name of God and doing what is right with a mind single to the glory of God. These guiding angels know us well because we have associated with them for a long time.

Our familial relationship did not begin with their birth or ours. I sensed this eternal connection while I was viewing my premortal childhood home. Our relationships are ordained, and they are eternally significant. Our relationships began long ago in the household of God, before our birth and before the creation of the world. We have loved one another a long time and have served one another in unending ways. It is probably also true that while they were mortals, we lovingly ministered to them. And now they are ministering to us in the same office.

Everything God does is according to law and according to agency. God does not gift us with things we have not qualified for in some way. This is also true of angels. Some angels have greater abilities because of their greater diligence and because of greater righteousness while they were mortals. Some angels are learning, while others are quite accomplished. Some have great faith, while others are of less faith.

Looking at this phenomenon from a parent's perspective, it gives us the ability to bless our children and grandchildren after we leave mortality. These spiritual gifts and strengths become the heritage of our grandchildren, because when they choose the light, we are there waiting anxiously to pour out the gifts we ourselves obtained in mortality, upon them.

This is also the reason that drunkenness, abuse, crime, war-mongering, mafia, and other dark traits that may corrupt political power, run in families. These dark tendencies are passed down through the ages. When our ancestors find themselves in the next life as unhappy spirit beings who are still addicted, pain-racked, miserable souls, they seek to make others miserable like themselves. When their children and grandchildren follow their example, then the dark "gifts" are passed down through the generations. This may explain why some families have been royalty for hundreds of years, or wealthy and oppressive from the beginning of time, or any other dark familial trait.

It may also explain why prophets and apostles tend to be related, and greatness runs in families.

At last I realized that this was the message of this whole experience, to see how darkness infests mortality through evil "angels," and how light is amplified in our lives through obedience to God and the ministry of angels of light. I started seeing glimpses of how people's choices were making this happen.

Light, Darkness, and the Earth

I saw that the earth itself had been created perfect and is fulfilling the measure of its creation. Everything about it—its placement in the universe; the distance from the sun; and the bringing forth of life, fruit, and beauty—is all created by and maintained by the continuing presence of the light of Christ.

People institute governments, false religion, false science, and false teachings. They build cities where evil easily thrives and provide universities and schools to promote such things—the entire collection of the "philosophies of men," their lies, their religions, their rationalizations and sins. As these constructs and pollutions of man spread across the globe, they cover the world with darkness, and the earth responds with upheaval, devastations, floods, famines, pestilence, and death.

All of this is like a blanket of darkness that spreads itself across the face of the earth, dimming the light of Christ that reaches the earth. This diminishes the power that keeps the earth orderly and a fit habitation for mankind.

There is a process given to the earth whereby it cleanses itself. When evil overtakes it, natural disasters, plagues, and upheavals begin in random places. When evil on the world becomes so great that the light of Christ is dimmed, it will produce eruptions, extremes of weather and temperature, storms, floods, earthquakes, and other destructive events. There is a direct correlation between the choices of mortals and the condition of the earth. This is why there will be so many natural disasters and death caused by these acts of nature in the latter days—because mankind by then will have veiled the earth in darkness.

This isn't to say that the earthquake or flood is aimed like a missile at the evil, or that the places where disasters happen needed cleansing most. The whole of humanity suffers when darkness reigns.

Enoch saw the earth weep because it was overwhelmed and covered by evil in Enoch's day. It wanted to rid itself of evil and rest in the millennial day.

If it was tired and sick in Enoch's day, imagine how weary it is today.

Immediately following this view of the earth and the effects of spiritual light and darkness, the scene changed once again.

I began seeing the earth going through the prophesied latter-day destructions. The first thing I saw was the signs of the Second Coming being made manifest in the earth. These signs were in the form of events in the heavens and on the earth. The most visible of these were the unending natural disasters. Other signs were wrongly interpreted by mankind to be unexpected but normal upheavals in the earth and celestial events among the stars and planets.

I could see growing evil in the hearts of mankind. I saw that the earth was in great trouble. It was suffering, dying, losing its ability to sustain life on its face. It was like a tropical flower that had been moved into a basement devoid of all light and was dying in the darkness. It could not live without the light that gave life to everything, and made it beautiful and useful to man. Every part of the earth was in great tribulation.

Flying across America

I began moving across the world, flying as if I were in a fast helicopter, close to the earth. I could see every detail below me. I was not in any machine, of course, but I saw it from that perspective. My spiritual companion was with me and guided our flight. We moved in and out of the cities across North America.

I saw that whenever this time was that I was being shown, the financial structure of the world had completely collapsed. Every bank had closed down and money was worthless. People were learning to trade and barter. Manufacturing and industry were at a virtual standstill. There were no raw materials and no money to pay the workers. Factories and global businesses shut down overnight.

All of the utilities were in chaos. People tried to keep the necessities of life running, but they were sporadic and mostly off-line. There were blackouts everywhere, some of them lasting many months. Almost all water was not fit to drink because of acts of war against this country. People suffered everywhere.

My flight across North America began in Salt Lake City. There had been a massive earthquake in that area in the fall of the year. I tried to determine which year it was even while I was in the vision, but I could not. I looked into shop windows for a calendar or date. I even looked at people's watches to see if they showed the year. I was not allowed to learn when these things might happen. All I can say is that Salt Lake City looked in that vision much as it does to-day. There were models of automobiles that I did not recognize, and other small changes, but I considered it as having happened not far into the future.

The fault that runs along the Wasatch front had moved dramatically, causing a great deal of damage to cities along the front. In the third part of this experience, which I will relate in the next chapter, I went back to Salt Lake City and found myself in my own life, in my own body, living through these very events. So I will come back to those events when I relate the third part of this visionary event.

The Next Spring

I saw that the next spring after the destruction in Utah, there was another devastating series of earthquakes that occurred along the west coast of North and South America. The western coast of California, Mexico, and all the way to the tip of South America, was shaken so badly that much of it broke away from the mainland and formed a series of islands off the coast. Seawater rushed in to fill in the canyons between land and island. Major cities were shaken to the ground, with inland areas suffering less damage. The same quake extended up the coast of Canada and continued all the way to Alaska. I didn't see the effects of the earthquakes north of the continental United States, but I assume the destruction was undiminished.

This earthquake sent tidal waves across the world. I was not shown what occurred in South America, Europe, Asia, or Africa. But I assume this was a worldwide catastrophe. From events that I will relate in the next chapter, I assume that Europe was not as badly affected by the earthquakes as North America, because those countries sent large amounts of relief and supplies to America after the earthquakes.

Two Months Later

About two months later, another earthquake opened up a narrow canyon approximately where the Mississippi River is now, though it deviated eastward where the Mississippi presently merges with the Ohio River. It followed the Ohio into the Great Lakes. The Ohio River and the remainder of the Mississippi River rerouted itself into this canyon. It created a huge new lake and river system approximately where the Mississippi River is now. This canyon essentially created an eastern and a western United States, which figured into some international intrigue later on.

I next "flew" over the lower part of California and toward the Gulf of Mexico. Almost all of California was in ruin, with less destruction further away from the coast. I saw that a great landmass had risen up into the Gulf. It extended from Mexico to Florida and consisted of a few large islands that replaced the water of the gulf. I did not think to look toward Cuba. In some places, the new land met Mexico, Texas, and Florida, but there was also a large waterway separating most of the new land from America.

I did not see where the land came from. It either rose up from the Gulf floor, or was pushed north by the earthquakes from South America. The land was not barren all over, but large parts of it had trees and other vegetation. Some parts of it were just muddy islands. I am at a loss to explain where it came from.

This great landmass created a tidal wave that did a great deal of devastation as far north as Chicago.

About two-thirds of the Gulf was now a series of large islands. I did not see the damage this caused worldwide, but I can only assume it was extensive.

I then "flew" across the upper part of Florida and up the east coast of the United States. The earthquakes had not reached here as strongly, so the infrastructure was more intact. But there had been a biological attack, and there was more death in the eastern and northeastern parts of the country than in those areas stricken by the earthquakes. I saw bodies stacked in town squares and cities abandoned because of the stench of death. There were marauding bands of people plundering and stealing in every major city. They were murdering everyone they found to preserve remaining resources for themselves. It was like survivors in a lifeboat throwing the weakest among them overboard to leave enough food and water for the strongest. It was a gruesome scene.

The scene was violent and disgusting. During the writing of this book, I was shown the text of President John Taylor's vision of similar events, where starvation and death were everywhere. I was startled by the similarities, though the suffering was seen more graphically in President Taylor's vision. (See Appendix A for the complete text of the dream.)

Foreign Troops

I saw foreign troops landing on the east and west coasts of America. There were tens of thousands of them. They came in large ships, some of them former cruise ships with naval escorts. They landed with thousands of vehicles, most of them laden with relief supplies, but also with large tanks and missile launchers. They wore blue-green helmets, and I assumed they were international relief troops. My mortal body is color blind, and I am not sure if I saw the color of these troop's helmets correctly in the vision. I didn't see many troops in the large cities like Boston, Chicago, and New York because there was almost nobody there to relieve. Those who had not died were trudging west to escape from the cities.

In California, some Americans tried to fight the troops because they saw them as invaders. There were a few battles where the local people lost the battles and were subdued. The foreign troops did not punish the survivors; they just asked them to cooperate, fed them, and released them. This won over the minds of the people. I also saw that the foreign troops had come with the expectation that they would have to kill locals, even though Americans were in no condition to resist them.

CHAPTER SEVEN

TRIBULATION AND FULNESS

Earthquakes and Floods

My next realization was that I was in my body, standing in the parking garage beneath the present Church Office Building. What I mean by "in my body" is that I was no longer "flying" across the continent, but I was now a participant in the vision. It once again felt real to me. I had possession of all of my senses and was experiencing these things in perfect detail. As in everyday life, I was subject to the events around me.

Even though what I saw next has yet to occur, I was nevertheless there, dressed in a business suit, carrying a briefcase, and walking through this familiar underground parking garage. I had parked there many times when I had attended my monthly meetings appertaining to my calling.

In my new circumstance, I remembered that I was just walking from a meeting with a member of the Quorum of the Twelve. I was feeling content, with the Spirit warmly present upon me. I had just reached my car, which was a different vehicle than the one I presently drive (in 2011). I had just about reached the car door when the ground started shaking violently.

I thought, *This is a bad earthquake! I don't have time to get out of this parking garage with my car! The building will fall on top of me before I get out!*

I was only twenty or so feet from the exit, so I dropped my brief-case and ran for the exit. The ground was rolling violently beneath me. I fell down many times, but when I stood I was not injured. I reached the road, which was North Temple, only to see water gushing up out of the ground.

I have to pause in my narrative a moment to say that I have been sick all of my life, and running even that short distance would normally have exhausted me. But in this vision, I was not tired, not injured by repeated falling, and not particularly afraid. I realized I was different; my body had been upgraded in some indefinable way. Even though this all felt real, I knew I was experiencing a vision, and I wondered if my upgraded body was an effect of this vision. I didn't understand what I was being shown until much later.

Now, back to North Temple. The earthquake had broken up the streets, and where there were cracks in the road, water was shoot-ing into the sky. Water was also gushing from manhole covers, storm drains, and cracks in the earth. It was shooting up with sufficient force that water was spraying everywhere, completely soaking me. It was fresh water, surprisingly clean and clear. Everywhere I could see there were geysers of water spraying with a deafening roar into the air. I asked myself, "Where is all of this water coming from?" I can only guess at the answer to this question.

I turned east and ran uphill. Water was roaring down North Temple in a flood, which grew deeper each moment. Water was now up around my calves, and I ran uphill against the current with surpris-ing energy. The eastern side of Salt Lake City is several hundred feet higher than where the temple sits, and I was running for high ground.

The ground continued to heave, and I fell down many times, but each time was uninjured. I saw cars with people in them being swept down the street along with furniture, parts of homes, dead bodies, and trash of every type. It was a sickening scene. There was nothing I could do to help them. I fell one more time and was myself swept away into the swirling flood. I held onto debris and kept my head above water.

All this time I was wondering where all the water was coming from. The water was shooting up about six feet into the air. It was all astonishing.

I found myself flowing west toward the old Union Pacific train station. There were people standing on the stairs watching the flood flow around the building, trying to help anyone that floated near. I floated toward them and someone pulled me onto the stairs, and others helped me stand up. I found that my trousers were ripped completely off of me. I had no shoes. I was standing there in my shirt and tie, socks, and underwear.

The train station was flooded by about a foot of water, which went down to a few inches as the hours passed. The survivors with me included women, children, and men. We watched the flooding until the sun began to set. We realized we were going to spend the night in the station, and we tried to prepare a dry place where we could sleep. We tried to sweep the water out of the places we needed to be, and we packed blankets under the doors to try to hold back the water that was still flowing over the sill. To me the train station felt like a sinking boat just before it goes under. There were still a few inches of water flowing over the tunnels.

We found dry places and sat on the wooden benches to try to get dry. I remember being quite cold and trying to sleep on these benches. In one of the storage areas, we found some small blankets, probably left over from the days of passenger trains. We also found tiny pillows previously used for sleeping on the train. We huddled together and tried to cover ourselves with these.

Someone found a storage room filled with workmen's coveralls. They were faded blue, like a janitor's uniform. They were clean but not new. I also found a pair of shoes that almost fit.

The next morning we found that the floodwater was going down. There was a lot of pooling and an amazing variety of debris everywhere, including dead bodies and body parts, which was disturbing.

I engaged myself in helping those in the train station, trying to provide for our immediate needs. Someone found a kitchen and some kind of mush, which we mixed with water and ate cold with our fingers. All telephone and cell phone services were down. There was no electricity or running water, so we were truly in the dark.

At about two or three that afternoon, I decided to make my way back home. It should have taken me half of a day of brisk walking, but my journey took three full days because of the devastation, the breakup of the roads, and the fallen trees and buildings. I had to keep detouring. Anytime I found someone in need, I joined them in their work. They offered me food and assistance as I made my way home.

The devastation was awesome and terrifying, but there was no looting or selfishness. The city had changed; old landmarks were gone. I found myself disoriented because signs, buildings, and even trees I had used to guide myself home for many years were now gone. I had to keep asking for directions and to find out which roads were open. I traveled south a long distance before I could again turn east for a while, and then north back toward my home. I probably walked twenty miles to cover five.

I looked up and saw that the mountain behind the city had collapsed. The tops of the mountains had fallen upon the upper parts of the city, burying most of the large homes on the benches above the city.

When I finally made it to my subdivision, I walked up the street I lived on. I could see no people anywhere. They had all abandoned their homes. The houses were shifted and pushed off of their foundations. My house was so twisted that I could look down into the basement from outside. I realized that it was no longer habitable and was dangerous to enter. I did not find my wife or any family members. I went back later with help and went down into the basement to recover our food storage and a few personal things, but I never did enter the upper part of my home. I just walked away.

The whole quake had lasted only six to eight minutes, but it felt like hours. The flood waters rose for about eight hours and then began to subside. After that, water remained in the streets and pooled in low places for several weeks. The pools of water quickly became fetid and septic. There was water flooding into Salt Lake City from the Bountiful area. I'm not sure if a reservoir had burst, or what might have caused that. There was flooding from the south where the Jordan River was running over its banks, I presume from Utah Lake being inundated by water from the reservoirs above Provo and other areas.

All of this water drained into the Great Salt Lake, moving the salted water in a tidal wave out into the desert northwest of the lake. The lake was at least twice the size that it is now and had risen about twelve feet in depth. Low-lying farms and homes were gone. In some places, water was covering I-15. The whole airport area was flooded, and it was months before military planes could land there. I don't believe commercial air services were ever restored.

Most of the inhabitants of the area generally did not believe that this was a "sign" of the coming of Christ. They just considered it a natural disaster. A strong core group continued to listen to the Holy Spirit and to believe and correctly interpret the "signs" we were seeing. But there were many, both in the Church and out of the Church, who were angry, were despairing, and had little hope.

The leadership of the Church was stricken just as hard as the general population, and since all communication was down, it was several weeks before we heard anything from the official lines of the Church. Those members of the Twelve and other quorums who had been away on assignment were cut off by the collapse of communication worldwide. The first thing we knew of the Church was that some of the food we received from the foreign troops was marked with the Church logo. This comforted us, but it was still weeks before we were assured that the Church leadership and its local and international organization had not collapsed altogether.

We didn't know if the Prophet or any of the Twelve had survived. This scared many people and prompted some to stand up to try to reorganize the Church according to their own ideas.

Those who had the Spirit knew that the process of rebuilding the Church and restoring the quorums of the priesthood was underway, but we knew almost no details. The Church's reorganization was hampered initially by not knowing who had survived there in Salt Lake City and across the globe.

Without the voice of the Prophet among us, a feeling of discord and strife grew in the Church. People grew angry about almost everything, and some were selfish with the remaining resources. However, many were stalwart and faithful through all of this discord and strife.

The local churches of all denominations, including stakes and wards, rose to the occasion, organizing relief efforts among their people, housing and feeding people, providing comfort and safety. The Church had a prominent role in the rebuilding effort because the

Church and her people were so well prepared, but every other church joined in a united effort. I was among those who went door to door, digging out the survivors and burying the dead. Sometimes we were moved upon to give priesthood blessings, and those who had faith were saved, some with miraculous recoveries. But mostly we buried the dead and brought food and water for those who were without means.

I was actually amazed at how many good Latter-day Saints had little or no food storage. We didn't judge them. Those with faith, who had stored food, gave it away freely and joined the work of saving those who suffered and of preparing for the fast-approaching winter. We rushed to close in the damaged homes and to find a means of heating the homes. We took materials from damaged homes to repair the standing ones. Many families moved in together into one home. It was a herculean effort.

About this time, a large column of military vehicles arrived in town. They had come to help. They wore blue helmets and had international insignias on their doors, helmets, and uniforms. Our local civic leaders had tried to organize relief efforts, but that effort expired when the foreign troops took over. Only the Church and our Christian friends remained organized and committed.

The foreign troops were from many nations. Most groups didn't speak English at all. There were groups who looked Asian. We couldn't tell from their language or from their uniforms because they were all dressed alike. There were troops from European counties as well, but none from England that I met. There were also American service people from what remained of the US armed forces. Depending upon their rank, they were sometimes the leaders of these divisions; most of the time they were not.

They came in large, strange-looking trucks—much larger than those of our present military. Some of the trucks had four or five driven axles and were too wide to drive down a single lane of a highway. They had come from the west coast of California and made their way across a large area of devastation. Their vehicles were covered in mud and showed evidence of harsh use but seemed rugged and reliable. The trucks were loaded with a great deal of cargo—food, medical supplies, fuel, and other necessities.

We were grateful to see them arrive, but it was unsettling just the same. They took over several schools as their headquarters and used the gymnasiums to store goods, which they guarded closely. They also set up hospitals with real doctors. They were soon overwhelmed by the injured.

Those of us who were uninjured volunteered to help with the work. They were surprised by how many came to help. They gave us gloves and coats and welcomed us. They found heavy equipment and soon began digging large graves in the school yards.

There were many former missionaries among us, so we were able to communicate with these new arrivals to some extent. They informed us that much of Europe, Asia, and Africa had been spared from the major effects of the earthquakes and tidal waves. Most of the devastation had occurred in North and South America. They said they had arrived in California in hundreds of ships and had immediately worked with those people to stabilize things, and then they had headed east. They told us that a large relief effort had landed on the east coast and was working west. We learned that every major city they had come to was devastated. They reported, as I had seen during my "fly-over" vision, that the California coastline had broken off into a series of islands.

They also told us that more troops and supplies were on the way from all over the world. They said to us, "America has always been generous to us in disaster relief, and now it is our turn to respond." They seemed genuine in their desire to help, but I could not see light in their faces, and I deeply distrusted their long-term objectives. I think most of us felt that way.

Not many days after they arrived, they began clearing the streets of rubble and overturned cars so that relief efforts could move more efficiently south. I was on one of the first big trucks when we headed south to see how far we could get beyond Salt Lake City, and what relief efforts were needed there.

Initially the foreigners, and especially the few American servicemen in their ranks, were impressed with what the Church had accomplished. They said that no other city they had encountered so far had done so much, or was better prepared, for a disaster of this magnitude.

These new troops were a great asset to us in our efforts to

recover. They didn't take long to get organized and soon had relief teams going up and down streets, providing necessary assistance to the citizens. Troops also left from Salt Lake City to continue south on into the Utah Valley area, which was also hit hard by the earthquakes but had experienced only minor localized flooding when reservoirs had failed.

The local relief workers joined with various groups of these foreign troops. We worked with them and rode in their vehicles to and from assignments. We worked our way down side streets, through the residential areas, approaching Immigration Canyon. We stopped at every home to assist people, promising that other rescuers were close behind us. We were still in the residential area, a few miles from the Point of the Mountain, when I realized that the view looked wrong. There were no more trees or power poles to be seen toward the south. We slowed down and approached with caution. We could not believe our eyes. Ahead of us, the ground had fallen away.

I walked up to the edge and peered down into the hole. I'm guessing the land beyond had fallen fifty feet or more. The area below was under water, with total destruction. Nothing had survived that we could see.

We stood there pondering for a long time until the military leader told us it was time to leave. We backed away and turned around. The sun was just setting in the most beautiful sunset I have ever seen. The atmosphere was filled with dust, and it made the deepest reds and oranges imaginable. We were just pulling away when a hypothesis formed in my mind.

The earthquake had not been centered in downtown Salt Lake City, but here where this land had dropped away. Apparently it had been overarching a massive underground lake. There is a major fault that runs right along the base of the mountain, and lesser faults that fracture out perpendicular to that. Apparently one of these east-west fractures had given way and dropped this landmass into the underground lake. With no place to go but up, the water had followed earthquake fissures and then storm drains until it gushed up into the sky inside the city. I am not sure if this is actually what happened, but it is one possible explanation for the water coming from underground.

This fallen area eventually formed a new freshwater lake that emptied into the Jordan River and then into the Great Salt Lake, which was now filled with fresh water.

It took a couple weeks for the water to drain out of the city. We continually followed the water's receding edge, bringing relief efforts and burying the dead. When we could finally see the Salt Lake Temple and Conference Center, we found that the temple had been flooded about twenty-five feet deep, up to the round windows. It was still majestic and solid. The old Tabernacle was gone. Only a foundation and a few timbers remained. The Joseph Smith Memorial building and Church office buildings were still standing, but there was water damage on the lower floors.

The Conference Center had survived with little more damage than flooding of the parking areas and lower rooms. The main auditorium had flooded partially, but most of it was easily salvaged.

The flood receded quickly enough that nobody was stuck in the taller buildings more than a few days.

A Devastating Plague

About this time, a devastating plague swept across the nation. It came in three waves. Each wave was more virulent, killing healthier people, and killing them quicker. It swept across North and South America and around the world, killing billions. But the troops who arrived seemed to be mostly immune to it, though a few of them died as well. Of the total population before the earthquake, I estimated that 25 percent died in the plague. I knew as I was "flying" over it that the plague had been man-made, and the troops were inoculated against it, but it took many months before the survivors of the plague realized the true source of it. I will talk more about this plague in the next chapter.

The lawlessness began to ease as the marauders were caught and summarily executed by the troops. They did not have any regard for civil rights, or even human rights. They had a job to do, and they did it with brute force and little empathy, which may have been necessary in that setting, at least at first.

When the troops arrived in the Salt Lake City area, they were complimentary of the Church and surprised at how far the relief and restoration had progressed. But as the weeks progressed, they became less and less tolerant. They started taking advantage of any chaos that existed. Because of the collapse of civil authority, the Church had become the only organized group of people remaining. The Church had taken charge of rebuilding and reorganizing and did not stop just because relief efforts had arrived. This was the first city the troops had entered that didn't just give up and hand control of civil matters over to the foreign troops.

The organization of the Church seemed to thwart their plans to be in control. In a short time it became apparent that their primary goal was to establish their own government in place of federal and local governments. When they found the Church organized and functioning as a de facto government, it frustrated their plans, and it also created a split in their ranks, largely by national origin.

The few US troops among them refused to act against the Church, as did many from Europe. Quite a few of the troops who resisted were members themselves. The troops from Asia were not dissuaded and thereafter decided that the Church was an enemy that had to be shut down or destroyed. But they could not proceed to just destroy the Church because of the troops who did not agree, and because of the fact that nearly all of the remaining population were members of the Church, or indebted to it for their lives and welfare.

A considerable amount of printed propaganda began coming from what appeared to be the remnants of our Federal Government. They proclaimed with great fanfare that this was the beginning of a "new world order." They claimed that everything had changed in the world. For the first time in memory, the United States was no longer able to meet its own basic needs, and the rest of the world was welcoming us into this new world. The logic they used was, "Why else would they be here with food and medicine, instead of with guns and bombs." Our own government seemed to be urging all US citizens to just submit and accept the changes in civil authority.

It didn't take long for most people to decide our Federal Government no longer existed and that this propaganda was coming from the foreign troops themselves.

The attitude of almost everyone changed from relief and

acceptance to viewing these foreign troops as an invasion force. There was a huge growth of local resistance and distrust. Especially in the Utah area, people saw them as having come to destroy our liberties and our church—which turned out to be true. Some people began to quietly disobey their new "laws." However, those who listened to the Holy Spirit realized that resisting these troops was not the Lord's will. He had His own agenda, and those who obeyed Him just watched and waited upon the Lord.

The foreign troops at first waged a propaganda campaign, trying to destroy the people's trust in the Church. They did this by publishing lies and accusations. They infiltrated the local meetings or paid people for information on what was going on in the local wards and stakes. They would then create some sort of uproar, just to see who was loyal to the Church and who would be loyal to the foreign authority.

They passed laws declaring that the Church had no authority in civil matters. They then falsely accused and arrested key leaders for involving themselves in civic affairs. These were crimes against the new laws. Some of these leaders were publicly executed, which dramatically darkened the mood of the people toward the troops. In a short period of time, they effectively ejected the Church from all civil matters. Since they could not tell a "Mormon" from anyone else just by looking at them, they made it illegal for any American to be in a position of authority in civil matters.

The mood of some of the people turned rebellious, and along with the troops who had defected from the foreign forces, they moved from their homes up into the mountains. They took guns and provisions with them and periodically attacked the foreign troops. Their efforts were poorly inspired, and they were soon killed or captured, or they melted back into the larger society. The remainder of the people quietly turned their attention to prayer and faith, and they hearkened to the leadership of the Church. The Church began operating quietly to accomplish the Lord's mission and did not fear the troops, but they also didn't provoke them.

I never saw an official group of US soldiers or National Guard. I found out later that atomic weapons had been deployed to take out major defense installations around the nation and in Utah. There had been a first strike against the United States, and it came without provocation.

About this time, the same plague that had devastated so much of the east coast arrived in Utah as it spread across the nation. The foreign troops had brought hazmat equipment, as if they were expecting the plague, and few of them got sick. As I said, we found out later that the plague was man-made, and the troops had been inoculated against the pathogen that caused the plague.

The foreign troops were prepared in other ways. They had printed posters[1] that they required everyone to fasten to their front

door. The sign was a black circle with a diagonal line through it, inside of a wreath. The sign had the word "PLAGUE" in red letters printed behind the black line. There was a row of white, numbered stickers across the bottom of the poster. There were instructions on

1 When Spencer described this plague poster to me, I couldn't picture it in my mind. I asked him to make a sketch of it and realized he was drawing the UN wreath, and the circle with the diagonal line was an international symbol for "no." I drew the image above and showed it to Spencer. He said, "Where did you find that?" I asked, "Is this correct?" He replied, "It is exactly as I remember it! Where did you find it?" Since it was apparently accurate, I thought it of value to include it in the book. It is also of great interest that in John Taylor's vision, recorded in Appendix A at the end of this book, he describes seeing badges or signs of mourning upon every door, "in every land, and in every place."

the poster. We were to put a sticker on the left side of the poster on the black line indicating how many people were alive in the home. When someone died, we were to put the number of the dead on the right side of the poster on the line. We then changed the number of the living. The stickers could be reused as needed. It was a terrifying and grieving moment when someone had to change their stickers. People often stood around the front door, weeping and praying for strength just to move the stickers.

When the troops came, they drove by each house and aimed a reader gun at the poster. The gun was attached to a laptop computer that remembered each house by its GPS position. If the numbers had changed, indicating another death, they pulled into your driveway.

We were given body bags and were instructed to put our dead on the back porch or in the backyard, and they would come gather them up in the evening. When the plague was at its most deathly stage, it took days, or even weeks, for the trucks to make it to outlaying streets. They were most concerned about controlling the city center and only left that area when all of the dead had been collected.

When a person contracted the plague, they got many small pox marks on their skin, similar to pimples. These grew in size and quantity until nearly their whole body was covered by them. They grew very sick quickly. The itching and pain was severe. Shortly before death, the pox erupted and oozed. This fluid was extremely contagious. Everyone who touched it got sick.

We learned all this by sad experience. Many people who knew they were going to die zipped themselves into the body bags before the pox erupted, to spare their loved ones having to handle their bodies. These were dark times. The very young and very old died first. Those who were trying to help others and became contaminated by touching the fluid died next.

The plague ultimately killed more than half of those who were exposed to it. Some people survived by some natural immunity or divine intervention. Once symptoms appeared, a person would die about twelve hours later. The plague came in three waves, each one taking out the next weakest group of people. If you got sick and somehow survived, you became immune.

The soldiers who handled the dead were dressed in white

contamination suits. They took away the bodies of the dead to parks or football stadiums where they had dug large holes. The dead were then soaked with fuel and cremated. The troops did not speak to us since most of them did not speak English. They were detached and unsympathetic. They just had a nasty job to do, which they were determined to accomplish without contaminating themselves or becoming insane from so much death. They also didn't harass us. It was all impersonal.

When I had earlier seen these scenes while "flying" across the landscape, I saw city after city across the nation where these posters were on the doors. I didn't understand what they meant until I saw this latter part of the vision where I was on the ground experiencing it as a living person. I was left with the impression that between the earthquake and the plague, more than half of the population had been killed—more on the coastlines and fewer inland.

The scene became more and more horrendous as I watched time pass. In Utah, and other places where people had hearkened to the warnings to store food and prepare spiritually, there was hope. In other places, people lost hope. Some people intentionally contaminated themselves with the plague after watching loved ones die. In places where people had no hope, awful things happened that I think it best not to articulate. Suffice it to say that heinous crimes were commonplace.

In heavily populated areas, starvation and thirst drove people to do the unthinkable, fulfilling many prophecies of these times that Christ had referred to as the "Abomination of Desolations." Civilization came to a standstill to await the end of all life, and people despaired aloud, saying that Jesus Christ was delaying His coming until after the end of all life on earth.

Anywhere the Church was prevalent, the people were much better off because of the preparations of the people and of the Church. Food and water were still available. Large meals were prepared and served in public places, most often churches. People had at least one sustaining meal a day. Many came with more food than they ate, sustaining the relief effort and calming people's fears. Nobody was turned away. We divided what we had with everyone.

As long as the Church didn't take any part in civic decisions, the foreign troops allowed these efforts and contributed to the food that was served.

Churches—LDS and others—were divided off into family living quarters. The troops brought in water in large tanker trucks. Water was rationed, but it was plentiful. The food was simple. I didn't see much meat; it was mostly stored food from local people and the Church.

If someone grew ill, there was a protocol for a local doctor or nurse to certify that you did not have the plague, and then the foreign troops would take you to the larger hospitals.

The troops continued to assert greater and greater control, including establishing martial law and suspending civil liberties. The enforcement of their new laws was either by a warning, refusing further food and services to your family, or by execution. They did not maintain jails.

It was about this time that the plague hit Europe, Asia, and Africa. I don't believe it was ever started there, or intended to go there, but it got out of control and crossed the oceans. The devastation there was far more severe than in the Americas. The result over time was a complete collapse of society. We also heard of great natural disasters now taking place all around the world. There were hurricanes, tornadoes, floods, earthquakes, and disease. This was the time period when the landmass arose in the gulf, and the tidal wave swept northward.

Initially, America had been hardest hit by all of this, but when the destructions hit the nations who had released the plague and launched the nuclear weapons, it was far more destructive for them. Their entire governments, financial institutions, and economies collapsed. They experienced powerful earthquakes and continental movement, and rioting and war were far more devastating than in America. People were trying to leave those continents in droves. As I will explain more fully later, angels and translated beings ministered to the worthy and faithful and protected them as they began their journey to Zion.

The Mark of the Beast

In all of my visions, I never saw a mark upon people, or heard people talking of being forced to receive a mark or microchip in order to buy and sell. It was already true that we each had a number to our name, and that number was required for any large transaction, such as buying a home or obtaining credit. That may have been part of the mark.

But what I did see was that we had spiritually marked ourselves. This marking began perhaps thirty years before the tribulations, when the counterculture of political correctness began, and the assault on Christian values and traditions began. At first it seemed so ridiculous that it was harmless, kind of like a disease to which we were all immune. Soon, however, it was recolored to equal compassion, fairness, acceptance, tolerance, and equality. From there it evolved into a power with the ability to take any truth and repaint it as a lie, to take any lie and relabel it as truth. Subscribing to this thinking and tuning out the Holy Spirit marked us with darkness. It was a mark we placed upon our own soul. It was not visible to another human, but those who had marked themselves in this way could not discern the Holy Spirit, and they found themselves completely reliant upon the foreign troops, who truthfully had no long-term interest in their survival.

When the tribulations began, it was nearly impossible for those who had received the mark of the beast to see God's hand reaching out to lead them to safety. They were blinded to the only thing that could redeem them, and many were eventually lost.

Signs of the Second Coming

The winter that rolled in was mild. The sky was laden with ash, smoke, and water vapor. The sun still seemed as warm as before, but the weather was mild. Stunning sunsets and sunrises abounded. We often stood and watched them, wondering what they meant. The snows did not come at all that winter, which was a cause of great relief and of increased survival. Most people had no effective means of heating any of the buildings we huddled into.

The atmosphere of the earth felt different from then on. There was a cleansing process that was taking place. Even though we were experiencing great devastation, the water grew clearer and cleaner in the rivers and lakes. You could see a great distance to the bottom of the lakes. The earth was apparently being cleansed and purified. Many people commented and wondered at the great "signs and wonders" that were manifest in the earth and sky. We saw differences in the constellations, which made us wonder if the earth was being pulled from its normal orbit. This caused worldwide panic when it was first observed, but there was not as much fear among the Saints. We knew that God's hand was upon us and that these were the "Signs of the Second Coming" that the world had so long waited to see.

Raising the Dead Boy

One of my favorite memories of this time in the vision was of being in the basement of an older LDS church in Salt Lake City. We were singing around a piano when the Bishop's wife ran into the room and asked me and some others to come up and bless her baby, who had just taken ill. I hurried upstairs and examined the boy without touching him. I did not see the now-familiar signs of plague on him. He was about two years old with soft, blond hair. His light blue eyes were open, staring blankly. His little body was thin from poor diet. His face was mottled-looking, with veins clearly showing in his face, as if he had suffocated. He was not breathing and had no pulse.

We anointed the child with consecrated oil. His mother had asked me to pronounce the blessing. Several other brethren joined me. After a short pause to be sure I was hearing the Holy Spirit correctly, and to give my courage a moment to catch up to my faith, I said, "Tommy, in the name of Jesus Christ, I command you to be made whole. In the name of Jesus Christ, amen." It was a short blessing, just those few words.

The little boy instantly awoke from death, took a deep breath, and began to cry. His mother cried in joy and tried to comfort her son. His appearance quickly became normal, and in a short time he returned to playing.

Fulness of the Priesthood

We brethren who had participated in the raising of the young boy talked a long while about this, because we had given priesthood blessings hundreds of times since the disasters began, and we found that we had no power to stop the plague, and only occasional power to raise the dead. We had some wonderful success with other afflictions, but never such a miracle as this. The Spirit wrought upon us, and we realized that we now had the fulness of the priesthood. We rejoiced and quickly began going from person to person in the Church and community, healing most of them. Some we were not allowed to heal, because it was not the Lord's plan for them. We didn't ask why but gave blessings such as the Spirit dictated, and then we moved on. The Holy Spirit told us where to go and whom we could heal. From then on, 100 percent of the people we administered to were healed or raised from the dead. No words can describe the relief and joy we felt as we went from door to door. We were positive in our new gifts, and our faith in Jesus Christ was profound. We knew we could, and we did. We worked day and night to administer to the people, all the while admonishing every person involved to avoid revealing this change to the foreign troops.

Other groups of priesthood holders discovered the same blessing, and a great restoration of the physical and emotional health of the people quickly came about.

This new power gave great hope and courage among the Saints. This was a powerfully unifying event among us. It made us strongly cohesive—united—one in heart. Our courage and faith was not just restored, but it was amplified and made visible before all. We knew at that moment that we were going to survive, and that God was beginning to work miracles to save us. The day of miracles had begun.

At this time, we also had a surge in missionary work. Those of other faiths could see with eyes opened by the Holy Spirit that miracles were happening. We healed many of them and their children. They wanted to know what we had that made us different. We taught them, and many of them gratefully joined us and began their own miraculous ministry in the latter days.

We began getting regular instructions and updates from the Church. A list of casualties of the Brethren was published, and we mourned a substantial loss of our beloved leaders. I remember most of the names of the dead, and the survivors, because we repeated them among ourselves many times and prayed for their families. But

I have chosen to not ever reveal their names.

Life reached a sort of balance. The plague was almost over in our part of the world, though it still raged elsewhere. We had a degree of society restored, and we had this greater power in the priesthood. Our hearts turned to rebuilding, especially of Temple Square. I walked there hundreds of times to assist in the cleanup. The temple had been flooded about twenty-five feet deep, as I mentioned, and only temple-worthy workers were allowed to enter. My work inside the temple was a sweet pleasure to my soul.

There was a sense of unity and purpose among those that gathered to repair and reclaim the temple grounds that I had never felt before. There was no despair, no arguing, no contrary opinions—just brotherly and sisterly solidarity. Those whose voices rang angry did not join us in this part of our rebuilding.

It was now several months since the flood, and close to the first of October, but it was not cold. The sky was so filled with debris that it did not grow cold. I suppose this was a true manifestation of global warming. It probably saved our lives. We worked in mud and sodden buildings all day long, and yet we were not suffering from the cold.

I noticed that I had deep reserves of energy and more physical strength than I had ever had in my life. I took care to not display these strengths openly, but to work steadily, and when helping others move timbers or fallen structures, I was able to do much more than the others realized. I noted that many others in our groups had similar abilities. At least half of these were women. We quickly learned to recognize other people who were beginning to be changed. There was no glow or outward sign, but there was an essence or look about us that others like us could see. We did not speak to one another of what we were experiencing because none of us actually understood it.

General Conference

Near the end of the year, the Church announced that there would be a general conference and general funeral service for all of the dead, and for the lost General Authorities in the Conference Center on the first Sunday in October. We all rejoiced but also mourned for our lost loved ones.

All of my children had moved to other parts of the country before the tribulations had begun, and I had no idea about their welfare. I never saw my wife again. Lyn sadly perished in the flood that first day, and I missed her deeply. But I mourned her with a sense of great relief too. She was not well at this time. This new life would have been overwhelming for her. I was pleased she did not have to experience it, and I knew that she was fully engaged in blessing her children from her new position. I also realized that she was watching over me and that she was aware of the changes that were happening in me. I bid her tearfully good-bye, knowing full well that not long into the future, I would hold her again when Christ finally returned.

Representatives of the Church passed through the workers in Temple Square, and then from street to street, handing out tickets to this next conference. There were to be four sessions of conference. The tickets were torn strips of paper. The sessions were distinguished by white, blue, green, and red tickets. I was handed a red ticket, which signified the last session of the day.

On the day of the conference, since I had the last session, I climbed the stairs to the top floor of the Joseph Smith Memorial building and found a seat at the window where the restaurant is now. I was looking directly across at the angel Moroni and the grounds below. Every possible inch of ground was filled with people. They had tried to dress in Sunday attire, but water was scarce for washing and people looked a little smudged. This was the first time since the flood that I had been inside a taller building, and I was shocked by how much destruction was still evident as far as I could see.

The Church had set up large screens on the side of the temple and other buildings so that people could watch and listen to any session of conference they wished. There were far too many people for everyone to be seated, even with four sessions. The people extended out and down the streets. Everyone could hear the broadcast on loudspeakers, and most could see the screens.

Large areas were set aside for the preparation and serving of food, since it was almost all done communally now. The foreign troops vacated the area to make room. There was no need for police because the harmony and unity was so strong that even they could feel it.

There were no cars in the streets. Nothing was moving. The power had not been restored, but I could hear generators running near the projection screens and beyond the Conference Center. The building I was in had electricity, but most rooms were left in darkness. The day dawned clear and warm. The people below only needed sweaters and jackets.

The first session of conference was a funeral service. All of the names of the fallen General Authorities were read that were known. I was shocked at how many familiar names had perished; some of them were long acquaintances and friends. In the Conference Center were eighteen empty coffins below the stand, representing the many fallen who had been buried weeks or months ago.

There was an almost electric feeling of the Holy Spirit among us. We wept for the faithful dead, but we also sensed something wonderful was going to happen in this conference. There was no fear, no dissenters, just a sense of anticipation and powerful unity.

When the first session ended, the next group of faithful entered the Conference Center, and a slightly different session was convened. The dead were mentioned, but not memorialized. Speakers taught powerful gospel principles and instructed us on plans to rebuild and regroup.

The third session was in the late afternoon. It was different from earlier sessions as well and spoke of the future of the Church and the future of the world. They announced that the final session would not be broadcast and invited those gathered outside to return to their homes.

By the time the third session had vacated the Conference Center, the sun was low in the sky. I rode the elevator down, into the basement. I walked through the tunnel and came up right by the baptistery in the temple. I walked out that door by the flagpole and between the temple and where the Tabernacle used to be. I found many others with red tickets there, walking across the street. There was no traffic, so we walked across like the advance wave of an army. We were all dressed in Sunday clothing, but most of us were somewhat dirty and smudged from lack of water and conditions in the streets.

I walked to the Conference Center and showed my ticket. Brethren at the doors let me into the session and directed me to the main floor. I was pleased to occupy a seat closer to the front of the main floor. The Conference Center smelled damp but not musty. The floors were dry, but water damage was evident about ten feet up the walls.

The general authorities were already on the stand. Only one brother sat in the three seats reserved for the First Presidency. I recognized all of the Twelve who remained.

I continued to scan the seats to the right of the pulpit and recognized others of the Twelve, with many vacant chairs. To the left of the pulpit sat a number of brethren I did not immediately recognize. I continued to study them carefully. I could feel the Spirit growing stronger within me, and suddenly I realized that one of the people on the stand was Joseph Smith Jr., the prophet of the Restoration. Maybe my eyes came to him sooner because he was wearing a linen suit, white shirt, and a linen-colored tie. Everyone else wore dark suits. He looked quite different from the paintings and statues I had seen of him, but his identity came to me in a flash of burning revelation. I just knew who he was. He sat still, studying the gathering audience before him.

I thought I recognized John Taylor and Brigham Young, but I wasn't entirely sure because they were younger than they looked in photos I had seen of them. I became convinced that some of the others on the stand were resurrected beings, though I could not name them.

The conference started like any other. The senior remaining Apostle stood and welcomed us and announced the first portion of the meeting. Seated in their usual red seats were about half of the Tabernacle Choir. Instead of grouping toward the front, they sat in their usual seats, leaving obvious gaps between them in tribute of the fallen among them. They stood and sang. Prayer followed and the choir sang again. The power went off several times during the choir performance, which made them sound small, then large, then small again.

After this they named the new apostles who would fill the vacancies in the Twelve. I recognized some of these brethren but not all of them. They announced the new First Presidency, and the new Brethren moved to their seats. We were asked to sustain these actions, and did so with raised arms and with an exclamation of "Yes!" which I had never before heard in conference, but it was spontaneous and filled with joy.

The first person who spoke was my friend from the Twelve who had now been dead many years. It thrilled me to see him again, and I wept, because I loved him and had missed him, but also because of his being here, speaking to this conference with other dignitaries from former days. It was a powerful sign of these great times now dawning. He spoke of the fulfillment of all that the prophets had foretold. He testified of Christ in such powerful terms that I knew—everyone knew—he had seen Christ and been in His arms. He read scriptures about the fulfilling of the dispensations, but he changed some words so that instead of speaking of future things, they were testifying of present things.

Joseph Smith Jr.

The presiding authority then announced that we had a special person that was going to address us. He then introduced Joseph Smith Jr., who stood and walked to the pulpit. He was taller and broader of shoulder than I had imagined. He stood silently for a moment, gazing out across that vast assembly.

When he spoke, his voice was mild, pure, and unshaken. His voice had the power of absolute knowledge behind it. We understood that his faith and knowledge were perfect. He had a commanding use of the language and was able to speak with color and powers of description few people possess. Coupled with the fact that we were infused with the Holy Ghost, you can understand why we were so stunned by him. He wove the prophetic utterances of the scriptures and his own testimony together with such eloquence that no one could doubt or deny their truth and power. I am also certain that every soul present already flowed with light and truth, and his testimony brightly illuminated our understanding and gave us additional cause to rejoice.

It was so silent in the building that you could have heard someone inhale. They didn't even want the sound of their hearts to make them miss a single word. Every eye was glued upon him, captured by his presence. There was a luminescence of righteousness about him.

He welcomed us and bore his testimony of the Savior. He turned and recognized the living authorities and named each of them. He verified that they had been called of God and that he was not there to take over, or to be the current prophet. He said that he had his own assignment regarding the building of Zion, which would assist us in the great task before us, and that he would work through the ordained prophet and not on his own.

Adam-ondi-Ahman

Joseph said, "I would like to speak of an event that happened a few weeks ago in the valley of Adam-ondi-Ahman." He turned to the newly ordained prophet and nodded, as if seeking his approval. The Prophet nodded once in reply. Joseph then spoke for about ninety minutes, telling us about the great meeting of Adam-ondi-Ahman, which had just taken place. He rehearsed the events in great detail. He described how a temporary platform had been erected, and the only one seated upon it was Adam. The group was small, so there was no need for a PA system. He named each dispensation head, what he looked like, what he had said, and what he had reported.

Never before, in all of my hearing, has a more powerful testimony been born among men.

Joseph then said that Adam had received the report of every prophet, then Joseph himself reported last. He reported to us with great emotion that he then turned to Adam and testified in the name of Jesus Christ, that his work had been accomplished, not all completed, but his assigned labors were accomplished.

At that moment in the meeting, Joseph reported that Jesus Christ then appeared in glory next to Adam. Adam knelt and reported to Jesus Christ that the work had been accomplished. Jesus Christ then accepted his report and pronounced it good and commended them all for their faithfulness.

Then Joseph spoke about the gathering of the Saints in these times. He said that there was a gathering taking place in Salt Lake City, and, because of the recent events, that some of the faithful would be inspired from around the world to come to this place. He said that those who arrived here would be coming under God's banner, and that we should receive and care for them.

He informed us that many other places all over the world would become "cities of Zion" and safe gathering places for the Saints. He said that the "Center Place of Zion" in what had been known as Missouri, would attract those ordained to gather there, and when we were all gathered into these safe places, then the work of the Millennium would begin. He said that when all of the elect had been safely gathered into Zion, Jesus Christ would Himself come to rule and reign upon the earth.

When he said these words, a spontaneous shout of "Hosanna!" arose from our hearts and lips.

Joseph spoke about the restoration of all things, that all blessings and powers that ever were, from the beginning of time, were now restored in their fulness at this time. He emphasized that every gift embodied in the fulness of the priesthood, including the power of translation, was now restored in even greater measure than ever before on this earth. He said that even those miracles that we were beginning to experience among ourselves today would seem small compared with what was yet to be. This, he said, is what was meant by the "fulness of times."

We were amazed because we were wondering how this could be, what greater things could happen than were happening at this very moment? Here we were listening to a resurrected prophet and looking at resurrected prophets on the stand. We already had the fulness of the priesthood, though we acknowledged that we did not know what that meant exactly. We participated in miracles daily. We had all seen angels and were in the process of physically changing—we couldn't imagine anything greater. But it did not stop us from believing his words; we just couldn't imagine anything greater, and the power of his assertion burned brightly in our souls, illuminating our minds and elevating our hopes beyond the scope of human belief.

There was not a dry eye in the building. We all wept openly, joyfully, and with great hope. I was weeping so profoundly because I realized at this moment that everything I had seen, and all that I had been promised, was in that moment fulfilled. The promises had just been fulfilled. It was done. My journey, which I thought had been to bring me to this moment, was altered in my soul—my true journey had just now begun. The days and years of my spiritual infancy were over, and I was prepared. The hammer of the refiner's forge had fallen upon me until all of the impurities and the dross was finally gone.

I could not restrain my tears, relief, and astonishment, because here I was, sitting in muddy clothing, in a damaged building, with lights flickering, in a devastated world, where nothing of society remained. Yet I had at long last reached the beginning of the path that had so long been in my heart but so far beyond my ability to claim. Now in this unexpected moment, seated before resurrected beings from past dispensations, I had finally reached the beginning of my latter-day mission.

Joseph paused for a long moment until there was absolute silence. He seemed to be struggling with his emotions and kept glancing to his right. Finally he swept his hand toward the person sitting just to the right of the new First Presidency and cleared his throat.

I had no idea who this person was. He was dressed in a plain, black business suit and white shirt and red tie, which he could have purchased at JCPenney the day before the flood. His clothing was just as rumpled and smudged as any of us present. I assumed he was one of the former dispensation heads. I knew he was a resurrected being, and I also knew from his rumpled appearance that he had been assisting in the work of rescue and rebuilding.

The Son of God

Joseph said in a voice choked with emotion, "It is my great privilege to introduce to you Jesus Christ, the Son of God."

The man he indicated stood and began to brighten in glory. His countenance beamed, as did every part of His person. His clothing grew white as His glory overpowered every color near Him.

He had sat there the entire meeting, which was now well into the third hour, and I had not recognized him. I had seen His face and been embraced by Him several times, but I did not recognize Him until Joseph spoke His name. Then it was as if a veil had been lifted, and I recognized Him instantly and almost jumped from my seat to run to Him, but I did not. I just gasped in wonder along with everyone present.

He did not walk to the pulpit but merely stood there as every eye was transfixed upon him. He became the center of the universe, and stepping to the pulpit would not have changed that. The light that came from Him increased in intensity until it lit the entire Conference Center. It was so bright that every shadow was filled.

I realized later that what had happened during this long moment as we watched His glory increase wasn't that *He* was being changed—*we* were. We were being transfigured by the Holy Ghost to be able to see Him in His glory without being consumed by it.

All worry was taken from my heart and replaced with hope, joy, charity, love, surety, and pure knowledge. I finally knew that I was done with this mortal life.

I thought about those of my family who had died in the earthquake and felt total and complete peace. I knew they were happy and engaged in this same work. For those of my family who had survived, I knew exactly what I needed to do to strengthen and help them.

When Christ stood and was transfigured into His full glory, the whole experience of being in that room, in the presence of the transfigured Christ, began to change us. We knew we were being transfigured, and some of us were being translated.

I had a bright recollection in my mind of a sacred experience that I have not related yet, wherein the Savior had promised me that if I continue true and faithful in my present calling, that the time would come when I would be changed, like the ancient inhabitants of Enoch's Zion, into a life and body that could not die.

When our Savior spoke, the first word from His lips was my name! I was extremely startled until I also realized that every person present had heard his or her own name. As He spoke, I could hear and fully understand the words He was saying to me, but I was also seeing a vision of His description of my future mission. I saw my entire life from that moment forward, everything that I would do, everywhere I would go, every person to whom I would minister, and how it would all be. I later talked to everyone I could who had been in that glorious event, probably several hundred people, and everyone I talked to had heard their own name and seen a vision of their own life.

My first emotion was that everything I had seen over the many years, my many excursions beyond death, and the many visions and things that I had seen, were actually true. I had always believed that they were true, but that they were perhaps more of a metaphor than a vision of actual future happenings. I had always been faithful to that knowledge, but now I knew I had been shown actual events in my future. I knew it nothing doubting, and I rejoiced. The visions I had seen years earlier were to guide me to this moment. The visions I saw now completed my education and gave me all of the missing pieces. As I have said many times, I didn't understand big parts of what I had seen, and now I understood it all in sweet clarity.

This vision closed and Jesus Christ paused. In real time, I think only a few minutes had elapsed since He stood, but the visions I saw spanned years of time.

Jesus Christ then told us that He had been to the Father and reported on the work that the family of Adam had accomplished. The Father had accepted the work. He then turned slowly from left to right, silently blessing everyone in the congregation. He spoke to every individual's heart at the same time. His words penetrated every heart and mind completely, in an intimate and individual way. I knew, and everyone knew, He was speaking to them personally.

To be in the Conference Center and to see the fulfillment of all we had ever hoped for, believed, and desired now come to pass, turned our hope into reality, and our faith was made sure. Our knowledge of all that the prophets had told us for generations came to full fruition. It was overwhelming, definite, and empowering.

We saw the long-awaited Savior stand before us and speak the words we had only read before. His words welled up within us and sank deep within our hearts and minds. Yet now we knew with the greatest certainty that all He had ever spoken about these days and times, all He had told His prophets for millennia, had now come to pass and would all be fulfilled in our lifetimes, before our very eyes. He was our only reality. We saw Him! We heard Him! We saw the visions and shed the tears! We knew! We were united, knit together in the deepest bonds of His love, to never again be separated from Him.

As we closed the meeting, we sang "I Know That My Redeemer Lives." The words became powerfully personal and immediately fulfilled for us all.

> I know that my Redeemer lives.
> What comfort this sweet sentence gives!
> He lives, he lives, who once was dead.
> He lives, my ever-living Head.
> He lives to bless me with his love.
> He lives to plead for me above.
> He lives my hungry soul to feed.
> He lives to bless in time of need.

He lives to grant me rich supply.
He lives to guide me with his eye.
He lives to comfort me when faint.
He lives to hear my soul's complaint.
He lives to silence all my fears.
He lives to wipe away my tears.
He lives to calm my troubled heart.
He lives all blessings to impart.

He lives, my kind, wise, heav'nly Friend.
He lives and loves me to the end.
He lives, and while he lives, I'll sing.
He lives, my Prophet, Priest, and King.
He lives and grants me daily breath.
He lives, and I shall conquer death.
He lives my mansion to prepare.
He lives to bring me safely there.

He lives! All glory to his name!
He lives, my Savior, still the same.
Oh, sweet the joy this sentence gives:
"I know that my Redeemer lives!"
He lives! All glory to his name!
He lives, my Savior, still the same.
Oh, sweet the joy this sentence gives:
"I know that my Redeemer lives!"

(Text by Samuel Medley, LDS hymnbook 1835.)

As we sang with Him, tears rushed down our cheeks and His cheeks. He was rejoicing with us that His mission as our Savior was at this sublime juncture at last.

For years afterward, those who were privileged to be in that never-to-be-forgotten meeting of the Saints spoke of seeing Christ, singing with Him, working side by side with Him and not knowing it was Him. We spoke of feeling our hearts burn within us as He descended to bless us and heal us in our time of great need in this glorious dispensation of the fulness of times.

Changed!

The blessing He bestowed upon each of us was the ability and strength to complete this new phase of our lives with honor and righteousness. The powerful promises came back to me, both those I had seen in visions over the years and those I had received in the temple. These, and a thousand other realizations and truths, swept through my soul. I knew I was being changed, then and there, in fulfillment of those promises. From the emotion and rapt attention of the large gathering there—the powerful quiet and reverence, and the realization that we were hearing the very Christ speak to us and bless us individually—I knew we were all experiencing the same thing. We were being empowered to complete our missions, but I believe only a small percentage of those assembled there experienced this additional change into the translated state. I came to this conclusion in a later vision of Zion I will relate in turn. I believe that all of the Twelve were likewise changed, for they thereafter did marvelous things no unchanged mortal could have done. As an example, after this event I journeyed for most of a year to arrive at our next destination, and when we arrived, members of the Twelve Apostles were there ahead of us. We were the first to arrive, and there were no roads, trains, or air traffic of any form. They simply came and went by the power of God. This is why I believe they were also changed.

It would still take me years to learn the extent and the full power of that change, and how to bless others by what I now was given, but the change was complete in me—in that moment. My education in using it was just beginning.

CHAPTER EIGHT

THE JOURNEY BEGINS

Preparing Our Company

E arly the next spring, we made preparations to leave on the assignments we had received while in that last great conference. We had seen who would be in our company, where we would gather, where we would go, and the broader details of what we would do along the way. We didn't see how we would do all of it, but we knew, nothing doubting, that God would direct and enable our success because we had seen it. During the winter we had all been set apart by Church authorities to fulfill these great latter-day assignments from Christ. Everything occurred under the direction of the Church. Even though we had seen it all, we still had to be called and authorized to administer in Christ's name.

I gathered with those called to be in my company. We recognized each other and were excited to finally be gathering and collecting the necessities of the journey. I was assigned to a group of about 150 Saints consisting of men and women, not counting many teens, youth, toddlers, and infants. We were assigned to head north to Cardston, Canada, to a gathering place near the temple there.

Our leader was a local man whom the Lord had designated in the vision and whom the Church had called and set apart for this journey. According to the pattern we had been shown, he called two counselors, and then a council of twelve, and others to leadership, consisting of men and women. We called these twelve people "The Council" among ourselves. Each of these individuals had specific responsibilities that did not change. As they were inspired, some of them called additional councils consisting of three to seven men and women. Some teens served on these councils as well. These people served as counselors to one of the twelve, and as workers and organizers of the various tasks.

I was not called to be on the council. By this time I was a much older man, and I was asked to be a spiritual advisor to the whole company, sort of like a patriarch, or maybe a bishop, but I had no title and no authority. In this capacity, I spent most of my time in council meetings and counseling individuals. I was in a position where I only gave my opinion regarding something after I had been moved upon by the Holy Ghost and had been asked my opinion. Until then, I did not engage in the discussion.

Our company operated by common consent. Our leaders would consider some problem or need and discuss it until they arrived at a consensus. Then they prayed until they knew the mind of the Lord. I waited for them to ask me a question before I contributed. I replied with what the Holy Ghost was impressing upon me, or I gave them no opinion. After this process, the leaders presented the decision to the whole group, and they were asked to sustain the decision. After this, the council and their committees went to work to accomplish their tasks.

In the beginning, these decisions were lengthy and sometimes challenging. At times it was difficult to align our mortal thinking with the Lord's will, and we had to scrap our idea and start over. As we gained experience in this process, it became more efficient. We learned to listen more closely to the voice of revelation as we prepared our plan, and then the confirmation process was already accomplished. We felt inspired readily, and the people felt the same inspiration as they sustained the plan, and they were then inspired in their execution of the work.

I realized early in our journey that I was one of two people in our company who had been translated, and I was only one of twenty or so who had been in that great conference where we had seen and heard Jesus Christ, and seen our mission in vision. I realized that I had a much clearer view of what we needed to do and a more sensitive ear and heart for the word of the Lord. This process, this journey, this whole arrangement of councils and sustaining was engineered to refine us and to lift us all to knowing our duty without further need to discuss or design strategies and plans.

But for now, as we began, this was an inspired plan, and we all took our place, anxious to begin.

Other Companies

There were about fifty companies forming in various parts of the city. Some were headed to Mexico, others to California and almost every point of the compass. About a year after this, other groups were sent to other continents, but for now there was no commercial transport, and we were relegated to what remained of our world.

Each company had the same task: to find those whom God showed to us, assist them in their needs, teach them, strengthen them, and prepare them for their latter-day labors. In most cases, those labors were to build cities of Zion in their own location, not to trek to the New Jerusalem. It took many years and much teaching and testifying before the general population of the Church actually internalized this truth. Quite understandably, they all wanted to be among the "Saints" who came marching into Zion at long last—as did I.

Our company gathered everything they felt impressed to bring: clothing, bedding, food, and medical supplies. A few people brought military-issued weapons and ammunition, which our leaders elected to leave behind.

Our Big Truck

Two of our brethren showed up with a huge military vehicle and many drums of fuel on the back. It was one of the large vehicles the foreign troops had brought with them. It had a cab large enough to carry four soldiers in full gear, or six people in ragged clothing. It had a large flat bed, about twenty-five feet long, with a fabric cover that could be set up on steel hoops, which made it look like a mammoth covered wagon. It had four driven axles and large, high flotation tires. The front two axles steered, and the back two were fixed. The steering wheel was on the right side of the cab. I think it had been made in Asia, but I don't remember any insignias on the truck itself.

One interesting feature of the truck was that it had a large solar panel on the roof of the cab. The solar panel could recharge the battery, or another vehicle's battery. It also had an inverter which produced normal voltage, which we used to cook, make lights for the camp, or any other electrical device. When the truck was running, it had a large generator to make electricity at night, but we chose not to use it much to conserve fuel.

By the time we reached the end of our journey in Zion, this truck had served us profoundly and had saved many lives. It truly was a survival vehicle. It was built to handle anything. The truck itself was made of some kind of carbon fiber, which made it light and stronger than normal steel. The wheels were designed so that they always remained on the ground, even when crossing a tall obstacle, rock, or fallen tree. The truck was flexible and seemed to twist as it crossed obstacles, but the bed always remained flat and level.

Our leaders decided to take it largely because it came with its own fuel, and it had the capacity to carry almost all of our supplies. We didn't even ask how they had acquired this big truck but just accepted it as a gift from God. As our journey progressed, it figured prominently in our journey and in our success. Looking back at all that happened on our journey, it was the only vehicle that we did not get hopelessly stuck at least once, and the only one that did not break down. We found that it would run on anything from crude oil, spent vegetable oils, and cooking grease, to vodka, though we didn't find much of the latter fuel. We made full use of that ability. It was one of the few vehicles that left Salt Lake City, and actually arrived in Canada and most of the way to Missouri. All of the others either broke down or were discarded to save fuel along the way.

We also discovered that there was a water purification plant built into the truck. We could pour dirty water from a puddle, or even antifreeze from a car radiator, into it, and it would make fresh water for us to drink. This was a great blessing to our journey.

I remember when we discovered this feature. The system was near the engine and was not readily apparent. Because the writing was not in English, we weren't sure what it was or what it did. I watched one of the brethren pour dirty water into the square funnel. I stood there doubting that this was what it was for, or that clean water would be the result. About twenty minutes later, the most pure and refreshing water began running into a heavy plastic container at the bottom of the truck. Filthy water was draining onto the ground. I remember tasting it and marveling. I have never been good at mechanical things, and this seemed like a miracle to me. It wasn't until I was working on this book that I learned that filters with this ability actually exist. I was like a child watching something that seemed miraculous, but which others of our company understood.

We also had a number of four-wheel ATVs of the type where two to four people could ride on them. Many of these pulled trailers. We left behind smaller ATVs. There were some four-wheel-drive pickups that pulled large horse trailers so we could move the animals quickly if need be. At other times, the horse trailers served as shelter from rain and storm. We left with about a dozen horses and numerous dogs and goats. We did not bring cows, chickens, or other farm animals because the Spirit led us to leave them behind.

We brought a large quantity of food and other odd things, like farm implements, spare parts, and other items that the Spirit led us to collect. All of these things played into our ability to barter and trade along the way. This was all for our learning, to teach us to rely totally and only upon Christ. It was a hard lesson to learn because we had to keep relearning it on higher and higher levels.

We left Salt Lake City late in March on a beautiful spring morning. Flowers were just beginning to bloom. It was warmer than expected, and grass was green everywhere you looked. The spring had been quite rainy, and the world of plants seemed to explode with flowers and greenery.

We departed on I-15 heading north. We moved at a slow pace because most of our company was afoot. We were not in a hurry. Before we left that morning, we met in council, and after discussion and prayer, we agreed upon our route and our distance of travel. We were not just going to Cardston—we were the Lord's camp, and we were content to go wherever the Lord sent us and for it to take as long as it took.

We soon realized that the big truck and pickups could not travel at a walking pace economically. We sent them ahead and carefully calculated their best economic speed, which they used throughout the remainder of our journey. We caught up with them each evening where camp was already being set up. I was on foot as well and often helped carry infants or whatever else people needed. We were full of hope, and as our heritage song says, we did "with joy wend our way."

We often left the highway to travel on side roads because the earthquake had destroyed long stretches of the freeway, or opened caverns across it. Sometimes our foot traffic caught up with the trucks as they pondered how to cross some obstacle. Many of these obstacles were natural, but there were also those consisting of barricades made and defended by people, as well as other caravans along the way.

The first part of our journey was without worry, except that the Lord sent us around one area that had been hit by a nuclear weapon. This explosion had not occurred because of aerial strike, but by sabotage of a nuclear weapon stored underground at that place. I believe that many of the nuclear explosions across the country were a result of sabotage rather than a missile attack. A few days after we crossed into Idaho, we left all highways and went cross-country. Idaho had been rocked by several atomic weapons, all at military installations, probably also due to sabotage. We were completely responsive to the voice of the Lord and were led around those areas.

We learned by experience that the highways and roads were where most of our problems arose. If some armed band was accosting caravans and robbing them, it was on the highways. If there was impassible damage, it was on the highways. Our big truck was perfect for cross-country. It rolled across everything, including fences, leaving behind wide tracks for smaller vehicles and foot traffic. The further we went, the more we valued the big thing.

We also were not on a direct course to Canada. Each morning the council met and prayerfully planned each day. Some days we were given the name of a family, a person, or sometimes a ward or town to minister to. Sometimes it was just an impression to go toward a farm or town. We would determine by the Spirit how many were to go, and they would leave in the morning, taking with them whatever the Spirit directed. Sometimes we took items that the people we met desperately needed, and we were able to trade for more fuel or fresh meat or vegetables. Sometimes our mechanics went and traded for parts. Sometimes we would knock on a farmhouse door, and the people within had been warned by the Lord, like unto Lehi, to be prepared to leave. We would show up just as they were walking out of their home. Every imaginable thing happened as we traveled, and we learned to never fear because the Lord was ever present in our journey.

Gifts of the Spirit

The power of the priesthood was manifest often in healings and other miracles. Not everyone had the same gifts. We found that some had great faith to heal and others to prophecy. Even children and teens had their gifts, and we embraced all that came from God. There were those among us who had an ability I had not seen before, which was the ability to speak and teach with so much power that even our enemies were pacified, and their were hearts softened toward us. This convincing gift did not flow from powerful oratory or long and mighty speaking. Their words were just softly spoken, mostly without eloquence, but what they said could not be disbelieved when their gift was manifest. We found this to be a mighty gift and reserved it to those times when the Lord sanctioned its use, usually when we were trapped and had no other way to continue our journey.

My gifts grew along with most all of our company. Many of us developed the ability to read the hearts of men. We often met other caravans or small groups of people going in every direction. They would approach us with great caution because of our military truck. I was often in the group that went out to meet with these traveling bands. We found when we looked at them as we approached that we knew their intent and their needs. We also knew how to reply when they were lying to us.

As we left to parlay with them, we often were told by the Spirit what to bring with us to trade with them. Since we were in Idaho, quite often these were good Latter-day Saints trying to make their way to Salt Lake City or some other place. Often they were going to find their families in other parts of the country, or even trying to journey to Missouri. These we fed and shared provisions with, and sometimes, we invited them to join us. Sometimes we urged them to return to their homes and build Zion where they were from. They rarely followed our counsel, and I do not know what happened to them. But most often these chance encounters were not with people we were directed to gather. We were sent to those we gathered. We went to their homes, into their cities, and onto their farms under guidance from God. We went to them.

Build Zion Where You Are

When we first entered a city, we would go to the local leaders of the Church in each town. Often, the leaders asked us to speak to their people, and we would spread the word. We would meet these people outside of town, build a big fire, and have a true "fireside." We told them what had happened since the earthquake in Salt Lake and how the Lord was advancing the work of the latter days. Everyone was curious about what had happened in Salt Lake City, as rumors had circulated of both awful and glorious things. We were pleased to update their view of the work of the latter days and thereby give them a correct vision of the unfolding strength of the latter-day kingdom.

If the Spirit accorded, we told them who we were and what our mission was. The convincing power of God would move some of them to join us, and we welcomed them. However, much more often we taught them to continue building Zion where they were, and to prepare themselves spiritually to receive the Lord when He came.

I don't want to give the impression that everyone who was worthy was being gathered into our company. This was not the case. We had been authorized by the Brethren to represent the Church wherever we went, and most often the Spirit led us to counsel them to stay where they were.

Most of the local leaders we met already understood that they were to gather where they were and to make holy the ground upon which they presently stood. Their gathering place was there or somewhere nearby. We generally found the Saints to be in good spirits with strong hopes, and often, but not always, possessing a fulness of the priesthood, just as we had obtained it. If they were lacking, we counseled and admonished them to repent and live up to their potential. Almost without exception, they humbly and gratefully received our words and began their spiritual journey to Zion without fear.

The people of the Lord's church did not present a scene of starving people hunkering in basements, waiting without hope. Those who survived were chosen for these times before the world was created, and they arose with great faith and willingness to do the Lord's work. They were not lost, they were home. Sometimes all we needed to do was to point this out with the convincing power of the Spirit.

There were also gatherings of people not in the Church who were full of the Spirit and doing the Lord's work, increasing their faith and living without fear. We were led to these at times. When we were, we blessed and uplifted them and left them in the hands of God to continue their work. We fully expected to see them someday in Zion. But we first had to make our own way there and build it—this was the focus of our hearts and minds.

While among the Saints, we always traded with them. We occasionally had just what they needed, and they had things we were in need of. One thing we were always bartering for was fuel, and we found people willing to trade because you can't eat fuel, and there were no roads to drive on. We found we could get used engine oil and inedible deep fryer oil for almost nothing, yet our faithful big truck could burn it all. It just gave off an interesting exhaust that smelled of french fries. We always continued our journey with sufficient for our needs. I don't recall ever exchanging money, gold, or silver. These were relatively worthless. What mattered was food and necessities.

During this leg of our journey, I don't recall ever seeing a miracle to provide loaves and fishes or fuel. We had the mind-set that the Lord expected us to provide for our needs, and that He would lead us to obtain them. We developed complete faith in this process. We learned much later, however, that this is a lesser law, and that we were really being brought to a greater faith that would allow us to rely upon Him for everything. We learned this in greater degrees as we continued our journey to Zion. We were taught it in as many ways as it took until it was a perfect and powerful truth—until we simply had nothing but Him, and it was enough.

Changes in the Earth

The earth had changed dramatically. The landscape had changed. Mountains had been flattened. Valleys had been heaved up. Rivers had changed course and created new lakes. Roads that used to lead to a city now led to a canyon or into a lake. Most roads were no longer passable, and for this reason, most cars and trucks had been abandoned. Horses became the gold standard of transportation. In the devastated areas, if you had a horse, a warm shelter, and something to eat, you were wealthy.

But there were also areas of the country we passed through that were pristine. There were towns and communities in out-of-the-way places that had not been devastated, and where basic utilities had been restored. Sometimes we were invited into homes to shelter and sometimes into stake centers to take showers or eat. The smaller towns were succeeding more quickly at reestablishing law and order than the bigger cities. They all came to the point of guarding their borders day and night to secure their peace. We had little trouble convincing these guards to let us enter. They welcomed us, and we blessed them, taught them, shared news and meals with them, and then left them without fear into the Lord's keeping.

I found it interesting that many of the bridges were still intact. The roads leading up to them were often broken up, but many bridges somehow survived. We spent about 40 percent of our time on old roads, and the remainder going cross-country. We found the open land easier to navigate and with less human interference.

Our habit was to camp far outside of a town or city and to send a small unarmed group into the city to trade or to gather people in. We proceeded with a great deal of caution, and not until we had obtained the word of the Lord to guide us. The larger cities were far more dangerous to approach or enter.

Our groups always returned with what we needed. They also often returned with stories of miraculous interventions where the Lord had preserved them and provided the object of their mission. Sometimes they returned with stories of marvelous healings and other blessings they had left upon the people who had been kind and receptive.

When bridges were gone, we had to divert far from the bridge to some place where the slopes were gradual. There we could descend into the valley, ford the river, and then trudge back up to the top. There were times when some of our vehicles became badly stuck or swamped in the rivers. Sometimes we pulled them out with the big truck, other times we left them behind. If a vehicle broke, our mechanics fixed it with parts we had, or we left it behind.

We passed many abandoned vehicles. There was little fuel, and nearly half the population as before, so perfectly serviceable vehicles of every type just sat where they ran out of fuel. Upon occasion, we left one of our damaged vehicles behind and claimed better ones we found abandoned on the roads and fields.

When we approached larger cities, we occasionally came upon foreign troops. We would stop and let them approach us. Most often we had known before the start of that day's journey that we would meet them. We had a show we put on for them. We acted the part of wanderers with little or nothing among us, basically headed north with no real destination. We actually were not a threat, and we made sure this was obvious. It wasn't a difficult part to play. We appeared to be a caravan of a few strong leaders, leading crying babies and tired women, complaining teens, and stumbling old men to an undetermined new home. In fact, the only small deception was that we knew very well where we were going. The rest of what they saw was the truth.

The odd thing was that they never questioned where we had gotten our big truck. They even searched it occasionally, but never seemed to actually see that it was one of their own. It seemed almost invisible to them. The foreign troops would check our identity and look for military-grade weapons. They were rough and authoritative, but not hostile at this point. They didn't care where we were going as long as we were not breaking their new laws.

We had a few hunting rifles, but we never hid them. The troops didn't care about such things.

I should mention that we never fired those weapons at people. If we were approached by a hostile group, sometimes we would display them as a show of force, and they would leave us alone. But I do not recall ever firing them, except if some individual did so to obtain food. As time progressed, we ceased killing game for food because it no longer felt necessary.

We went up through Idaho in a zigzag fashion, following the voice of the Spirit, gathering those we were shown. Our group was growing in size, with more mouths to feed. But our biggest effort was in teaching those who joined us. These new people soon caught the spirit of our camp and became considerable assets to our company. Everybody had a job, and everybody worked unselfishly. Even the teens and youth worked hard, sometimes after a little complaining, but we just smiled at them, praying silently, and they joined in willingly after that.

The leaves were just beginning to change color when we passed into Montana. There was a lot of damage in the cities here, more so than we had seen in Idaho. There was also a lot of lawlessness and chaos. Various gangs claimed regions of the cities and defended them, not letting people in or out without their permission, usually after paying tribute. The roads into the various parts of the city were heavily guarded. There was an economy of sorts working there, and some basic utilities had been restored. These bands or gangs preyed upon the people, taking part of their food in exchange for protecting them from other gangs.

We exercised due caution to avoid conflict with these bands. We were constantly on guard from those who feigned friendship or need in order to steal from us. We used the priesthood and relied upon the Lord to direct us to safety. Each night we set up watches that rotated every four hours.

When we determined by our spiritual gifts that people came peacefully, we fed them and shared our basic supplies. We rarely told them who we were or where we were ultimately going. All of these groups had their own destination and left us within a few days. We gave them what they needed, and if they had faith, we healed them by the priesthood. If a group we encountered was LDS, and the Spirit led us to, we would disclose who we were and where we were going and invite them to join us. But most often, they also went their own way.

Every day we cooked large community meals and ate together. It was basic food without frills, often without meat, but we thrived because we were being changed, even though most of our company could not yet understand what we were being changed into.

Zion in Canada

It took us all summer and fall to arrive in Cardston, Canada. Remember that even though I was experiencing this "on the ground," it was still a visionary experience. I was not actually there. My body was lying in my bed waiting for my spirit to return. My spirit was being shown these things in vision. My reason for reminding you of this is that time was compressed for me. In the beginning, I saw every day and every step of our journey. The closer we got to Canada, the more I just saw important events and major places. The vision began jumping forward, skipping periods of time. This left me without a clear concept of how much time had elapsed. The passage of time got even more confusing when we finally arrived in Zion, but I will save those details for the proper place in the story.

We found a large gathering of Saints in Cardston, not far from the temple. I estimate there were 20,000 people there already, and more were arriving daily. They had erected a small city on a large tract of farmland a short distance from the temple. It was all organized and orderly. There were many local people who were expecting us and who had prepared to receive us. The land we settled onto held a few scattered buildings, barns, storage facilities, and homes on the property. These became parts of the new town, the stores, and meeting places.

This settlement was not destined to remain a tent city, though there were many tents, travel trailers, motorhomes, and every other type of shelter imaginable in the beginning. The Brethren were following a plan, building permanent housing and other structures. There were large stores of food and water. A clear river ran to the east of our camp and provided a source of water. The city was lit by electricity, with streetlights and lights in tents and trailers. I knew that the electricity was being produced somewhere in the camp, but I do not remember hearing a large generator running. I don't know where it was coming from, and I don't recall seeing the power flicker or fail. There were hospitals, schools, cafeterias, and every other needed service and facility.

We were arriving nearly a year after this gathering had begun, and things were more permanent and orderly than they had been a year ago. The Church had taken charge and the tent city quickly evolved into an organized and safe place with basic needs filled. Men and women were put to work building a permanent city here.

There was no money—they had all things in common, and they were happy. The people welcomed us without suspicion. They had been expecting our arrival for days. We were the first to arrive, but other groups that had left Salt Lake City at the same time with other assignments began arriving every few days. They had left as hundreds and were arriving as thousands. Some had come through California, Oregon, and Washington, and had inspiring and interesting tales to tell of their journey. We greeted these almost as Alma and the Sons of Mosiah. We fell upon their necks and rejoiced, glorying in the work our God had accomplished by their hands.

The camp was enclosed by a fence, but not a barricade or fortress like we had seen in cities in Montana. Here there was safety and peace. The guards at the gate did not carry weapons. If defense was necessary, it was by divine intervention.

I was aware that there were other gathering places like this throughout the United States, Europe, South America, and anywhere the stakes of Zion had been fully organized prior to the earthquakes. The power of God had infused the Church, which had arisen to full capability throughout the world. The Church had a worldwide communication system in place, and they led us with inspired counsel and kept us informed of world events.

We were shown a place to camp and were given food and places to sleep. We did not stay as a company but spread throughout the city on various assignments according to our several skills and abilities. I was invited to go with our "twelve" to report to the Brethren in Cardston. We walked a modest distance to the temple, where the Church leadership had offices. We were surprised, though perhaps we should not have been, when we met with two members of the Quorum of the Twelve Apostles there in the Church offices in Canada. What amazed us most was that they had not traveled with any of the companies, and there was no such thing as commercial transportation nor any road system that connected us. They had arrived months ahead of us. How they had traveled here was unknown to anyone but themselves. It was never explained to us how they got there ahead of us—though years later when we finally arrived in Zion, such things were commonplace and no longer surprising at all.

We reported on our journey. We had kept records of every city we ministered to and every person who had left with us, joined us, died along the way, and finally arrived with us. They thanked us most warmly and gratefully, and like we had heard about Adam-ondi-Ahman, they accepted our report and told us, "Well done."

Conference in Cardston

By the end of that fall, every awaited company had arrived. The Brethren in Cardston announced that we would enjoy another conference that October. A large section of sloping pasture land was identified for the conference. A temporary stage was erected with lights and an adequate PA system. The conference was literally "standing room only," as there were few chairs. People brought blankets to sit upon the hillside or they stood. We felt it a sublime privilege to be there, and I heard nobody complain.

When we had arrived in Canada, we had rejoiced as a company, and as reunited friends. Now we met and rejoiced as a city. I imagine there were 30,000 people gathered in that field, and the spirit of unity and joy was powerful. There was mourning for the dead, lost family in the earthquakes, and sacrifices on the trail to this part of Zion. But our minds were focused on the joy of these times that had been so long anticipated, seen in vision, and written of in scripture. Our hearts were one in thinking, "It has finally occurred. It has finally happened. We survived! We survived the cleansing. We survived the journey and here we are!"

We all felt anxious to leave Cardston and get on to Missouri to build Zion, usher in the Millennium, and receive Christ when He came. Much of the talk and speculation prior to conference was regarding who would leave first and how soon. Many expected this camp in Cardston to be temporary. I think everyone there expected to continue walking on to the New Jerusalem.

Conference began with a large choir singing the hymns of

Zion. The senior member of the Twelve then in Cardston conducted. The first talk was teaching us that few of us were actually going on to Missouri, and that this place would be developed into a city as glorious and large as the Center of Zion. This caused some disappointment as people realized they were not going to be sent to Zion. We learned later that some groups were being sent to Asia, Europe, and other faraway places to bolster the Saints, and to build up Zion cities across the world.

We learned in this conference that there was already a group who had arrived in Zion, as well as some members of the Twelve Apostles, and that the temple construction there had already begun.

One of the Apostles stood and reported on the great conference in Salt Lake City and on the changes in the world. He spoke about our duty to build, beautify, and maintain these various new "cities of Zion" that were even now being built.

There were several groups who had arrived from South America, and they stood and reported on their journey. They did not speak English, but everyone understood them, and they understood us, though they insisted they were speaking and hearing their own language, even as we were hearing and speaking English. From then on, we no longer thought about language in the same way. We accepted this change as one of the miracles of the latter days and vital to our missions to gather in from all the world into Zion.

The groups who had come through California and other paths reported briefly on their journey and told of the miracles of faith they had enjoyed. The also mentioned the vast changes in the landscape and sweeping changes in society. There was no mention of the foreign troops or what they were doing because it was inconsequential and all subject to God's plans, not their own.

The conference lasted all through the day. It was approximately October, but it was not cold. The weather was mild, with even just a sweater being overly warm at times. Even the nights and evenings were mild. We all watched and wondered at these changes.

After that conference, the Saints were strengthened. It had given us a much broader view of what was happening and what we were going to do next. The difference in us was like reading stories about the exodus of the Children of Israel, and then hearing the same story from someone who had actually been there. Every heart there turned to viewing these days as the end of times, not just a global earthquake.

Waiting in Cardston

There was a lot of conversation about how soon the Second Coming was going to be. There were so many visible changes in the earth, our priesthood, and our bodies, that the people had a hard time telling where we were in the overall scheme of things. There were so many opinions about how these times were unfolding that we could not reconcile it with our present circumstances. Like I said, I was constrained for the most part from speaking of the timetable I understood, because it was not my place to "reveal" such things to other people.

We couldn't get information then as we can now. We no longer had computers, TVs, or radios. The Internet had disappeared. We not only craved knowledge of these times, but we also longed to know what was happening in the rest of the world. All of us knew someone, somewhere, who was missing. Most of us wanted to know whether the United States had survived as a nation, and what the foreign troops were really up to.

People were putting the pieces together, but not necessarily in perfect order. Some people thought the Second Coming had happened in Salt Lake City when Christ appeared in the conference there. Depending upon how much a person had studied and understood the doctrine of the priesthood, and depending upon how powerfully the Spirit had worked upon them in the years prior to this day, some of our group were infants in their understanding. Their ideas did not cause contention, but it made it harder for them to see their own future unfolding.

Many sermons and special meetings were held and dedicated to these subjects. Our leaders urged us to not worry about the times, world events, national intrigue, or wars, but to wait upon the Lord and just keep moving forward.

Significant things had happened in the last year, so there was no sense of doubt that we were on the cusp of the Second Coming. We knew the times were advancing rapidly.

During the conference, we had received our assignments and had once again been divided up into companies. We were anxious to go forth and finish our assignments, to create our part of Zion so that the Second Coming could occur. We had received our marching orders, and at least for now, it was enough to prepare to leave as soon as we got the word to head out.

The civic authorities in Canada and the foreign troops there were initially pleased that we were taking care of ourselves and were not a drain on their resources. However, as our numbers grew larger, they became concerned that we would gather in more people than we could support and would begin asking them for food or resources. Canada had been hit hard in some areas, especially along the coasts, but in Cardston there was far less damage. The temple there had suffered only minor damage.

We considered Cardston a permanent dwelling, and the locals considered us temporary. There began to be some conflicts where local people tried to steal food or start fights. Our leaders released the people after giving them food and an invitation to return any time for more. We considered that these altercations were staged to try to give the foreign troops cause to enter our little city and establish martial law, and also take control of our stores of food. They wanted us to disperse, and if we had no food, they reasoned most would leave.

However, they never succeeded in finding cause against us. Our leaders were inspired in every reaction and had been planning for this day for decades. We planted fruit trees and grains on large tracts of ground and raised animals that produced milk and cheese. We had a huge workforce and could accomplish anything we began in just a few days or weeks. Many buildings were being constructed. These were not clapboard structures, but permanent buildings of fine workmanship made of wood, brick, and stone.

During one of the meetings, the Brethren showed us a series of large maps that had been drawn long ago. It showed Zion in Missouri as the center of a bull's-eye, with scores of concentric rings drawn outward from that hub. All across North America there were cities indicated along these lines and rings drawn around those cities indicating their planned size. The end result was that the whole continent was covered with evenly spaced cities flowing outward from the center place of Zion. The whole face of the continent was more flat now, with remaining mountains more like big hills than great obstacles to man. There were only small roads drawn to connect all of the cities to one another, and to Zion, but no highways or rails. The city plan included farms, commerce, temples, and every other necessity for a Zion society. Each city could live independently with this plan.

I was interested that there was almost no indication of industry on the map, and few roads. Rather than it being an omission, as I initially wondered, I later came to understand that by the time Christ returned, and this plan was developed, that there would be no need for industry or roads because the whole world would be living in a millennial condition. There would be no death, no disease, and no needs that could not be met either by cottage industry or by calling upon the power of God.

An Evolving Society

Society was changing; at least it was here in the Cardston "City of Zion." The world outside was still in great chaos. Everywhere governments recovered, they began exerting control, usually in the form of martial law, which led to conflict and civil war. Throughout the world, wars began over everything imaginable. Ethnic and traditional hatreds still smoldered, and old borders and treaties had ceased to exist. Even with more than half of the world population gone, these wars outside of Zion ultimately cut the remaining human population by half again.

Here in our little part of Zion, our hearts were changing, our bodies were changing, and our spiritual IQ was changing. We still had a fulness of the priesthood, as we first discovered just before the first great conference, and we were learning every day what that meant. It took us years to understand that we had to evolve into Zion, not just march to it. It was a process that involved stripping away everything belonging to the world and replacing it with total faith in God. We had to learn that we did not need anything from the telestial world. All we needed was complete faith in Christ. It was a hard transition to make, but it was one of the reasons our journey to Zion took so many years—not to cover the distance, but to evolve spiritually so that we would be worthy to be in Zion when we actually arrived there.

As an illustration, I am reminded of an event that taught us all a great deal. On the first leg of our journey, one of the brethren on the council was a diabetic from childhood. He was able to secure and bring with him a supply of his medication. But after a few months, he ran out. He grew sicker day by day until he could not function and could only eat tiny amounts or his blood sugar went dangerously high. He lost weight dramatically and struggled for months. We all began to expect him to die soon.

He asked for, and of course, received several priesthood blessings, but he still did not improve. Our ability to heal had been manifest nearly 100 percent of the time we called upon God. We had seen many miracles of the priesthood and could not understand why this faithful brother, whom we knew to be righteous, did not recover immediately. We had seen him work miracles himself and knew he was worthy of the blessings we were calling down upon him, but he did not recover.

Then, one morning, he got up out of bed and announced that he did not need medication any more. He ate a normal breakfast and was fine ever after that. We asked him what had changed—why he was now healed.

He replied, "While I was dying, all I could think of was, 'Why hasn't the Lord led me to more medicine so I can continue my mission for the Lord?' I had to get very low and near death to realize that I was asking for the wrong blessing. I had been in the Conference Center when Jesus Christ showed us all our future labors in vision, and I knew I would arrive in Zion with this company. But I was trying to have the Lord make me arrive on my own terms—which was with my medicine. I humbled myself and told the Lord I would go anywhere He wanted, to Zion or to Heaven, and I would go on His terms."

He continued, "It just came into my heart that I already knew I would arrive in Zion, and if the Lord had not yet provided medicine, then I obviously didn't need it. I knew it was true. I felt vitality come back into my body, and I got out of bed. The power of God and of His priesthood are manifest in me, and I'm perfectly fine now. I just had to learn that the Lord was my salvation, not a bottle of medicine."

We had the priesthood power, but not the spiritual maturity and understanding to use it flawlessly. Like this fine brother, we had to learn how to be of perfect faith, and how to release our grip on "things" as our salvation.

There were other lessons we had to learn before we arrived in Zion. If we had fully understood what we had, we could have just "traveled" to Zion in a heartbeat by the power of God. That knowledge was not revealed to us because we had to walk there and in the process to be stripped of everything we had except a few rags of clothing before we learned to rely totally upon God, and to use His priesthood to provide things we had always previously relied upon society and hard work to provide. The law of "by the sweat of thy brow" had been amended, but it would take us years to grow into that sweet knowledge.

Our society was also evolving in the sense that there was not a plan for highways, airports, or trains, because in time the Saints would be taught to travel from place to place by the power of God. We knew this was how some of the apostles and other leaders had come to Canada for the last conference, but we did not yet know how to access this blessing for ourselves.

There was also no plan for permanent utilities because cities of Zion were to be lit by the power of God; communication and information was to be implemented through a Urim and Thummim each person would possess, and millennial bodies did not thirst, hunger, or produce waste—hence, there was no need for utilities.

Society was also evolving into an almost pre-industrial age because in time, quite a long time, actually, we eventually learned that we no longer had to manufacture anything. In our evolving Zion in Cardston, we built medical clinics and sawmills and many other small industries to support us now, which some of us knew would eventually have no practical use to us at all. I will have much more to say about this later.

In the meantime, we were just waiting to be told it was time to leave Cardston. I waited too, and I served in the temple or anywhere else the Lord called. It was a marvelous time for me. Having been sickly all my life, to now have the power of God and changes to my body giving me unending health and energy, I now felt like a toddler who was learning how to walk. It was a time of wide-eyed discovery for me, and I loved every minute. More than that, I loved the Lord, and grew deeply attached to those with whom I served.

We stayed through the winter, or perhaps it was several winters. I'm not sure. Once again, my view of these things began jumping larger and larger periods of time more frequently. I understood it all clearly when I was in the vision, but when I returned to my mortal identity, it was far more than my mortal mind could contain, and some of these complexities were lost to me.

The winter was mild, in the fifties and never freezing. Most people spent the time building and working for our common welfare. All of the work was organized, and people rotated from job to job every few days unless they had a specialty, such as medicine or some science. Since I had been an ordinance worker in the temple, I served in the temple day and night, working to complete many thousands of ordinances for people who had arrived, had been taught, and were now ready.

There was also a lot of conversation and curiosity about when and where the return of the "lost" ten tribes would occur. We knew some companies had been sent to foreign countries, and we speculated that they were gathering in these lost groups. When we gathered for conference or other meetings, we were hungry to learn from these other companies. With all of this wonderment and delightful speculation, there was no doubt all would come to pass as prophesied. We just wanted to know how far things had progressed.

During this winter, many small groups arrived. There were companies from Europe and Asia, and a large company who came across a new land bridge from Russia to Alaska, and then down through Alaska and Canada to Cardston. They may not have known who they were, but their patriarchal blessings revealed them as being from one of the so-called "lost" tribes of Israel. They weren't actually lost; they just didn't know who they were until they arrived.

The people who had led them to Cardston were literally angels. To the refugees, these angels were just people who came, gathered them, taught them, baptized and ordained them—all during their years of exodus. Only a few righteous leaders truly understood who was leading them. To my eyes, they were translated people—some from thousands of years ago, some from these very times. By the time they arrived, these people had been through the very refiner's fire that we had all experienced on our journeys. They began in trucks and arrived in rags, but they literally glowed with righteousness and faith when they arrived.

Even though I was seeing this in vision, I tell you these are times I will never forget. Whether in the body or out, I was there, and it was magnificent.

Around the first of April, another conference was held. We received our assignments and destinations to various "cities of Zion." We received a detailed report on the New Jerusalem. We were amazed at how much work had already been accomplished in Zion and how long the leadership of the Church had been planning and preparing to build in what we used to call Missouri.

Many were surprised at their assignments, but there was a growing spirit of righteous willingness among us. One of the difficulties was that the concept of "walking to Zion" in Missouri had been such a part of Mormon culture for so long, that now it was hard to imagine going anywhere else. I didn't hear of anyone refusing or complaining about their new missions. They just made preparations to continue on.

Because I had been in the great conference in Salt Lake City, and had seen the vision of my future mission, as had many people there, I knew a great deal more about our journey beyond Canada than those who had not enjoyed that prophetic experience. When the Spirit moved me, I shared my knowledge, but mostly I was constrained to be silent.

I was continually watching and listening to find anyone else who had been in that conference. During the many conversations I had with these blessed people, I found that everyone had seen a vision of their own future. Our individual visions were personalized and different from one another. We told our stories, and by fitting together our various views, we were able to discern a broader picture of what was going to happen, and it was literally stunning to behold.

Those of us who had experienced the actual physical change of translation were somewhat different than others. We had clearer views of things and greater spiritual gifts. Unless we were speaking to another translated soul, we kept our translated status and these greater views to ourselves, as the Spirit seemed to require.

We were learning that translated people didn't get tired like normal people. Everything took less effort and taxed us less. We recovered quickly and could work long and hard and then recover in a few minutes. We still ate and slept, but we talked amongst ourselves, wondering if eating and sleeping was even necessary. After a big day's work, I felt hungry and tired but much less than in my previous life. I chose to eat, but it was different. I needed less food, slept better and far shorter, and felt absolutely wonderful. I could awaken in a second, even after just a few minutes of sleep, and feel perfectly awake and ready to go forward. At the end of the day, I was no more fatigued than when I slept a full night. I found that injuries, cuts, and scratches healed as fast as I wanted them to. There was no pain, only a realization of the injury. If I ignored it, it healed in days instead of weeks. If I wished it away, and prayed to the Father, it would heal in a matter of minutes. I expected in time to be impervious to injury, but I wasn't at this time.

I was physically stronger day by day. My mind grew clearer and much quicker. Things that would have taken me long study before now came to me in flashes of understanding. I grew in my ability to understand complex situations, and I could instantly come up with complex answers that were completely correct and inspired. My hearing was acutely attuned to the word of the Lord. Revelation became constant and unending. I no longer experienced temptations of any kind. I no longer walked through mists of darkness. I didn't hold onto the Iron Rod because it became a part of me, a part of my soul, what I was.

My capacity to love was profoundly enhanced, which made meetings and partings even sweeter, and more difficult. If anything had the power to make a translated soul sorrow or feel pain, it was this infusion of charity, because my heart wanted everyone to be blessed, uplifted, and supplied with every need. This wasn't always possible, and people I loved sometimes chose to transgress, and this caused deep sorrow at times.

Every new gift I had was focused upon our new mission. The constant companionship of the Holy Ghost was an ever-present reality, and we knew the mind and will of the Lord. There was no guesswork and no more fear.

Science and math and even my professional training all seemed to become less important. If you're looking for a solution that would take five engineers with super computers, and the answer just enters your mind as revelation—there is no point in checking it against mortal sciences. You already had the answer. This new thinking was not an upgrade to our IQ; it was a lifting of the veil to reveal what we already were. Some of us had participated in the creation of worlds before we were born, and those divine sciences we understood then were slowly piercing the mortal veil, replacing mortal sciences.

It was fascinating to watch our society leap forward, even while becoming simpler, less industrial, and non-commercial, with no consumer mind-set.

We would come to discover the truth of all these questions over time. For now, it was like slowly unwrapping presents on Christmas morning—seeking to enjoy the process of discovery as much as the presents inside.

To my spiritual eyes, translated people just looked different. I could discern them far off. So when I had the chance to talk with another newly translated person, we occasionally took the time to discuss what this all meant, and what experiences and new priesthood gifts we had experienced. We compared our experiences from the great conference and tried to piece together a larger picture. The more I learned, the more I realized that even with this great view of my own life ahead, I knew but a tiny part of the whole. It was a good grounding and humbling realization for me.

We also knew that even though the gift of translation had been fully given to us, that we still were in the process of becoming, of learning our duties and our abilities and when it was appropriate to use them. When I met an old translated being, there was a power and righteous serenity about them that I did not possess. Seeing and experiencing their highly developed state motivated me to yield to whatever process I needed to endure to become fully evolved in my new status. I knew I was changing. I also knew it was going to take years for the process to be fully implemented.

There was a direct and constant influence of the Holy Ghost

in the camps that could not be denied. It was a new phenomenon among the Saints that had begun that day of the great conference. Everyone was adjusting to this new level of spiritual power. There was a lot of conversation about whether this was the "millennial state" or if it was part of the process to the greater change of translation.

About this time trans-oceanic travel became possible again via ships at sea. The different cities of Zion around the world had been established and fortified. Many groups from Canada were assigned to travel to these smaller cities and to gather the elect along the way. Companies also left from Salt Lake City and other Zion cities to go forth and gather. This work was all directed by the Apostles from Salt Lake City. The Church had a working telecommunication network before the tribulations began, but we were learning to use a more perfect system. It began to function because the power of God was being made manifest in greater degree among us. Just as the two Apostles had arrived in Cardston by divine means, man-made communications systems slowly became obsolete.

Leaving Cardston

We prepared to leave throughout that winter. It was March when we bid our new homes and new friends good-bye. We were headed to the Center Place of Zion in former Missouri, and we left with a song in our hearts. Our company was smaller, perhaps three hundred people, including families. We took our big military vehicle loaded with supplies, as well as a few pickups. Fuel was not abundant, but in Canada there were a few refineries still in operation and we traded for fuel. We left feeling fearless. We had seen so many miracles that we could imagine nothing but the Lord's constant care and protection. We feared neither man nor army, seen or unseen.

I was called in and sat with one of the Apostles then in Cardston. He greeted me most graciously. He was a newly translated soul himself, and we greeted each other with an embrace like brothers from childhood. He set me apart for my new assignment at the temple in the New Jerusalem. This was the reason I was in this company and not going somewhere else. I knew all of the live ordinances from my prior service in temples before the tribulations and while in Canada.

I was assigned to take this knowledge to Missouri, establish the ordinances, and train others. I was of course thrilled. It was a part of my journey that I had not foreseen. I had seen in vision that I would arrive in Zion, but not what I would do once there.

As we had done in the first leg of our journey, we began with a council meeting, which quickly resulted in our knowing the mind of the Lord and destination of our first day's journey. We presented this to our camp, and it was sustained. We knelt in prayer, ate breakfast one last time in Cardston, and left out of the southern gate. We were headed back into Montana. The trucks trundled along a little faster and were soon out of sight. We walked and sang and wondered.

This leg of our journey felt simplified. We were not assigned to gather as many. We were not carrying as many supplies, and we had fewer belongings. We were well past the "work it out in your own mind, then ask if it be right," phase of revelation. We awoke each morning knowing the will of the Lord. We knew what to do, how to do it, and how it would come out. We ceased to make mistakes. We were always where we needed to be, at the right moment, with the right words and the power to accomplish the Lord's will.

We could approach a total stranger and know their exact circumstances and needs. We could say, "Your husband is at home dying. Your young son died just last night, and your husband asked you to go get help. You are hungry and exhausted and terrified. We will help you, but we need to come to your home and give him a blessing and raise your young son from the dead. Will you take us there?" They felt the love and faith in our voices, and miracles occurred.

After experiencing these types of miracles day after day, we looked forward to each new morning with joy. We just kept thinking, "Behold the majesty of the Lord!" and we went forward without fear.

For me there was a dual identity. I was in that company, participating in these glorious days, but I knew in my heart that this was a vision. Boy, I did not want to go back into my mortal body! I wanted to be in the company of Zion. Even though I realized that I was seeing a future event, it was so real that I was living it—I was there and it was reality. It was so real that it was hard to remember that my real reality, my true self, was lying in a bed in Utah, and my spirit was seeing future events.

Those of us who were translated soon paired off and took the opportunity to speak of our blessings. The other person in our company was a woman in her fifties. I'll call her Rachael. I had actually known Rachael from her youth. My relationship with her was like father to daughter. I had been involved in her youth as an advisor and confidant. We had both been in the first great conference and had both been translated that moment. She was humble about her gift but had some difficulty accepting that she really was ready or that she was the right person for these gifts. She wanted reassurance and instruction from me on how to progress, which I did not have. We were in the same boat, so to speak.

She woke up each morning almost expecting her gifts to be gone. Finally she realized that these changes were permanent, and she ceased to worry.

From then on, she was inspired, intelligent, and organized. She was the women's leader in our group. She was like a Relief Society president. She counseled with the women and gave out daily assignments. She was also a spiritual leader. I remember talks she gave to the whole company. There were times when her words rallied the group and gave us all courage to face impossible obstacles, depending wholly upon the Lord.

She was married, and her husband was with us. He was a great man, one of our council. His responsibility was the youth of the company. He was a man of faith, but he was not translated like his wife. This gave him some doubts about his own righteousness. He was not slack or faithless or doubting in any way—he just questioned his own capacity and wondered why he could not do the things he wanted to do. He felt like he was of less worth, which in fact was not true. His condition and his calling were perfect for him, and it was all engineered to bless and prepare him for his full endowment of power. He came from a background of success and confidence, and his journey was taking him through humility and reliance upon the Lord. His wife came from a background of humility and doubting her worth, and her journey was taking her to see herself through the eyes of God and embracing her own worth.

From this point on in the vision, the journey was shown to me as a series of snapshot scenes. I was no longer participating in the events, but was watching them from a distance, as if on a large screen. The vision was still showing me things that would happen, but I was no longer an actor, I was now a spectator. Each of the following vignettes occurred this way.

The First Vignette

The first vignette caught up with my company just north of Wyoming. I don't know how much time had elapsed, but it must have been at least a few months. The season was later in the year.

I saw that they had been attacked several times by the foreign troops with the blue-green helmets. They were trying to stop our journey into Missouri. I don't know what their motive was. Perhaps they also knew of the city that was quickly growing there and feared that it would become a source of political solidarity that could challenge their dominance. I was never told why, I just saw that they robbed us of food and fuel, killed some of us, and tried to intimidate us into turning back. They had blown up bridges to stop our progress, and they threatened to kill us all if we did not turn back.

It was at this time that we were also attacked by a band of armed thugs who attempted to rob us, but we had nothing. Instead they kidnapped some of our beautiful young people. It was an awful, horrifying moment, but instead of intimidating us, it did the opposite.

The foreign troops were trying to taking over the government of the nation and all local governments. The Latter-day Saints were the largest organized body of people remaining from the old world, and thus they saw us as their biggest threat even though we gave them no reason to fear us. Their assignment was to break down all organized groups, including all religious organizations. Our aims were manifestly not political, and they knew this. We had been instructed that we were not to take part in any political process, or to give our allegiance to any government entity no matter who it was.

Our vision, or the vision the Lord had instilled in our minds, was that we were preparing Zion for the return of Jesus Christ, and that He would soon reign as King of Kings and Lord of Lords. We were not trying to rebuild the nation; we were trying to build the Kingdom of God. We knew He would subdue all enemies under His feet when He came, and we need not participate in that process. We were united in our great relief that this was the case. We were sick of the world and everything we left behind. Our only desire was for Christ to come and end this telestial world of tears.

The foreign troops knew we had a plan, which we were accomplishing. They perceived that we were organized, well governed, and determined to accomplish this plan. They also knew our plan had something to do with Missouri, so they took up position to stop us. They didn't even know why we were going there, but they believed stopping us would destroy us. They didn't realize it wasn't our plan, but God's, and they were powerless to stop us.

It was disconcerting to me to jump from seeing our company as a joyful and powerful company of Zion suddenly reduced to a ragtag group of struggling survivors. The change had happened quickly. I saw myself among the group, and I was now watching myself in these circumstances as if in a 3D diorama. It made perfect sense in the vision, but is a little hard to explain or even fathom as a mortal.

The foreign troops' aggression proved our earlier realization that they really were our enemy, and they saw us the same way. We went to great lengths to avoid them and not meet or interact with them. They, on the other hand, began to hunt us. They grew from harassing and robbing us to setting up ambushes to destroy us entirely.

In addition to the foreign troops, there were armed bands of thugs. These bandits were generally defectors from the foreign troops or were brigands from all around. They were well supplied and heavily armed. They had robbed many times and kidnapped some of our youth.

We were just struggling to continue our journey. As I looked upon my little company from the distance of the vision, I saw that this opposition had the opposite effect our enemies hoped. I saw our spiritual strength growing and our courage and reliance upon God and the priesthood increase dramatically.

I saw that there were great miracles in the camp. Tiny supplies fed many people, and they did not dwindle with use. Water was found or provided by miraculous means. We were led to areas by the Lord that exactly met our needs for that day. We grew from courageous to fearless in spite of the overwhelming obstacles and losses we faced.

As soon as we ceased to fear, we awoke one morning to a new phenomenon. There was a pillar of light in the front of our camp and one at our rear. The bright light was a pillar about thirty feet tall. It was observable to our enemies as well. It was a literal light and was visible by day and by night. It went before us and behind us, and it terrified our enemies.

The light didn't come from heaven or from the earth. It was self-contained, as if the power of the light was the light itself.

At first, we did not know what its function was. Some in our company wondered if it would make us more visible to our enemies, but this fear quickly evaporated. We could walk up to the light and touch it. It was comforting and healing. We would take those who were injured, ill, or starving and exhausted, and we would leave them within or near the light, and they would quickly be healed. The light also healed sadness, fear, and confusion. Before the light began, we often felt discouraged or saddened by loss. Now we felt great comfort and peace to go with our previous fearlessness.

We no longer met in council to decide our day's journey because we knew in our souls the way we should go, and the light led us that way. We weren't following the light, we were following Jesus Christ. The light was a living manifestation of His love and protection. When it stopped, we stopped. When it moved, we moved. The light led us through the wilderness of our need. We miraculously rescued those who had been kidnapped; healed them body, mind, and soul of their recent abuse; and rejoiced with them. They became some of the strongest among us. They never spoke of their captivity other than in grateful terms for the experience and subsequent total healing.

The pillars of light were bright enough that they lit the entire camp at night. It was becoming winter, but the lights radiated sufficient heat that we no longer lit fires. We ate our little bits of food and then slept within the light, and we were filled and renewed.

I will never forget one event I saw shortly after the pillars of light joined us. We were walking toward a valley between two hills. We saw that a band of heavily armed thugs were blocking the valley through which we needed to pass. It was the same gang who had earlier kidnapped some of our youth. There was a moment of panic, particularly for those who had been kidnapped and abused by them and then miraculously rescued, but the fear quickly left us. We knew too much of God's power to be afraid anymore, and we had consecrated our lives to Christ, which meant we did not fear what the world could do or how our lives might end. I tell you, we had no fear.

Our enemy could see the pillars of light, but they thought it was some trick we were producing ourselves. The pillars of fire stopped, and we knelt in prayer. Our leaders went out to talk to them. They said they only wanted our food and supplies. We tried to negotiate with them but could not meet their demands. We knew their hearts. They intended to kill us and retake those whom they had kidnapped, no matter what we gave them.

The light led us forward and they stood their ground, ready to fire at us and the light. As soon as the light approached them, they were overpowered. They could not move or act. They were frozen in place with a look of astonishment on their faces. Their eyes were following us, but they could not move their bodies or limbs to lift or fire their weapons. We just walked around and through them and continued our journey.

I don't know what happened to those evil people who had threatened us so many times, but we never saw them again.

This experience again solidified our faith. We knew that the pillars of light weren't just there to guide us, but they were also there to protect us. We also began to realize that the power of the light, the ability that it had to protect us, was entirely based upon our faith and unity. It was very much like the Liahona, which operated according to Lehi's people's faith and diligence. As our faith and confidence in God grew, the light became brighter, taller, and more powerful.

I kept thinking that my faith couldn't get any stronger. When we began healing people 100 percent of the time in Utah, I thought my faith was perfect. When we were directed to obtain our every need on the trail, I thought my faith was perfect and couldn't get any stronger. When we beheld the miracles that saved us along the trail, I thought my faith was perfect and couldn't get stronger. When we saw the pillars of light and recovered our lost people, it was so strong that I did not see how it could get stronger. Yet every time a challenge and loss stripped us of something we needed, our faith grew stronger still, rendering that thing unnecessary. And still I considered my faith as perfect and as great as it could become. But I was mistaken in this assumption.

Along with the protection from the pillars of light, we walked in the light of revelation. Nobody doubted ever again. Even our children received revelation as often as the adults. They spoke the words of Christ and prophesied. They changed at this time. They became a blessing to the camp instead of a burden. We still took care of them like children, but they had a purpose for being in the camp, and they fulfilled that purpose. They often sang in times of trial and threat, and their little voices sounded like angels and actually gave the adults greater faith and unity, and it terrified our enemies. When they heard the children singing like angels, they knew we had no fear and that they could not prevail.

The Second Vignette

My next awareness was that a long time had passed. I saw that during the intervening time our company had almost run out of fuel, and we had abandoned our vehicles except for the big truck. All of the other vehicles had been destroyed by our enemies, broken down, or abandoned due to the lack of fuel. Our big truck just seemed to keep going with the needle hovering just above "E." It just kept going and going.

Almost everyone was afoot, with small backpacks on their back. Even the children carried little bundles with their own food and clothing. We were moving slowly now.

My first view was that we had entered a mountain pass. I don't know where it was. On our right were tall cliffs. The stone was dark, with trees and bushes growing out of it. We were standing in tall grass and bushes at the bottom of the cliff. On the hillside to our left, a long row of military vehicles came into view. They had been waiting in ambush. Troops took up position at the entrance and exit to the canyon, trapping us inside. There were trucks with machine guns, several huge army tanks, and half a dozen trucks with rocket launchers. They were mocking us and threatening us, telling us that we were all going to be dead in a few minutes. They taunted God and said that this time, even God could not save us; they were more powerful than God.

These troops were from almost every nation that had survived—Asia, Russia, Europe, and Africa. The soldier who was taunting us was shouting in broken English through a large bullhorn.

They began to fire upon us. People from our company began to fall.

Rachael, the only woman who was translated, got up onto the bed of our big truck and cried with a mighty voice that could be heard above the roar of rockets and machine gun fire, "Behold the majesty of the Lord!"

The pillars of light grew brighter as the enemy fired every weapon they had. The pillar of light before us seemed to arch backward to meet the pillar from behind. The rockets and bullets they shot at us began bouncing back at the enemy. A huge explosion rocked the enemy in a ball of fire, and then there was thundering silence and gray smoke on the hillside.

The pillar of light returned to its normal size. We rushed to our dead and injured and immediately healed them. There were only two people who we did not immediately heal. The first was a middle-age woman who was almost blown in half. She was alive when we came to her. God did not instruct us to heal her. Her journey was finally over, and she died praising God. The second was a young man whose hip had been shot away by a large-caliber weapon. It was Rachael's son.

She ran to her son, weeping for his pain, but having great faith. All of the Council was there, as well as myself. I knew I could heal him, but I did not have permission from the Lord to do so. Rachael looked at me and requested that I ask the Lord to heal him, then immediately realized by the same Spirit that I was not the right person to ask. She looked at the president of our Council. He shook his head and turned to Rachael's husband, the boy's father.

He called him by name, "Brother Zachary, it is the Lord's will that you heal your son."

Zachary was a great man, and a member of the Council, but he doubted his spiritual gifts, largely because, as I earlier explained, he was not translated, and his wife was. He also knew that his wife had greater power with God than he did to heal their son.

Nevertheless, he knelt and placed his hands upon his teenage son. In just a few words, he invoked the priesthood and commanded his son to be made whole in the name of Jesus Christ. He did this with deep humility and even deeper faith. The Spirit was brightly upon us, and we all felt the power.

Immediately the young man's leg began to rise up. It looked to my eyes as if it were inflating. All I could think to say was, "Praise God!" and I think everyone there said the same. In less than a minute, his leg was completely normal. The color instantly returned to his face, and he opened his eyes.

"Thanks, Dad," he said. Then looking up to heaven, he said, "Thank you, Father."

We helped him stand on his new hip and leg. His pants were nearly completely blown away by the explosion, but he just stood there looking down at his leg with a funny expression on his face.

"What's wrong," Rachael asked with an almost comical laugh born of powerful relief and joy.

"Mom, I can feel my leg, but I can't figure out how to tell it to walk." He laughed, and tried to take a step. His leg wobbled out from under him, and he was caught by his parents and myself.

After many attempts and much amazement, he still could not walk, so we loaded him onto the truck. It took several weeks for him to learn how to use his new leg. There was no pain and no lack of strength, he just looked like a baby learning to crawl, and then to toddle, then to walk and eventually run. His father was constantly by his side, encouraging him and supporting him as he learned to use his new leg.

Rachael and I spoke privately about this odd event. We had never seen or heard of such a thing. It soon became obvious to everyone what was happening and why this had occurred. Brother Zachary was experiencing his son's healing in slow motion, giving him weeks to process what had happened, to see his son's new limb over and over until he could not doubt that it was a miracle of profound degree, and that it had occurred by his own hand and by God's grace. By the time his son was able to walk and run again, Zachary was changed. He no longer doubted his spiritual standing with God. His faith had caught up with his body on his journey to Zion.

A few of us climbed the hill to where the foreign troops had been. All that we found was a city block-sized piece of charred ground. All that remained of the enemy was melted metal and a fine gray powder that had once been soldiers and weapons.

We moved out of that little valley, and as we departed, the rock wall on our right collapsed down upon the army, burying all evidence of their existence. We stopped on the other side of the valley, knelt together, and sent prayers to heaven of gratitude and rejoicing.

The Third Vignette

The scene changed, and I again found myself looking at a distant time. Our company was about a day away from entering Zion. We had come a long way. We left Cardston on trucks with good supplies and confidence. We arrived at Zion on foot and in rags. All of our vehicles were abandoned and our supplies were gone. Even our pockets were empty. We had been stripped of everything we relied upon, everything that had produced our earlier confidence, even food and clothing. It was this process of sacrificing everything earthly that had sequentially taught us to totally trust in God, to have utter confidence in Him, rather than in our "things." We arrived with a pillar of fire before us and a pillar of fire behind us, and we lacked for nothing. We had been beaten down, and in that same process we had been elevated to the stature of Zion.

I saw that we were singing and rejoicing, but we were also tired—physically, emotionally, and spiritually. Rejoicing was the only emotion we had left.

The next day, a company came out of Zion and brought us food and brand-new clothing. We hugged them and laughed and praised God with them. We spent some time washing and dressing in the new clothing. Later that afternoon, we entered Zion in a long parade with a pillar of fire and angels leading the way.

We found the New Jerusalem sitting upon a low plateau above a bend in a new river that had formed during the tribulations. Everywhere one looked were thousands of people happily engaged in the construction of all types of buildings. The whole city was being constructed according to the pattern that Joseph Smith had drawn while he was still alive in Nauvoo.

There were about 3,000 people in Zion. They stopped to welcome us and to express rich love. This was no ordinary construction project. We saw miracles everywhere we looked. Women were carrying large timbers as if they were toothpicks, and men were moving dirt with shovelfuls that landed upon the pile like truck loads. We were sure that many of these workmen and women were translated beings and angels.

They took us to the foundation of the new temple, which was constructed up to the second story. The construction was of a metal shell, like a modern-day skyscraper. I couldn't make sense of the shape of it at the time. It was not a typical, rectangular building. It appeared circular in design. They were using modern electric tools, but there were no tractors or dozers. I saw a large overhead crane moving the metal beams. So far, there was no stonework on the temple

We met people from almost every ethnic background. They fell upon our necks and kissed us. They had awaited us with longing and anticipation. Unknown to us, the Lord had included people in our group with special craftsmanship skills needed to complete parts of the temple, and also those of us who had authority to officiate in the temple.

The Fourth Vignette: The Temple

This last vignette jumped forward in time to after the main structure of the temple had been completed. I have never seen such a building. It was round in shape. The center spire was ornate and beautiful. Extending out from the center building were twelve covered walkways, each leading to twelve outer temples that connected into an outer rim of temples, giving it a wagon wheel shape. The twelve outer temples were dedicated to each of the twelve tribes of Israel and had been built exclusively by those people. Each outer temple was detailed slightly differently to represent the ancient origins of each of the tribes of Israel. The temple belonging to Ephraim was facing exactly east, with others in order of spiritual heritage around the outer rim.

The outer temples were offices, chapels, and ordinance rooms. Between the spokes leading to the center structure were lush gardens, each planted with native plants from their homelands and beautifully manicured grounds. The center building contained the Holy of Holies at its center, where Jesus Christ would dwell when He came to His temple. There were a series of offices and ordinance rooms opening into the Holy of Holies. Around these offices was a circular hallway, with offices facing outward into the courtyards. Everything was magnificently beautiful.

The statue of the angel Moroni stood upon the tip of the spire facing east, but his trumpet was no longer to his lips. The bell of the trumpet rested upon his right toe, and his outstretched arm held the tip. He no longer had it to his lips because it had already been blown.

When I first saw it in this vision, I beheld that two of the twelve outer temples were still under construction. It was a beautiful, divinely inspired structure—the only temple like it ever to be built.

Stone had been imported from somewhere in Canada. It had been brought by the power of God from a vein of white stone that had been discovered just shortly before the tribulations began. The stone sparkled like diamonds and shone like mother of pearl. It was a precious stone that had previously only been found in pebbles large enough for small jewelry. This vein in Canada was a hundred yards wide and thirty miles long. The stone itself was almost as hard as diamond, and it was the most beautiful substance on earth. It could only be cut efficiently by the power of God.

I found myself sitting in the finished temple. Because of my calling in the temple, I had been assigned one of the offices that adjoined the Holy of Holies. The office was quite large and slightly pie shaped with the narrow end about fifteen feet across. The depth of the room was about forty feet, with the back wall around thirty. The architecture was elaborate, with high-arched ceilings. Everything, including the pillars that supported the ceiling, were made of the same white stone, but the stone in this office had streaks of silver that moved slowly within the stone. I'm not sure this material can exist in a mortal world.

I was standing before an arched window about fifteen feet tall and five feet wide. The white arched frame was thick and beautifully constructed, as was every other part of this room. To my right was a moderate-sized desk made of beautiful white wood. The surface of the desk was wood as reflective as glass. There was nothing on the desk but an opened set of scriptures bound in white.

The window was not made of glass and was not transparent. If it had been transparent, I would have been looking into the Holy of Holies, as it was set in the wall that separated my office from it. The window had the appearance of a lens, causing some distortion to the reflection of my office as I looked at it. I understood that it was a Urim and Thummim, a "portal" as we called them. It brought light into the room as well as being indispensable at that time for most of the work the Lord assigned us.

To my left, beside the portal, an ornate, arched white doorway led into the Holy of Holies. I never tried, but I understood that I could not open the door from my side.

Behind me sat a long conference table made of a stunning, dark wood. It looked as if it was made from a single tree that had been asked by God to assume the shape of a table. The table surface was wood, but also was as reflective as glass. There were fifteen comfortable chairs around the table, three at my back, and six on each side. The same type of chair lined the walls on both sides of the room. On the far side of the table was a large double door that opened into a circular hallway through which I came and went.

The portal belonged to me, and spiritually speaking, was a part of me. After I learned to use its full capabilities I was able to see anything I wished. It could only be used for inspired purposes and in fulfilling the assignments of the Lord.

By looking into the surface I could view any event or place merely by wishing to. At first, I could only view things as they presently were, but over time I learned to use it to see the past and the future as it pertained to my assignments. I could also contact other translated people and see them through the portal. If necessary, I could speak to them and they to me. If I walked into the glass, I would instantly be taken to that location. I could hand things to them and receive things from them without actually going there myself.

Like the pillars of light that had protected us on the last leg of our journey, this portal also had a healing and rejuvenating property.

Being near it, or especially passing through it, would heal anyone's body and soul who came with me.

This portal was tuned to myself and would only respond to me—though it would show other people what I was seeing if I included them. I could also bring other people and other things through the portal with me if it was the Lord's will.

I had the impression that it was alive—a living thing, full of truth and understanding and immense power. It was not a person, or a soul, but it was living in the way that the earth is living. It contained all of the history of the workmanship of God and could show it to me when my requests were righteous.

I also knew that it was eternal in nature and had been a part of my life before I was born and would be a part of my life eternally thereafter. It operated exactly as the one I had seen in my premortal room. I could view or study anything I wished merely by wondering about it. If I needed to handle something, it would present a solid representation of that thing, which I could handle and operate.

I fully understood that it was for the work of the Lord and not for my entertainment, and that I could not, nor would I ever consider, entertaining myself with it or gratifying curiosity. The only limitation to the portal was my own faith and my understanding of how to use it. No matter how many wonders and gifts of God we obtained, it required experience and inspiration to use them fully. I do not recall ever receiving something from God and immediately having full command of it. It took personal diligence and spiritual effort to grow into these gifts.

I used it many times to go on assignment for the Lord. Before I left, I took time to study everything and everyone I would minister to, including their history. This information came to me merely by wondering about it. I took it in with my eyes and with my soul in floods of information. When I was prepared, I would walk into the surface of the portal and it would take me there instantly. I could complete my mission, and merely by wanting to return, I would take one step and find myself back inside my temple office.

The vision flashed forward to a time when I was seated with my back to the table facing the portal with two other translated brethren, one on my left and one on my right. I knew them, but I don't recall their names. We were waiting for Jesus Christ to come in to give us an assignment. I vividly recall waiting with excitement, speaking in soft voices to one another and wondering what this assignment might be because we generally received our assignments without a personal appearance of our Savior. I had seen Him in the temple many times, and each experience changed me, leaving me feeling more joyful and more awed by His love and glory.

A moment later, the door opened and He walked into my office. We stood as He entered. Our hearts were kneeling before Him, but He had asked to not fall to our knees before Him as we were now His friends as well as His servants. We felt comfortable and loved His presence. He was dressed in a beautiful white robe across his right shoulder and pulled up on his left with a clasp. He was in His glorified state. Three translated men followed Him through the door. Christ did not introduce them. I knew exactly who they were in the vision, but as happened many times, I am not allowed to remember now.

He stopped in front of the portal, just a few feet from us. He paused for a long moment while we felt His love and glory. He told us the time had come to begin blessing other people in Zion with the gift of translation.

Initially, He had only given it to a few other than the Apostles in that first great conference in Salt Lake City. Jesus Christ and the three with Him laid their hands upon us one by one and ordained us to this new priesthood privilege. In each case, Christ spoke the ordinance. This was a day we had long awaited and hoped for but had not anticipated this soon. We knew that this signaled a great acceleration in the gathering of Israel and the formation of the 144,000. We wanted to shout for joy, but we did not. Christ knew our joy and smiled at us broadly.

When we were all ordained to this new power, they asked us to sit. They stood between us and the portal. Each of them stepped forward and told us why we had each received this blessing early in the first great conference four years ago. They showed us our future missions in vision. We saw everyone to whom we would minister. We didn't need to jot down a list. It was impossible for us to forget.

It was a tearful time, with profound humility and profound rejoicing. It was a time I will never forget. We were in total awe that we were here, in this great latter-day temple, in Zion, speaking with our living Savior, being ordained to this office.

After the three had spoken, Christ instructed us to go to each of these men and women we had just seen and teach them what they yet lacked. When they were prepared, we were authorized to bless them with this additional gift of translation. This was a day of days because prior to this moment, every translated person throughout history had been personally ordained by Jesus Christ. From this day forward the power of translation was entrusted to mortals. Following each new person's translation, they would then go through a somewhat abbreviated learning process similar to the one we had endured during our long journey to Zion to learn the extent and proper use of their powers.

Jesus Christ and His three companions lingered with us, rejoicing with us. They were in no hurry to leave. They wanted to be there with us until our rejoicing and our transformation was complete. In all of the history of this world, such a gathering had only rarely occurred, and they waited with us. Visions surrounded us, angels appeared and taught us. We were fully enveloped in glory.

When it was time to depart, Jesus and each of His companions embraced us one more time before returning back through the same door. We sat at the table for a long while, rejoicing and discussing what had just happened. In time, the Spirit let us know that it was over. We prayed together and left to begin our work.

We quickly found that all of our senses and sensibilities were amplified once again. From then on, when we went to those we were to bless, we could see the whole process of their lives. I had enjoyed this gift a few times while out of body, but never as a mortal. Now it was with us continually. We knew how to minister to these righteous people and how it would affect their lives. It was a beautiful vision, full of joy and peace for them, and we rejoiced to be a part of it.

This amplified gift of knowing people this intimately operated on everyone we met, not just the candidates for translation. Being able to completely understand people like that is a gift that comes with being translated, and that grows more powerful with experience and further blessings. It took us many years to understand and implement this new gift.

We immediately began to fulfill our new commission, seeking those we should minister to with this new gift. The first people who were blessed had journeyed with us from Utah to Cardston, and then on to Zion. These people were fully prepared and only needed to be ordained to this calling. Zachary is a good example of those who were fully prepared and who immediately began their new ministry as a translated being. There were many we ministered to in other companies who now were building remote cities of Zion. We literally ordained thousands to this calling. We didn't require a list. Our gifts made it impossible for us to forget. After this initial calling, we were shown many others who were less prepared, but they learned quickly because they had us to teach them, where we had learned by prolonged and sometimes harsh experience. We and others commissioned to this same work continued this labor by use of the portals for years. We did not stop until our number reached, and then exceeded 144,000.

Everyone had an assignment in the New Jerusalem. There were those responsible for clothing, or farming, or engineering and construction. As the years progressed, most of these people became translated beings. The work they performed was accelerated, inspired, and beautiful. There were great technological and scientific advances that blessed our lives. These advances were all spiritual in their nature and depended upon increasingly greater manifestations of faith to operate them. There were no advances in electronics or anything the world had invented before.

Electronics and earthly sciences seemed like primitive stone tools to us. We were intensely interested in the gifts of God and the changes in our hearts and bodies and priesthood power. Our old "ruggedly self-sufficient" attitude now seemed barbaric. "Self" seemed barbaric. We wanted to be one with Christ. We wanted to search the depths of our blessings and to rejoice in the abundance of our new spiritual world. Those things that were revealed to us gave us far greater gifts than anything electronic, mechanical, or scientific, as you will come to understand.

My job in the temple was to maintain the purity and consistency of the temple ordinances. After I had done the initial training, this did not occupy much of my time because our people's hearts and minds were perfect, so I spent most of it gathering people to Zion.

Gathering people was completely dependent upon inspiration. I would be given a name by revelation of a person, family, or company who needed my help. I would study them through the portal until I was inspired with the perfect way to help them. I would then go through the portal and assist them. I often healed them, raised their dead, and provided for their needs. Sometimes they saw me as a wonderful stranger who just happened upon them, and sometimes they guessed at my true nature. It wasn't until they were prepared that I revealed why I was there and where I was from. Sometimes, they never knew where I came from, and they never knew my name.

It took years in most cases for these people to evolve. We went to them many times and taught them many times. Many of these people, perhaps even most of them, were not LDS, especially since almost all of these had been gathered by the initial companies from Salt Lake City shortly after the tribulations began.

Some of those to whom I now ministered were in groups, some were families or individuals. When they were prepared, we showed them how to begin their journey to Zion, and we pointed them in the right direction. I often returned to them at critical moments to defend them and deliver them by the power of God. But they had to make the journey afoot, just as we had.

CHAPTER NINE

THE MILLENNIAL DAY

The Cavern

As this scene closed, I found myself standing on the Pacific seaboard. A boat was coming toward me as the sun was rising, revealing it a little at a time. It looked like a modest-sized, ocean-going fishing boat with nets and buoys dangling from the sides. I was the only one on the shore. The rest of my company was on the boat. Our company consisted of myself and eighteen others, mostly priesthood brethren with some women who had been prepared to bring our next group to Zion. All of us were aware that I was the only translated person among our small company.

My companions had made all of the arrangements, including the boat. I had received an assignment to meet them here and had come through the portal only days before. Most of the accompanying crew were not from Zion and had been sent from various cities of Zion to make preparations and to pick me up and accompany me on this mission. I stood in the bow of the boat, leading us forward because I had seen the route during my preparations at the portal.

We traveled north for weeks, far beyond the United States, past Canada, around Alaska, and up into the Arctic regions above Canada. We passed many large islands and went through narrow channels. We were far enough north that we should have been in harsh arctic weather, but there was no snow on the ground, and the land we passed showed new growth of grass and bushes that had not been there before the tribulations. As I have mentioned, the weather around the globe had changed. The winters were much milder, and the ice pack in the far north had mostly melted, exposing ground that had been frozen and buried beneath ice for millennia.

I was wearing a gray business suit with a white shirt and tie. In my current state, I did not experience any weather as cold or hot. It was all warm and pleasant to me. Though it was winter by the calendar's reckoning, it was in the fifties and sixties. My companions were from much warmer places and were not translated as I was, so they wore coats and warm hats and waited in the cabin for me.

After many weeks, we arrived at a place where the sea crashed against almost vertical cliffs. There were three rocky peaks of gray-blue stone, which I had seen through the portal. It was a clear landmark that we were in the right place. A man-made road had been carved into the face of the cliff that climbed from a rocky beach to the middle of the three peaks. We were well behind some large islands, and the ocean was subdued as we arrived. The boat continued past the cliffs and slid onto a narrow rocky beach. Once on land, my companions led me a little inland to where a road had, centuries ago, been beaten into the sand by many feet and many vehicles. We turned left and continued up the road we had seen carved into the cliff face. It was wide and smooth, though obviously of ancient origin.

It felt like springtime in the air, but it should have been sub-arctic winter. I also knew that this road, the three peaks, and where we were going had been under a hundred feet of ice for several millennia. Only since the temperature of the earth had warmed, and the ice had melted, had this place become accessible once again.

We stopped at nearly the center of the middle peak, which towered above us. The road continued upward but got narrower just past where we stopped. The men who accompanied me had brought shovels and picks. They took off their coats and chipped away at the stone. They were not chipping away natural stone, but a type of concrete with one side skillfully colored to match the cliff, which covered the entrance to a large cave.

The opening to the cave was about the size of a four-lane highway once we got it uncovered. I stepped into the entrance of the cave, and even though I had seen these things through the portal, they were much larger in real life than I had interpreted. There was a row of yellow lights about head high going down both sides of the tunnel. The tunnel was arched overhead, carved out of natural stone, but the floor was flat and smooth, apparently made of the same material we had just chipped away from the entrance. The entrance to this tunnel had not been opened to the outside world for many generations of man.

The cave curved gently downward a long way, disappearing into an apparently endless row of lights. My escorts set down their tools, dusted themselves off, and followed me into the mountain. I stopped to study one of the lights on the side of the tunnel, which looked like a roughly cast piece of glass. It was about the size of a basketball and gave off a steady light without heat. I picked one up and was surprised at how light it was. I determined that it was not attached to the cavern by wires or any power supply I could see. I learned later that they were much like the stones the Brother of Jared had asked the Lord to illuminate. They were not electric, but powered by God.

We walked about a mile, continually descending. The tunnel grew ever brighter as we approached a large cavern at the bottom. My first impression of this cavern was that it was miles in diameter. The ceiling was dotted with the same glowing stones, but they were almost as bright as the sun in this great cavern. The air was moving gently, and it had a pleasant smell of flowers and plants, like a sunny meadow just after a rainstorm.

When I could finally see into the cavern, I saw thousands of people gathered together. They were all facing away from me, looking at a man who stood upon a ledge carved into the rock wall. He was preaching to them with a voice that naturally amplified across the cavern. He was speaking a language I had never heard, but that came to my ears as English with an Irish or Scottish trill.

There were men, women, and children gathered before me. Just before entering this great cavern, there were several large boulders that had fallen during the earthquakes. I stepped beside one of these to listen and to pray for guidance.

The man addressing them had long, white hair and a long, white beard that flowed neatly to his chest. He held in one arm a large book, to which he gestured from time to time. He was teaching them about the changes the earth had recently undergone. He thumbed to various pages and read prophecy in their scripture regarding these days. His words were powerful, and the language was beautiful. He was speaking of things that we, myself and my companions, had just seen. He spoke with power about the New Jerusalem, from where we had just come. Everything he said was exactly true, and it thrilled me with the Spirit.

He was reading in a formal, poetic style, something like in Psalms, talking about the ice melting and highways being cast up in the deep. He read about the changes in the earth, the growth of grass and flowers once again in the desolate north. It came to our ears as the most beautiful poetry. His voice was singing more than speaking. It was magnificent—and we wept. I wept because it was so beautiful and because it was a third or fourth witness to why we were there. I had seen visions of these things years ago. Recently I had heard the words that Christ had spoken to me in person. I had studied these people through the portal. Finally I was hearing a prophet I had never known, reading from scripture I had never heard of, speaking prophetically of work I was even then doing, all coming to my ears by the power of God as the purest poetic English.

His words were being read from scripture thousands of years old, which no man but these few had ever heard, and it was prophesying about why we were there among them, though they had not yet noticed us. It was overwhelming to us all.

The people paid rapt attention to him. Their faces were clean and bright. I immediately recognized the glow of the Holy Spirit all about them. He thumbed to near the back of the book and read to them a long prophecy from their scripture, speaking of these times, prophesying that someone would arrive from the outside world who would lead them to the New Jerusalem, which, he added with great emphasis, would be "Above!" He meant, upon the face of the earth. The people laughed and cried, some prayed in a loud voice, thanking God. Others merely bowed their heads and wept. Their whole manner was of praising God, rejoicing, and weeping for joy.

Silence came over them and their prophet began teaching them of the blessings they would receive in Zion. He emphasized temple blessings, and the sealing of families forever. He promised them that shortly after they arrived in Zion, Jesus Christ would return to the earth to wipe wickedness from the earth, once again making it possible for these people to live where the sun shines, where rain falls, and where the stars are visible in the night sky.

After more joy and clapping, the prophet pointed directly to where I stood, next to the great boulder. He cried, "And here is the very messenger from God the scriptures testified would come! Today, the scriptures are fulfilled!" he cried, tears streaming down his face, pointing directly at me.

Thousands of eyes turned to look at me. A gasp of wonder arose and I stepped away from the boulder and took a slow step forward, still praying mightily under my breath. In my heart I was not fearful, but I was deeply intimidated. I had not watched the portal long enough to see all things, and this surprised me.

The people were beautiful, with high cheekbones and green or brown eyes with turquoise streaks. I had seen eyes like this only once before, long ago when the beautiful angel had come to tell me I was not going to die. In that instant I realized why she had come—because these were her people, her descendants.

Their hair was dark, almost black, with some brown-headed people, but no blond or red. Their complexion was swarthy, somewhat like present-day Jews. The men were broad shouldered and generally a little shorter than I am at six feet tall. Most of them had long hair, which they pulled back into a ponytail or a knot.

The women were about the same height as the men and beautiful. They wore their hair long in various ways, with many intricate types of braids and styles of hair. Their skin was flawless from generations away from sunlight. Their eyes were bright with wonder and free of judgment. I found my heart swelling to embrace them with love.

They all wore the same color clothing, which was the color of gun metal. It looked uncomfortable, but I learned that it was soft to the touch. They had other colors of clothing, but this was their formal attire that they wore on Sabbath days and for special occasions. The women wore dresses or tunics of this material that came to their knees. It was beautifully embroidered with flowing designs including mountains, birds, and trees—all things that they had never seen in their lifetimes. The men wore loose pants that were gathered at their ankles. Everyone wore light sandals on their feet.

As they turned their faces toward me, I had the impression that there were about 20,000 people looking at me. It was like standing in the Conference Center at the pulpit, though I have never had that experience; that was how many faces I beheld.

I had a bundle of books slung over my shoulder that I had been handed by the presiding Apostle in Zion. It contained all of our latter-day scriptures, a book describing temples and temple ordinances, a bundle of loose documents, and another old book that I have since not been allowed to recall the contents of. The books were bound on all sides by a leather strap with a shoulder strap to carry them. It was an unusual way to bind books. But when I was finally allowed to view their scriptures, they were bundled in the same way. It was a sign to their eyes that what I had brought them was indeed scripture.

The people parted, and I walked slowly forward. It was a considerable distance from where I stood to the platform where the prophet was speaking, maybe as much as a quarter mile. The people watched me intently with tears running down their faces. I walked past vegetable gardens lush with fruit and vegetables, past small parks with benches, common areas with beautifully crafted wooden chairs, and playgrounds full of toys. The people were standing in and through these places, watching me approach. I walked past them and smiled, though I felt like I just wanted to run to the stage.

I had learned that they had preserved a form of Old Testament doctrine. They did not have the New Testament and did not know the events of Christ's life. They spoke of Jehovah, and knew Him as Jesus Christ; however, they did not know many of His teachings. They worshiped Him as their Creator and Savior, but did not have a fulness of the Gospel. They did not have temple ordinances or an understanding of many sacred things.

Jesus Christ had visited them in their cavern world in the days after His resurrection and had promised them that He would return. He promised that before He came back to cleanse the world above, He would send messengers to teach them the fulness of the Gospel and to deliver them from their self-imposed exile.

They fully realized that this long-awaited moment had just arrived. They had been blessed with a long series of prophets who, for thousands of years, had preserved their sacred and secular history and kept their doctrine pure. They had the Aaronic priesthood and the appropriate ordinances thereof, but only their prophets held the higher priesthood. They knew of, but did not perform, temple ordinances. They had waited for many generations for this very day and this very moment. To them, it was somewhat like when Moses came to Egypt to deliver them from Pharaoh.

I will say it again: I was intimidated by the enormous challenge before me. Each of these people had to be taught the gospel, baptized into the latter-day Church, ordained to the priesthood, and prepared for the temple, all while on a long journey to the New Jerusalem to receive their blessings in the temple. Beyond that, they had to be taught the principles of Zion and integrated into the latter-day work.

As I walked forward, I was praying hard that I would say and do the right thing. Then I remembered who I was, who had sent me, and all that I had seen. The fear immediately left me, and I walked quickly to the front and climbed a narrow stone stair to join their prophet. I approached him and before I spoke, I handed him the bundle I had been given to deliver. He took it and held it over his head, and cried, "Here I hold the fulness of the gospel!" Then he turned and embraced me.

After the rejoicing gave way to silence, he asked me to address his people, and he stepped back with a sweep of his hand. There was no lectern or pulpit to separate me from these people. My heart filled with love for them as I stepped forward, still unsure what I should say.

As I opened my mouth, I knew they would understand my every word. The Holy Spirit fell upon me, and words began to flow into the perfect acoustics of that great cavern, and into the perfect innocence of their souls.

I began to teach them what had just happened in the earth. I told them of the collapse of society, of the earthquakes and floods. I bore powerful testimony that what I had just heard their prophet say was true, because I had seen everything he told them with my own eyes.

I spoke about Jesus Christ, about His life and Atonement. They wept and rejoiced. Their manner of worship was rather loud compared to my experience, and I had to stop frequently to let them cry out in joy. I found that I enjoyed their spontaneous expressions, for they were borne of the voice of the Spirit.

I spoke of the Apostasy and then of Joseph Smith's restoration of the latter-day Church. I told them about the Bible and held it up. I spoke at length about the Book of Mormon and held it up. I spoke of the current stature of the Church and told them of the hundreds of temples and the great latter-day gathering that was currently under way.

Lastly I spoke of the building of Zion, and that it had not been interrupted by recent destructions, but had accelerated because of them. I told them of the great conference in Salt Lake City and of seeing and hearing Jesus Christ address us in that meeting.

I told them that I had been sent by Jesus Christ personally, and by the Latter-day Church in Zion, to prepare them to return. I then opened the scriptures I had brought and read to them many scriptures and preached to them with the power of God. I do not know how long I spoke, but it was at least several hours.

They were thrilled to tears, weeping and praising God. Some fell to their knees, their strength consumed by their joy. They knew that their promises were about to be fulfilled.

I opened a small book on the top of the bundle I had brought to them. It contained maps and instructions on what was going to happen next and how to find their way to Zion. It also described their duties and their mission after they arrived to finish preparing the world for the return of Christ. I spoke of the portion of the temple that only they could build, and I held up a drawing of it.

I waited for silence to fall upon this large assembly. I then called up the other eighteen who had accompanied me. I introduced them each by name and told them what each person's calling was to be and how they would assist them to return to Zion. Each of the eighteen bore brief testimony to the group.

Their prophet came forward and handed me a copy of their scriptures and genealogy with great solemnity, almost ceremonially. He said, "I entrust these sacred things unto you. Take good care of them and take them back to the Prophet in Zion. These are our only copies, written by the hands of our prophets. Report to our new prophets that we are the children of God, and we have anxiously awaited this day when we could receive our blessings in Zion and in the temple. These are the records of our generations, and the history of our people. We desire that we and our ancestors may have our temple work done as soon as we are prepared. Tell them we are coming."

My next realization was walking with them up the wide tunnel. I was leaving with them to come out of their cavern home. They walked toward the daylight they had not seen for generations with determination, but there were also fond glances back at their home for all of living memory, and many tears of different types. In their lead walked their aged prophet, his face glowing in the Spirit, and in the sunshine he was beholding for the first time in his life. The last of their people took the glowing glass from the walls of the cavern and, after wrapping them in cloth, carefully placed them in a hand-drawn cart, leaving the great cavern in blackness. A few workman remained behind temporarily to seal the cave behind them.

The others of my party worked with the people to divide them into companies. They had built handcarts and small wagons but had no animals to pull them. By this time I knew some of their names and had grown to love them very much. They were truly a delightsome people, innocent and unpolluted by the world. They were like children in their faith and in their understanding of the world outside of their safe home in the earth. I wept as I thought about leaving them, but I knew they had to undergo their own journey to Zion, so they would be prepared when they arrived.

I didn't go with them. I hugged many of them, accepted their kisses upon my tears, then walked a short distance away until I was out of sight, and I returned to Zion via the portal. When I arrived I handed these books with their genealogy and scripture to the First Presidency of the Church, who by this time had relocated to what had formerly been known as Missouri, but no more. The world now called it Zion, the New Jerusalem.

Their Arrival in Zion

My next vision brought me to the day my friends from the cavern arrived in Zion. It was many years later. I had returned to them several times to encourage and minister to them, but the greater work had been accomplished by the eighteen who had walked with them to Zion.

We knew they were coming, and I went up and stood upon a low hill at the edge of the city. We had laid out a banquet to welcome and refresh them. They dropped their bundles and handcarts as soon as they saw us and ran into our arms. I wept as I embraced those I had come to love.

They were tired and ragged and had triumphed over much opposition. Their numbers were fewer. They had paid the price of the righteous journey. Their aged prophet had survived the journey and was walking in the lead when they arrived.

Joseph Smith joined us in welcoming them. He taught them about his role in the restoration of the gospel. He told them which tribe of Israel they were from, and he read from their own scriptures to instruct them. They were thrilled to know they were looking at a resurrected being in Joseph Smith, but they did not seem surprised. Our current prophet addressed them, as well as prophets who had ministered to them in past dispensations. These were prophets I had never heard named before, but they were well known to those who had arrived, and they gasped with wonder as each former beloved prophet was introduced.

When the people were fed and prepared spiritually, we brought them into the city. There was another long table set up near the temple with thousands of small glasses of water on it. They gathered and the Prophet explained that they were going to drink of the Water of Life.

"The Water of Life"

During the construction of the temple in the New Jerusalem, we had uncovered a natural spring. When we consulted the plans, it was actually marked on the drawings, along with designs for tapping the water that flowed from it. When the temple was completed, the water flowed from under the temple and out into a beautiful fountain we called the "Fountain of Living Waters" just outside of the temple. Near the fountain, a large and magnificent tree stood, which we called the "Tree of Life." It had not grown there but had been transplanted fully grown from a terrestrial sphere. Such a tree had never grown on earth before. We just observed it there one day, and like all other living things in Zion, we understood its complete history and everything else about it. Until being transplanted into Zion, it had long been a feature of Enoch's city.

The tree bore twelve kinds of fruit, representing the twelve tribes of Israel. Each type of fruit had a unique healing and sanctifying property that we used in ways I no longer remember. I do remember looking at the tree for many hours, wondering and marveling that such a perfected living thing could now be on earth.

Even the leaves had healing power. If a leaf or fruit was plucked from the tree, it almost immediately grew back. Taking a single leaf and placing it in the soil in another place caused the ground to heal, lush vegetation to grow, and the area to begin to change into the millennial format. One of the great purposes of the leaves of the tree was to heal the water from the resultant contamination of war and radiation. Just before and after the coming of the Lord, we took many leaves to the far-flung cities of Zion to begin their transformation into the millennial form, and eventually we carried them into all the world.

Eating fruit from the tree instantly changed one into the terrestrial or millennial format. We did not guard the tree because no unworthy person could enter Zion or in any way approach the temple and the Tree of Life unworthily. Those whose eyes were opened so that they could see the things of God and angels, saw mighty angels guarding the Tree of Life, just as the Father had commanded in the Garden of Eden.

The tree glowed with the glory of Jesus Christ both night and day, and was stunningly beautiful, much more perfect than any tree previously upon the earth.

The water from the fountain flowed around the tree and by so doing obtained the living properties of the tree. The water was thus "healed" of its telestial condition and became terrestrial in nature.

We built an open aqueduct to take the water down the center of every street in Zion, so that every person could freely partake. The channel was slightly raised and was built of beautifully carved stone overlaid with gold. We built smaller streams to take the water into gardens and orchards on the far side of the city. When the streams of water reached the edge of Zion, they went underground to nourish the land.

We channeled another stream from the fountain into the new river that flowed around Zion. The banks of the river began to return to life, with lush vegetation and flowering trees and plants growing spontaneously on the river banks, slowly moving inward across the denuded landscape. I might remind you that it was just under two years since the tidal wave from the Gulf had passed through here and had killed almost everything, including salting the earth so that it would hardly sustain vegetation.

The water was different from normal water. It was more clear and delicious and had a reflective property that caused it to scintillate in the sun. At night, it sparkled and glowed. Our prophets read the prophesies to us regarding this spring, of which a fragment is found in the last chapter of the Bible. A similar stream was eventually found in old Jerusalem. God had provided these waters by His power for the perfecting of Zion during the Millennium.

We found out soon that rubbing a little of the water on a wound would heal it in just a few minutes. Drinking it once healed any illness you had. Drinking it several times healed any disease and started to change you. Drinking it for about a week permanently changed you into the "Millennial Conditional," which was a change similar to translation, but without the spiritual gifts. From then on, your body never aged. You became impervious to sickness and disease. Injuries healed rapidly. In time, people became impervious to injury and pain. People who were old gradually grew younger-looking, and young people stopped aging at about thirty. It was all extremely thrilling and humbling to discover. We partook freely, rejoiced, and gave all glory to Jesus Christ.

We began calling it the "Water of Life," because it gave us life. We also named the fountain it came from as we did because we fully understood that it came from Jesus Christ, who is the Fountain of Living Water. The title "Water of Life" was a constant reminder to us that it came from our Savior.

Once we fully changed by drinking the water, we literally never thirsted again. We quit drinking normal water. We drank from the stream every day, but it was not necessary after the change had taken full effect.

After we drank, hunger was no longer an experience for us. We ate when we wanted to. Those who were not translated still needed to eat, but in much smaller amounts and far less frequently.

Just as amazing was that everywhere the water fell, the grass and trees and flowers began to grow and bloom in spontaneous abundance. Soil grew rich, and even rocks and stones were changed. Wiping the water on concrete or stone changed it so that it was perfect, no longer seamed or cracked or worn. It just became flawless, beautiful, and impervious to everything telestial.

We began watering gardens with it, and the fruit grew to enormous size. I once saw two men carrying a bunch of grapes attached to a pole between them. Each grape was the size of a watermelon. The men were changed themselves, so the enormous fruit did not burden them. They were carrying it to rejoice, and to parade it up and down the streets glorifying God and rejoicing in a loud voice, inviting everyone to come and taste the divine nectar of God's grace.

We soon learned to pick fruit when it was small and easier to eat, rather than allowing it to get so big. We found that after picking a fruit or vegetable, it soon grew back, so that trees were continually laden with fruit, and plants continually produced vegetables. We hardly ever actually planted new gardens. They just produced as if they were exploding with joy.

You could eat one small piece of fruit, and it would satisfy hunger and thirst for days. This food was fully absorbed by our bodies and produced no waste. It supplied everything our bodies needed to live without disease or death.

We found that the fruit was alive, and if you left a fruit on a cabinet or table, that it would remain fresh and delicious indefinitely. The food also had healing properties. Eating one piece of fruit could heal a common ailment, and repeatedly eating it would change you further. But only drinking the water changed one into the millennial state.

Even the grass, trees and animals became "millennial." The water was changing everything around us.

Becoming Ageless

People in Zion no longer aged unless they were children. The children would mature until they were approximately thirty and then become ageless. There was no infirmity, no disease, no sickness, no threatening injuries, and virtually no pain.

But there was a difference between the young and the old that we could see. Because our eyes were opened to spiritual things, and because of the constant presence of the Holy Ghost, older people possessed a look of wisdom, knowledge, and experience. They spoke differently and possessed knowledge of how to use the priesthood that younger people did not. They had greater experience, faith, and wisdom. We all looked the same age over time, but there was a difference that came with age that was revered, honored, and sought after.

The older people also remembered what it was like to be mortal, old, sick, or diseased. The younger people had not experienced these things. It was not uncommon for these older citizens of Zion to be asked to teach the young people what mortal life had been like so that they would value their millennial blessings.

We learned to communicate as much by the Spirit as by our voices, so the older generations were able to teach these things with great clarity, transferring the knowledge of these principles of mortality powerfully and clearly to their students.

A Blessing to Be Simple

After the living waters had healed the soil and the people, then came the times I referred to earlier, when there was no need for businesses, stores, utilities, manufacturing, commerce, industry, money, banks, borrowing or lending, or most any other convention of present mortality. The millennial state freed us from all of these entrapments of Babylon. Everything we needed was provided by the power of God that was initially only present in Zion, and later, in the cities of Zion. We were free to work exclusively for God, and that is exactly what we did—and it was the greatest of all forms of living.

There was no money system, and gold, silver, and precious stones only had value as adornments for temples, churches, works of art, and as pavement for streets. We had all things in common because we had all things we needed. We were all wealthy beyond what any mortal king had been, and none of it mattered to us. A dump truck full of diamonds would have been spread on wet concrete as an adornment of Zion before it appeared on someone's finger or neck. The concept of ownership and acquisition of "things" as part of our identity slipped from our social paradigm.

Pillars of Fire

This was all still before the Second Coming. The Lord had ordained for us to begin the millennial day within Zion and her cities while war and chaos reigned everywhere else. We were surrounded by war in our own land. The foreign troops were advancing their agenda, and we ignored them. They had no power over us; though they tried repeatedly to enter Zion and exert authority over us, they were always disappointed in their goals. We did not have to call down fire on them or guard our gates with anti-tank weapons. We lived within the safety of the power of God. The same pillars of fire that had accompanied us across the wastelands of America to Zion now blazed above the temple and at the twelve gates into Zion. Pillars of fire were often seen above homes or other places where the people were worshiping God, teaching by the power of God, or learning in humble obedience.

As the Living Waters changed everything within the walls of Zion, the city began to glow with an internal glory. Buildings glowed; streets glowed; and sidewalks, lawns, and flowers glowed. The most beautiful sight of all was the mighty temple there. The light of the whole city seemed to be drawn toward the temple and then thrust upward above the temple, where it punctured the sky like a mighty pillar of fire and extended beyond the vision of man into the heavens. To those who knew not why these things were happening, or who militated against her, Zion was truly as terrible as a great "army with banners" as foreseen by Isaiah. Yet, she was also as peaceful as a dove.

Expanding Zion

Our whole society was engaged in expanding Zion, which meant that the lands around us had to be prepared to become Zion. As time advanced, word spread around the Americas, and then around the world, that in Zion there was peace, safety, and food, and if you did not wish to be at war, that you had to pay whatever price it took to go to Zion and her cities. We no longer called this place Missouri; it was becoming known worldwide as Zion, the New Jerusalem, The City of the Living God.

As a result, people arrived at the gates of Zion every day. We could not admit them until they were prepared. In fact, they were not able to enter because of the pillars of fire guarding Zion. Our Savior visited us in the temple in Zion, and resurrected and translated beings walked the streets of Zion. Notables of past generations were seen every day, and only the pure could be there without being consumed by the pillars of fire.

At this time, Jesus Christ was not seen outside of the temple. After the Second Coming, our Savior actually lived in the New Jerusalem and was not an uncommon sight within the city. He would visit homes and families and bless them with His presence, love, and glory. As that day approached, the worthiness requirements to dwell there became much more celestial. We all knew this, and we accepted the standard of worthiness presently enforced as a minimum requirement. We also embraced the changes that were coming about in our collective holiness that would ultimately enable the Christ to walk our streets, which we lovingly paved with gold so that they would be appropriate places for His holy feet.

When people arrived in Zion, we had a large company assigned to greet them, give them food, and show them where they could camp outside of the city. Nobody was turned away, even those we knew had evil intent just by looking upon them. There was no need to deny them. They could not harm us, and they could not enter Zion. Our job was to love them and teach them so that they could have the opportunity to hear the gospel taught to their understanding.

The only food we had was that which we grew, which I was

describing earlier. Even a small meal of these foods would heal sickness of any kind. A steady diet caused health to be restored in a few days. But we learned that outside of Zion, the further changes did not occur that would have made them "millennial" in nature. We also heard stories of people taking the fruit of Zion to far-away places to try to sell it or use it to try to heal distant loved ones. The further away they took it, the less powerful it was, until it spoiled like any other fruit and was useless to them. The power of the fruit was not in the fruit—it was in Zion.

Still, when they saw that their wounds were rapidly healed and their bodies rejuvenated, they immediately wondered what powerful technology or miracle medicine we possessed. One of two things happened: either they made plans to steal whatever technology they were imagining we had, or they immediately felt the Spirit of God and made plans to join us. Those who wished to join us were taught and baptized, and they began their long journey to Zion while still camped outside of the city.

Beyond these camps of people who were seeking help and healing by being in proximity to Zion, there were other large camps of people who feared Zion, and who had at some time fought against us and attacked us during our journey to Zion. Many of the inhabitants of these camps had come to America as occupying troops, but had become disillusioned with the invaders and had deserted. They were still fearful and terrified of us because their weapons were useless if we chose to attack them. We never would have, but they lived in suspicion and fear. They were also terrified of their former comrades, and they lived in a buffer zone of fear on every side. Yet they stayed and ate the fruit of Zion, and they knew not how to either leave or enter.

The world was flooded with rumors of Zion, of our long life and physical strength, and they did not dare approach us. Yet they made their camps and established their tent cities near us because there was peace here. They were still hoping to discover or steal whatever made us mighty and prosperous. Some could not believe it had anything to do with the power of God. In time, they sent formal ambassadors to Zion asking that we teach them how to live in peace, health, and prosperity, but that they wanted nothing to do with our religion. That created some interesting teaching moments.

So here was the sifting of the wheat from the tares. In the world, we had continuing wars and abominations, which could be likened to hell or perdition, where the devil reigned with blood and horror. We had an outer circle of camps around us of people who saw us as mighty and terrible, who still lived by the sword, but who sought the peace of being near to Zion. They rejected anything spiritual from us, but valued the few benefits of their proximity to us. This might be likened to the telestial world.

There was also an inner circle of camps of people who were trying to enter Zion by learning and repentance, which was somewhat like the terrestrial kingdom, where the people benefitted from the healing and spiritual power of Zion.

Then there was the celestial center called Zion, where angels commonly walked the streets, resurrected beings taught classes, and the glory of God lit streets paved with gold.

People progressed by defecting from outer camps and seeking refuge in a closer one to Zion. It was an interesting process. People were wary of approaching a city gate. We sent missionaries out into the closer camps every day and taught with power those who wanted to partake. We organized and held sacrament meetings in the closer camps as the need arose. It was the greatest missionary work the world had ever experienced. All who were called to be missionaries loved their assignments and produced a great harvest among these people.

It had taken those of us inside Zion an entire lifetime to qualify to be there, and the laws that governed righteousness and worthiness were still in force. No one could be admitted into Zion until their hearts were pure and they were worthy to see and participate in the things that happened every hour in Zion. Their great advantage was that they were being taught with great power, and they could see the pillars of fire and experience the healing of their bodies. Those whose love of truth and of Christ were still glowing dimly in some recess of their soul found their progress reduced from decades to years or months, and their conversion was profound and permanent. Some people arrived fully repentant and full of faith, and their transition into Zion was swift.

As these people joined us, the land upon which they had camped was used to enlarge the borders of Zion, but this time, with them inside. Those who could not change were obligated to relocate further away from our borders.

To our complete astonishment, there were many, many people who chose to oppose us, rather than join us. It was hard to watch, knowing that the times of cleansing by fire were coming sometime soon, and these people had defined themselves as those who could not survive His coming in glory.

Return of the Ten Tribes

I came to understand over time that the ten tribes returned in four distinct ways.

First, for years, the tribes of Ephraim and Manasseh have been gathering themselves into the latter-day gospel through their own conversion process. People from all over the world have gathered by uniting themselves first with Christianity, and ultimately with the latter-day Church. These were the times of spiritual adoption where all who aligned themselves with God were adopted into the blessings of Israel through the latter-day Church.

Second, the work of gathering dramatically accelerated through use of the portals after the early days of Zion. I was a part of this gathering and worked for many years along with unseen angels, translated people, and even some resurrected people who had been assigned to facilitate the return of a specific tribe. These were gathered as Jeremiah foresaw: one of a family, two of a city into Zion. During this stage of returning, we taught and gathered all who had faith in Christ, both from within and without the latter-day Church. We led them to one of the many cities of Zion, where they would thrive through the remaining tribulations until Christ came to deliver us all. This process was completed just shortly before the Second Coming.

Third, groups of people were led by God, which is to say by His angels, specifically by we of Zion, from their long dispersion among the nations, back to the New Jerusalem and to the other cities of Zion across the globe. These people at times had their own prophets, their own scriptures, and their own traditions. We taught them during their long travels and baptized and ordained them to the priesthood as they became worthy. I have referred to the tremendous effort in

Zion to teach and perform ordinances for these throngs of people as they arrived.

Most of them were from scattered places, like Northern Europe, Africa, Asia, India, the Middle East, and the Slavic regions where they had fled to escape thousands of years ago. Even after they arrived, they sometimes struggled to identify themselves with Zion. Even though they may have made the physical journey to Missouri, they struggled to make the spiritual journey to Zion.

It was also a tremendous effort to teach them and to strip them of their uninspired traditions, clothing, jewelry and body piercings, and so on. They were like newborn spiritual babies who had to be taught in every point. The Saints worked hard to teach them, but it was a difficult transition, and the times were short.

For instance, they wanted to decorate themselves to celebrate their conversion, and we were constantly correcting them. It created a little bit of a comic situation because they showed up with these traditional mores recycled to represent Zion, and we had to teach them otherwise. The Saints were making all of our own clothing, and there was a humble simplicity about it. The clothing was beautiful but had no brand names, and only modest "bling." When these people from other areas saw this, they often tried to "dress up" their new apparel with their traditional jewelry and markings.

Fourth, there were large groups of people who wandered to Zion simply to survive. The kingdom of Satan was so awful, so grossly and horribly disturbed, that even some who had at first embraced the wars and political intrigue, who had willingly received the Mark of the Beast, who had by chance and cunning survived the tribulations, were beginning to repent. They could see that the powers of darkness were being challenged and broken down. Like rats leaving a sinking ship, some of them ran to Zion. They were taught, but it was difficult for them, and the times were short. Most of them could not make the life changes, embrace the gospel, repent, and become pure in the time that was left. When the hard times came, or a test came upon them, they often did not survive the trials, but fell away. It was hard for them and spiritual mortality was vast among them.

All of these groups were gathered prior to the Second Coming, but all these people constituted only a fraction of the remaining population of the world. There were millions to whom we did not minister who were yet worthy to escape the fire of cleansing at His coming. But without the protection of Zion, they struggled tragically until He came.

After Christ came, our attention turned to these greater throngs of lost children of God. To them we took healing, the message of the gospel of Christ, and hope. It would yet take a thousand years before the majority of these embraced their millennial privileges and partook of the full goodness of God. Even when the Millennium had nearly come to a close, after nearly the whole earth had received her millennial glory, there were tiny pockets of good people whose agency had allowed them to choose against joining themselves to Zion.

Portals Among Us

We were busy expanding Zion by gathering in the elect all around the globe through the portals. By this time, every translated person had his or her own portal, but there was a learning curve to using it. For an inexperienced person, they could only travel so far and would have to walk or obtain other transportation to go beyond that. Some newly translated people would go out on their missions and then become overwhelmed by what they saw, and with fear or sorrow in their hearts they could not return via the portals and thus pollute Zion. They had to begin their journeys back to Zion afoot, awaiting the time when they could regroup their faith and overcome their fear so that their portals could bring them back home.

All of us began serving the Lord in this way, with little knowledge of what we were doing. We all went out and taught and blessed those to whom we were assigned and then brought them home by boat, on foot, or by whatever means were available. As we learned how powerful our gifts were, and as by greater faith and greater experience in obedience we obtained full use of the translated state, we began to be able to bring the pure among them through the portals directly into Zion. Those whom we gathered this way were perfectly pure in heart prior to our coming to them. Any self-interest or impure desire would simply stop the portal from working, and we would have to leave them to find their own way to Zion.

Even for us, the first citizens of Zion, this was our journey—the systematic stripping away of everything we possessed, and everything we thought we needed to survive. It was this process that had purified us and taught us how magnificent life is with total confidence in our loving God. It was the only way to learn this exalting form of purity. Those whom we found ready to join us, the very "elect" of God, had submitted to this purifying process already during the course of their lives, and we brought them to Zion singing songs of everlasting joy.

These pure hearts were the ones whom Isaiah proclaimed we would bring back on our shoulders into Zion, singing songs of everlasting joy. These did not sleep or slumber or come in haste and did not unlatch their shoes. We brought them through the portals with joy into Zion, but they were the vast, vast exception.

We also learned that agency was forever in force, and being translated did not eliminate the possibility of incorrectly using our agency. I don't have knowledge of any translated person turning to evil and losing their status and their salvation, but I did hear of a few who learned by hard experience that they had to diligently maintain their stature of righteousness or the gifts and the portal would cease to work.

If our assignment required us to assume a new identity, passing through a portal changed our appearance. We almost never arrived at our destination in our Zion identity. I did not look or talk like Spencer. My clothing and my appearance was changed. I had a full knowledge of who my new persona was and how to be that person, including history, memories, and language. I could be anything the Lord needed me to be to accomplish my work.

It may seem strange that we were changed, but history is filled with stories of angels appearing in many forms, sometimes as old men, young women, or even a child's playmate. Yet we know that angels are ageless and not old or young, so they obviously come to us in the form that blesses us most. The only difference here was that we were now those angels. Male angels always appeared as male, and females always appeared as female, but in any guise we were inspired to take.

By studying each mission beforehand, I was fully aware of my next identity, and I was prepared to minister in that way. When I returned to my temple office, I was myself again. I never had to go change, bathe, or rest.

Sometimes I was sent through the portal to a time that was earlier than that present time in Zion. I went back to answer prayers, to fulfill promises, to keep covenants, or to adjust some past event in the lives of those to whom I ministered. I sometimes spent long periods of time on a mission, even months and years, but when I returned to Zion, I returned just a few minutes later than when I left. What I am alluding to is that when we learned to utilize the portal fully, it was limitless in power. It gave us godlike abilities because we were acting in His name, and He invested in us His power to fulfill His express will and command. As had been promised in many scriptures, we were beginning to receive all things that the Father has, and one of those things was this grand power of the portals.

Another unexpected result of this use of time as a tool was that when my vision of these things ended, my mortal mind could not contain the complexity of what I had seen, and I forgot many of the details. However, while in the vision, it was simple to comprehend and to execute. The constant companionship of the Holy Ghost made it impossible to forget some detail, or to make an error or omission by forgetting to do something.

Because the portal gave us a "new" name and identity during our ministry, when those people finally made their way to Zion, they did not know me. Many times I grew close to those I had served, even rescued and raised from the dead, and yet they did not know me after they actually arrived. I was not allowed to run up to them and embrace them and welcome them to Zion.

In a few cases, the people thought I had been Elijah, Moses, or some other prophet, and that was their story when they arrived in Zion. I didn't care about being recognized for the service, but it was hard to see them again and yet act like I did not know them. It was unlawful for us to tell them about our service unless the Lord revealed it to them Himself—which He occasionally did, just to add to our joy. In time, long after the gathering, these things were no longer veiled, and we knew all things about all people and had a thousand years to rejoice with those we had gathered.

There were three ways I could receive an assignment to use the portal. The most common was from Jesus Christ Himself. My office was in the temple, and only one door separated us. If He needed me, He came to me through that door. I always knew when He was coming. I never went from my office into the Holy of Holies. The second way was by a calling from the Prophet or one of the Apostles. These calls were to more local service, dealing with some need within their stewardship. They could have gone themselves, and often did through their own portals, but delegation is a true principle, and others were often sent.

The third way I might use the portal was by a prompting from the Holy Ghost. This usually happened when I was initially sent by Jesus Christ to begin a work. I would then return to Zion, and the Holy Ghost would prompt me when I needed to return to them to rescue or assist them in continuing their journey to Zion.

As my spiritual maturity grew, I found that I needed less and less to "see" or "preview" my mission through the portal. My faith and my ability to receive revelation, and to be guided in the moment, became much more powerful than sight or prior knowledge. I began to love this later and higher form of service. I would walk by faith, watching the miracles unfold as I ministered to these people. I never felt alone, lost, or without the power to do what the Lord had commissioned me to do. This was to actually have the mind of God, to be One with Him, and to act the same as if He were there Himself. This was thrilling to me and much more powerful than seeing beforehand and knowing what to do.

Two Prophets

It was at this time that two prophets were called in Zion to go and alter the course of the Jewish people. I knew who they were at the time, but I have not retained that memory. I believe they were members of the Quorum of the Twelve who were then serving in Zion. I know that they studied their mission via the portal in the temple, and they were prepared for their mission and their sacrifice. They left with great courage, knowing their task was pivotal and that it would cost them their lives. They were ordained by Jesus Christ Himself to this great calling before a large assemblage in the temple, and then they departed from our sight through the portal.

Dealing with Warfare

By this time there was no warfare near Zion or those camped around her. There was some violence in the outer camps, but we didn't police them in any way. The only time I actually experienced full warfare was when I went through the portal on assignment. We often found ourselves under attack or being threatened by unredeemed people. We had learned over the years how to deal with warfare.

At first, the power of God was not in full display, and we wrought miracles to stay out of sight and out of conflict. As time progressed, we were allowed to deal with people as the Spirit directed, often in miracles that all could see. Just by a thought, I could move people far away from me. They found themselves in a new place completely at a loss to explain how.

We could become invisible if need be. It wasn't a form of invisibility where light passed through our bodies, it was that those who sought us simply could not comprehend that we were there. A digital photo probably would have captured our presence, but their minds were blinded to our presence. Many times we walked right past the people who were hunting us. They could even bump into one of us, and they did not comprehend it. Sometimes soldiers walked past me like I was a lamppost—stepping around me, but not seeing me. I was completely protected, as were the people who were with me.

At times our enemies would approach our group. I would speak to them but they did not seem to see me because they didn't reply or even look at me. They sometimes saw the group I was leading, but they never saw me. I would say to them something like, "There is no one here," or anything the Lord led me to say, and they would leave. We were never in any danger, but those with me trembled with fear because they were still on their "journey to Zion," which involved long experience in learning to completely and absolutely trust the Lord.

I could also create an illusion if need be. If we were standing before the soldiers, I could cause them to "see" us suddenly turn and try to run away in a different direction. They would fire and be satisfied that we had been eliminated. After such an illusion, they could no longer see us, and we would leave. They couldn't even hear our voices or noise of our departure, no matter what it was. These things were continually amazing to me, and I always glorified God in my heart, and I plainly told the people what had happened so they could enhance their faith in Christ's protection and love.

There was a law we followed. It was not a rule, but a law. When an individual or group threatened us, we knew their hearts. If there was any hope, even the slightest hope that they could be saved, even in the most telestial sense, we did not harm them. When we were confronted by people who were fully ripe in iniquity, and who would never repent, then we were free to deliver them from mortality. Their death would then be a blessing to them because they could no longer add additional iniquity to their divine ledger.

In the beginning of our work of gathering, we most often hid behind God's power. Toward the end, we were most often granted permission to display God's power. Instead of hiding from them, we started them on their immortal journey. When we did this, it was not a bloodbath and rarely a consumption by fire. They just fell to the ground and slipped into the eternities. When this happened, we felt happy for them to be freed from the torment of their own delusions. With God they would eventually see clearly once again and could choose to cease heaping condemnation upon their souls.

Teaching with Power

In the beginning of our gathering, we were sent to people who had already prepared, many of whom were Latter-day Saints, but also many who were the honest in heart from many Christian faiths. Every person we led to Zion, no matter what their background was, had to be taught and prepared to enter the sacred parts of Zion. They had to be changed. Their "journey to Zion" didn't end when they arrived; there was still a great spiritual journey to accomplish.

For this purpose, we set up schools in Zion that anyone could enter. These were beautiful buildings with special classrooms, meeting halls that resembled chapels, and other rooms, including baptismal fonts. More than half of the current citizens of Zion worked in these schools to teach those who were coming to Zion. I was not a teacher. I was a gatherer and an officiator in the temple.

Just like in a university today, there were levels of students. The new people were there because they had been brought to Zion by miracles and preserved by angels who confessed openly that Christ had sent them. These new people wanted to know who we were, and how we had done what we had done. They could behold the glory of Zion and the perfect health and beauty of our people, and they wanted to know why this was and how to become a part of it.

Our teachers taught with power, opening the scriptures and speaking the language of Zion, which every person heard as their own language. There were few stumbling blocks to accepting what was being taught. The Spirit of God was upon us all, and there were pillars of fire and the glory of God throughout Zion. It was a missionary's dream assignment.

There were thousands of baptisms and ordinances every day. We limited the size of meetings to hundreds rather than thousands, and people were sometimes obligated to wait to be taught, and wait again to be baptized. As people progressed, their experiences grew greater and greater. In time, angels attended the meetings, and translated people taught classes. Resurrected beings showed them visions of the truth of the history of the earth and their own lives.

No ordinance was performed before the candidate was prepared. The blessings were immediately bestowed. When someone was baptized and given the gift of the Holy Ghost, they immediately received a full remission of sins and the Holy Ghost as their constant companion, causing them to be immediately changed by the Atonement of Christ. Cries of delight, prophetic utterances, visions, and miracles immediately became a part of their lives. When someone reached this point, the Living Water began to change them into the millennial format.

All of this teaching effort was highly organized. It was truly the school of the prophets, because people emerged from that process fully worthy, with great views of the future. Once people were taught and changed, our concerns for and about them ceased. They were true for the remainder of eternity. We were able to trust them with the most sacred assignments, and they could fulfill them with inspiration and exactness.

It is important to note here that there was a waiting period to these things, and these initial changes marked the beginning of their journey. There was a waiting period requirement for their spiritual growth—not just as a matter of policy, but to grant them time to grow in their gifts. After baptism, there was a period before they were ordained to the priesthood. There was a waiting period before they were able to enter the temple. There was a longer waiting period before they could enter the holiest parts of the temple and be fully endowed. There was a further period of growth and preparation to be in the presence of God.

These greater and spiritually lofty gifts of God were obtained at great cost before the building of Zion, and being in Zion and experiencing these miracles did not change the price of admission into the presence of God.

The temple experience was much the same as today, but with some modifications to bring it into the Zion format. There was no movie because every person saw the actual creation and Garden of Eden teachings in vision. When we progressed from level to level, the room changed from telestial to terrestrial to celestial. And the veil of the temple was not fabric, but the actual veil of heaven.

The City of Enoch

I am not sure how many years had passed by this time. It was still pre–Second Coming. In my visions of these times, I was not shown the return of the City of Enoch. I just knew that they were among us and working on the same labors as we were.

The City of Enoch now occupied some, or most, of the new landmass in the gulf. The details of their return and the particulars of their mission were not revealed to me. There were people from his city among us, and Enoch was a frequent visitor to Zion and was fully involved in the work of preparing the world for the Second Coming. People from Enoch's Zion were often leading far-flung groups to Zion. We considered Enoch's city as one of the great latter-day "cities of Zion."

Because of the enhanced spirituality we enjoyed, upon meeting people, we knew immediately where they were from and whether they were translated, resurrected, or mortal. We didn't need to ask or discuss it. When we met people from Enoch's city, we understood their life's experience and their whole journey to that moment in time. We knew everything about them, and we met them with reverence.

In like sense, they knew everything about us, and honored us for our obedience. It made for a lovely society, and a lovely social pattern, because we all understood, loved, and honored one another. We all had interesting stories and had paid an extraordinary price for our blessings, and our sacrifice was known and honored by everyone we met.

When we spoke to mortals of our lives and experiences, they often saw the events we were describing in vision as we described them. When speaking to a spiritually mature person, we also had the ability to exchange information without using words, speaking spirit-to-spirit, which we found was tremendously more efficient and much richer than the spoken word. In time, we began to only speak with our lips when we met someone we knew had not yet progressed beyond that limitation.

Spiritual Technology

When my friends arrived who had been hidden for thousands of years in the cavern in the north, they brought with them many craftsmen. Because of their long confinement without technology as we understand it, they had developed a more spiritual technology. It's difficult to explain without the use of visions and revelation. But when mortal technology begins to change something, it does it by cutting, carving, burning, melting, and pounding those things into some new shape. These people had developed a technology that exercised righteous stewardship over the object they wished to change. They still shaped it with their hands, but it was not by force; it was by love and divinely granted stewardship over that object. They knew they had obtained dominion over the earth, which their prophets had taught them included asking various objects to assume a new shape or new property. So their technology was spiritual in nature.

If they needed to shape a tree into a chair, they prayerfully and gently molded it into the shape they desired. There were no chips or sawdust. They did not pound and glue. They created amazing things, beautiful and intricate things, glorious and inspired things, by asking wood, stone, and anything else to yield to their stewardship over it. Just as the angels always asked me before they proceeded to take me on a vision or to give me some blessing, they had learned to ask—and to receive—the cooperation of all things of the earth.

This is how they made the stones that lit up. When they arrived in Zion, they brought all of this spiritual technology with them. They began teaching it to us, but it was not an easy principle to master. These craftsmen had been raised from birth to know they could work in these spiritual crafts, and they saw examples all around them of this workmanship and could watch their master craftsman working this way, and so they just did the same thing. Even as a translated being, it was hard to wrap my mind around asking a tree to become a chair or table, or a rock to glow. I never became accomplished in these things. In addition to being a spiritually difficult power to master, it also included artistic skill I did not have. Not everyone can mold a piece of clay into a beautiful sculpture, and not everyone can shape a perfectly compliant tree into a graceful chair.

They brought their few tools and their faith, along with their history of craftsmanship, and they began to finish the temple dedicated to their tribe, as well as to add beauty to the interior of all other parts of the temple. If they were to carve a beautiful scene into a wall or archway of the temple, they would study the design by running their fingers over the paper, spiritually ingesting the inspiration of the artist. Then they would stand before the wall and place their hands on the wall, moving them slowly across the surface, warming it and communicating with it, prayerfully asking it to yield to their stewardship.

In my earlier death experiences, I had experienced communicating with wood and stone, so I fully comprehended what they were doing. What they were also doing was communing with God and seeking His permission and the stone's compliance to mold the wall before them. It was a terrestrial use of God's creative power, the same power He used to form the earth and heavens. They were asking in faith for God to allow them to step into that creative role and change something that already existed. I watched with great awe as these spiritual masters worked, and I always felt the Spirit of God and observed a glow of righteous power where their hands touched their work.

When everything was right, they used their bare hands to sculpt the surface. If a line or image was too small or delicate for their fingers to form, they used wooden tools shaped with points and curves and square ends. These tools were ancient, darkened from handling, and beautiful themselves. A quick stroke a few inches long could execute an accent or line much longer than their stroke—like flinging paint across a canvas. Once they were prepared, and actually began to work, they worked quickly, finishing a scene or accent or flourish in a matter of minutes.

They also produced the stones that glowed—literally thousands of them. These were placed in every room in the temple and offices. They rested in beautiful sconces, upon candlesticks, or in fixtures in the ceiling. They responded to the desires of those in the room, becoming brighter or dim according to our desires.

These stones could be asked to shine with enough heat to cook, or to heat and cool a building, all without blinding you or even heating the surface upon which they rested. In time, every building and home in Zion used many of these stones so that we did not need electricity or fire at all.

Earlier in this book I spoke of my premortal room that was like a giant Urim and Thummim. I also mentioned that it was mine and was linked to me and a part of me. When a translated person obtained one of these stones, it too began to function as a Urim and Thummim. It exhibited the same power as a portal—to show us everything and to take us there.

In fact, the power of these things was not in the object itself, but in Christ and in our faith. Still, these objects increased our faith and served to empower us. Even knowing the truth of these things, everyone, including myself, initially found themselves better able to work powerfully with these spiritual tools.

We learned that these stones could function to contact anyone who also had a stone, so we didn't need any form of electronic devices or communication systems. While speaking to them via the stones, we had the same profound insight into whom we were addressing. We could hand them things or go there in an instant when it was in harmony with God's plan. The greater our righteousness and the more "one" our alignment was with heaven, the more latitude we had in using these gifts. The point in the beginning was to bring us to flawless obedience, perfect trust, and spiritual purity. Once accomplished, the purpose of everything we received was to enable us to serve God, and to beautify and enrich our lives. There has never been a happier time for mankind, and we had not yet entered the actual Millennium, or barely scratched the surface of our gifts. I once again found myself thinking my faith was now perfect, and life couldn't get any better—and I was still mistaken in this thinking.

Using the stones, we could view any unfolding event on earth, and not just see it, but comprehend the deep truths of what we were seeing. Some people among us were immensely interested in what was happening in the world. They had studied these events intently and were now involved in watching them unfold. Some were assigned to write what they saw, making an accurate history of these times. For myself, I was so busy with the tasks the Lord had given me that there was little time for curiosity, and I was pleased to have it that way.

Translated beings taught advanced classes on these stones, but powerful service depended most upon the individual's faith and their learning by personal exertion. There were some things the stones could do that you could be taught and some that could only be learned by revelation and by righteous experience. There were also spiritual gifts people just had or didn't have. Some people were adept at using them to see the future, while others were good at going from place to place by the power of God. Some people were content to use them to light their homes and cook their food.

These greater spiritual tools were known among us as "seer stones." Such a stone then became personalized to the owner, and it could not be used by any other person. Men and women received these blessings equally. Arriving at this point in one's progress, where we possessed our own seer stones, was seen as a great accomplishment. It was a fulfillment of promised blessings that we had received in premortality. When someone advanced to this point, there was often a family celebration. It was viewed as a holy calling, because it gave that person powers beyond this mortal world. It signified the complete evolution of that person into the full stature of Zion.

A seer stone was much more powerful than the stones we used to light, warm, or cool our homes and temple. Seer stones functioned exactly as a portal. When righteously used, we could see the past, present, and future. It could be used as an aid to learning to view and participate in historically significant events. It communicated to us the mind and will of God and eventually gave power to those who were called to actually go to other worlds if their assignments took them there.

To those who did not know about such things, those to whom we ministered, these things we did seemed miraculous to them. We were seen in many cases as angels, and in a real sense, we were.

Translated versus Millennial

I have drawn a distinction between those who were translated, and those who became "millennial" by drinking the Water of Life, and so there was a difference initially. But as the years advanced and the whole world evolved, the distinction became less vivid. Especially after Christ returned and the days of the Millennium rolled by, the difference almost disappeared. Everyone became perfect in their souls, and in their application of the gifts and powers of God. The only remaining difference was that "millennial" souls were assigned to this earth. They had work to do here. They bore and raised children here and labored to change the entire world into Zion. These were the people of the promise, those who had "inherited the earth," those whose children "grew up without sin unto salvation."

When people reached the age of a tree, which we observed was different for every person, being in the range of hundreds of years for most, they were simply changed one day "in the twinkling of an eye." They were resurrected where they were standing, and their labors on the earth came to an end.

To be resurrected in this fashion was not an unexpected event. They knew it was coming and often gathered loved ones near to share in the experience. There was no separation, no loss, no mourning, because these people could return to the millennial world as they wished. But now their labors were no longer earth-bound, but extended to the vastness of God's creation. The earth ceased to be their home at that point, and a place was ready for them in the presence of God. It was a glorious thing to behold.

Translated people did not have children and they were not earth-bound. Their labors were for a specific purpose, the building of Zion and establishment of the Kingdom of God. Sometimes their work included other places, even other planets and other people.

When their ministry was accomplished, and their time was over, they prayed to God and ended their translated ministry. They were instantly resurrected, and joined with all other such beings in the service of God. The eternal difference was that to be translated was a greater gift than any other course in and through mortality. Their joy was greater, and because of their long service to God, their rewards were the greatest a mortal may enjoy.

The Millennial Day

These times were the culmination of all of the promises that had been given since the beginning of time. It was amazing, awe inspiring, and glorious to behold how the Lord could bring all things and all the dispensations and their prophetic leaders and scriptures back together. It was fascinating, to say the least, to watch these things unfold during the restoration of Zion in former Missouri, and the Lord's promises concerning this place. But even more glorious was to see the fulness of times unfold before my eyes. Every gift of God was made manifest before us and was used every day. I must say that it never became commonplace, and we never grew accustomed to such things and viewed them with undimming wonder.

To see Zion arise in her beauty—this divinely beautiful city, rising up out of this wasteland—was something prophets had seen in vision and yearned for, and I was there watching it in person! This was the day of days for this earth, and I could practically feel the earth rejoicing beneath my feet.

The changes in the earth were amazing to behold. It was changing back into something like the Garden of Eden. The earth no longer withheld her abundance. We planted, and it grew rapidly and in perfect splendor. It produced the most beautiful fruit and crops man has ever harvested. Ever since the first day that we had channeled the Living Water to the crops, every plant and tree was lush and rich with fruit. We completely lost the desire to kill or eat meat. I don't recall being commanded to stop eating meat; we just no longer desired it. It actually felt repugnant to eat flesh. The animals were becoming "millennial" too and lived in harmony in Zion. We didn't have any lions in Zion, but they truly would have laid down with the lamb and eaten grass like the ox.

The fruit of one tomato had more nutrition and healing power than the human body gets in a lifetime of eating in our present experience, and such food was plentiful everywhere in Zion. We had people who loved to farm and garden, but farming was now in harmony with the earth and did not mean struggling against the elements. There was no need to irrigate, and there were no weeds, pests, or diseases. Fruit picked grew back quickly. Once ripe, the fruit just grew larger and never overripe or unusable. We learned in time to work with the trees and plants just as the stone cutters worked with the temple stone. We asked them to produce in a certain way, in a certain color or shape, and they responded to our stewardship over them.

But of all the changes in Zion, the most profound and beautiful changes occurred in mankind. What I saw in this vision led me to marvel that we have more capacity than any human mind can imagine. As we changed into the millennial form, we became almost godlike in attribute. Our bodies changed and we learned how to exercise our stewardship over them. Everyone was beautiful, natural, and glorious. We looked like gods and goddesses. Even the children and teens were perfect in body and in attribute. All of the unrefined and ungodly attributes of the natural man were completely gone, and only purity, power, beauty, and tremendous wisdom remained.

Everything changed. The laws of "nature" changed so that we again had stewardship over the earth, and she responded to our will. We beautified her face and created glorious edifices to God. Nature no longer wore things down. Buildings lasted forever. Things that dropped didn't break. Building materials changed from wood and stone to precious gems and gold. A mountain or boulder could be moved merely by righteously requesting it to move. There were few streets because we didn't need them. We traveled from place to place by the power of God and the portals. If we chose to walk or run we arrived refreshed and invigorated. The "law of opposition" was abridged. The so-called laws of physics no longer resisted anything we did. Physics no longer demanded an equal and opposite reaction—things only reacted to our righteous will. Everything we did was inspired and therefore always succeeded.

All of the powers of Babylon had been silenced. News, television, pornography, movies, government, political intrigue, international politicking, local and international corruption, buying, selling, social status, wealth, poverty, sickness, death—it was all gone. Nothing of it remained in Zion, though it still percolated in what remained of the world. The people of Zion listened only to the voice of the Lord. In that place, in Zion, among we few blessed and gathered, He was truly Lord of Lords and King of Kings—long before the global Millennium actually began, and before His return.

By this time, I thought over and over—what a wonder is mankind, how beautiful in face and form, how godlike in attribute! We never heard a dissenting or angry word. There was no selfishness or laziness, greed or self-promotion. There was no arrogance, false pride, or superiority. We were all remade into the image of our God, equal in our worth, beauty, and refinements. By the measure of mankind before this time, we were wealthier than any king because we had all things we desired, whether it was on earth or in heaven, and all things were subject to our command. We luxuriated in our lives. All of those things that had polluted our mortal world for so long were gone—extinct.

As the years advanced, we exited the telestial existence of man and the earth and entered the terrestrial phase. As luxurious and glorious as this life was, we knew that after the long millennial day, the earth would be changed into a celestial abode, and we would inherit it. It was a time we saw in vision and longed for.

The 144,000

The 144,000 consisted of all those who had been called to gather in the elect of God by use of the portals and seer stones. As more people were translated and gained the seer stones, they became members of the 144,000. It was not a calling from the Church because it involved no presidency or stewardship. It was the result of a lifetime of spiritual evolution. In the beginning, Christ personally attended to the translation of people. I recorded my own ordination to pass this terrestrial gift on to others and my assignment to do so. In time, many thousands were empowered to bestow this gift upon worthy souls, and they did, until all the world was changed.

Enoch and his people were a big part of this work and this gathering. They contributed 12,000 gatherers to our number and worked with great power in the world. We watched them with admiration and followed their example and learned from their use of their gifts. They were accomplished in their translated state, and we honored them.

Among the 144,000 were men and women. Our powers were equal. There was no difference. Women were High Priestesses, and men were High Priests, and we worked side by side. There was always one priesthood holder who presided over whatever we did, but in reality, Christ was our head, and we all followed Him.

We were sent as needed, sometimes just one of us, oftentimes two, and upon occasion, dozens of us were sent. We all had the seer stones, and we all understood the exact order of necessary events and the outcome of the mission. We did not all arrive at the same time or from the same place, but we all arrived when needed. We knew each other, even when we were in our new personas.

The women in our group sometimes did most of the speaking and convincing, especially when our mission was to families or struggling women and children.

Sometimes the brethren were called upon just to perform ordinances when the mission had reached that stage. Sometimes we posed as fellow wanderers, as husband and wife, or other roles. It was never the same.

Sometimes we were sent to gather children, in which case the sisters played an important and calming role. They were so filled with love and grace that the children instantly trusted them, and we easily accomplished our work.

It was just as common for sisters to work miracles as the

brethren. There was no difference between us in that regard. The only difference was that the brethren had the keys to perform ordinances or to preside when the Lord directed it.

Our translated stature gave us greatly enhanced senses. We could see, visually and spiritually, with great clarity and over long distances. We could see all of the spirits around us, both good and bad. We not only heard what was said, but knew their intent, their hearts, and their plans. We knew what people were going to say or ask before they actually said it and quite often answered their unvoiced questions to further bless and inspire them. We knew how every word would be interpreted, how each act would affect the near future. We simply knew by the power of God everything we needed to do.

Our intelligence was also dramatically increased. Like a chess grand master, we could discern complex solutions to anything we encountered—seeing the resulting chain of events long before they occurred. Actually, this was a joy to me; having done so much struggling to educate myself, I found I loved feeling my improved intellect absorbing vast truths and solving impenetrable mysteries. With all this, we also adored receiving revelation and confirmation from our God that our conclusions were true and celestially purposed. In fact, this super-human intellect was revelation to us—it was lifting the veil just a little and revealing who we really were.

Any grand miracle one reads about in the scriptures, which we rightly call miracles, was duplicated in far greater degree and with great regularity by the citizens and ministers from Zion. Miracles were routinely wrought that were far greater than dividing the Red Sea. We always marveled, but we were no longer surprised by such things. We were experiencing another reason this was called the "Fulness of Times"—because not only did we have all of these gifts and powers of God manifested hourly among us, but they were manifested with greater power and in a greater degree than ever in the history of the world.

Some members of our 144,000 were sent on assignments that took years as they actually walked every step of the way with their charges back to Zion. This was particularly evident in the gathering of some of the "lost" tribes. Some of my dear friends served in this very way, and their work was glorious. My missions seemed to be more short-term. I would go and work with people, then return to Zion for a while, and when the Holy Spirit moved me I would return to guide and encourage them.

Time was fluid for us. There were no deadlines. We could go to any group, even into their past, to prepare them, then move forward in time and visit them again, or do anything the Lord directed us to do to accomplish our work. But even among the 144,000, not all of us learned to use time in the way I just described. Everything depended upon agency and our diligence in learning how to use our gifts, just as has always been and will always be. Not every translated person had the same gifts or even the same interests. We grew as our agency and inspiration guided us until we truly came to "a measure of the stature of the fulness of Christ."

It was true that all of the rest of the world was moving forward in time as it is now, and as it continued throughout the Millennium. But for me and others of the 144,000, we could go for months or years and then arrive back a few minutes after we had left. Since we were tireless, and did not need sleep or food, we could continue this pattern of service without end, and we rejoiced in it. We grew weary neither in mind, soul, nor body. Every day was a Sabbath to us, and we communed with God and renewed our covenants with every breath we took. We met often, communing with angels and our Savior, but I do not recall attending an organized sacrament meeting.

It was only because of this ability to work with time, as opposed to being subject to it, that we actually completed the gathering prior to the Master's coming in glory.

Close to the end of our ministry to gather in the "elect," there was a large body of people who had the seer stones, and who worked with us. But I do not believe there were exactly 144,000 of us. That number evolved daily and may have actually exceeded that number toward the end. Our numbers were great.

The Second Coming

As I have mentioned, my perception of time was not as linear as it is now. A whole day in Zion could amount to years of service on the other side of the portal. I don't recall ever being confused about what time I was in on either side of the portal, but you have to remember that I was not actually in Zion—but in vision at my home in my bed. After the vision ended, and I had returned to my mortal body, the sequence and times of things became much more difficult to decipher.

For this reason, the exact timing of the Second Coming is indistinct to me. It was a while after we arrived in Zion, perhaps no longer than three and a half years. By the time Christ came in glory, the work of gathering had been completed. We had worked night and day for all of those years to finish the work. We had gathered into Zion every single soul Christ had sent us to in the entire world. We had not missed a soul. When He came, we were actively waiting for the day.

As I mentioned earlier, there were millions of terrestrial people, the good and honorable of the earth, to whom we were not sent. They would abide the day of His coming, but they did not partake of the protection and glory of Zion prior to His coming. We did no work among the warring and evil. We were only gathering the elect, those whom the Father had placed into Christ's power, "they that are Christ's at His coming."

Early one morning, we beheld billowing clouds crossing the sky from east to west. We did not sleep, so we often gathered to watch the sun come up. This was different. These clouds were pure white and billowing, rolling toward us from top to bottom like an unrolling scroll. There was no wind or lightning, and the clouds had no dark underside.

We had been actively watching for the day of His coming. Even minutes before we saw the billowing clouds, we did not know the day nor the hour when He would return, but the instant we saw it, our hearts jumped up into our throats, and we cried aloud with joy and relief. "He is coming! He is coming!" we cried with every energy of our souls. Every soul in Zion and all of her cities felt our joy and ran outside to see this long-awaited moment. All of the inhabitants of Zion and her cities were watching when He came.

We all heard a voice speak to us individually. I heard my name tenderly spoken. As before, everything that I am was contained within that sound, including all that Christ loved about me. It thrilled me with unspeakable joy. Everyone heard their own name at the same time. I immediately recognized it as the voice of Jesus Christ, as did all of my fellow Zion–dwellers. The good and honorable of the earth whom we had not gathered felt the spiritual magnificence of the moment and looked up. In an instant they began to rejoice as well, jumping toward heaven with their arms over their heads, as if trying to at last fly off of the earth and into His arms.

The benighted of the world perceived the sound as a mighty roaring and piercing sound somewhat like an enormous wind screaming as a devastating earthquake rumbling toward them. Instantly, there was crushing terror in their hearts. They did not know that it was Jesus Christ returning and would not have believed anyone who said so. They thought it was another devastation coming. Others thought it was a missile or new weapon. Some of the enemies of Zion thought we had finally launched a mighty weapon at them. As the cloud approached, it became apparent that there was a man standing in the cloud. Even a thousand miles away, every eye saw Him approaching in the clouds of heaven. Evil men fell to their knees and wept. Some took their own lives. The hardened among them turned their weapons toward the coming Christ and opened fire. It would be their last act of defiance.

We in Zion recognized His voice, and it was sweet and comforting to us. His voice told us to return to the temple quickly. By this time there were many temples across the world. Some were latter-day temples that had been upgraded to the millennial form. Most were new, built during this prelude to the Millennium. Each group gathered into their temple, some into dedicated church buildings, even in homes the inhabitants had made holy, and the Conference Center in Salt Lake City. There was room enough for all who heard His voice.

We dropped everything and ran. We didn't need to turn back to gather children or families, they all heard His call and came in that instant. Even infants heard and were brought by loving hands.

We entered the temple through the outer temple that was dedicated to our tribe of Israel. For me and my family and most of my friends, it was the outer temple for Ephraim on the east side of the temple.

We did not have time to change clothes, but each of us began glowing with purity that exceeded temple white. We were praising and singing and praying and rejoicing. The day was finally come—finally come, finally come!

We gathered in the large assembly hall where our prophets began speaking to us, reading scriptures, and rejoicing aloud in what was happening. We were all prepared, and we sang new hymns we had never heard before with a mighty fervor. To my ears, it was the most beautiful sound humans have ever produced!

Brightness and glory surrounded us, penetrated us, cleansed us even further. We were still in the temple, but the roof and part of the walls became transparent so that we could see the sky. We could hear angels singing with us and blowing trumpets that shook the earth. At last we saw Jesus Christ coming from the east, surrounded by billowing clouds and numerous angels all singing and praising the Father.

Even though He was still hundreds of miles away, we could see His face clearly. He was clothed in spotless white with a red sash around his waist. His face was not angry, but He was not smiling. He was coming to cleanse the earth.

He approached quickly and was soon above us. The temple was no longer visible to us. We were being taken up. We all felt the pull of gravity begin to release us. I saw the clouds growing closer, even as my soul expanded as broad as the universe—and then the vision closed.

This is all I saw. I could say I wish it were more, but in all truth, it was all I could take in. I was fully enraptured, filled with exquisite joy and rejoicing. Anything more than this would have been overwhelming and incomprehensible in my mortal state, and I would not have been able to retain the memory.

The Red Planet

From this point on, my experiences in this vision became small glimpses of the future. I saw that Zion had spread to fill the whole earth, and that the thousand years had nearly elapsed. I saw that there were small "nations," if you will, who had not embraced the gospel, but who had embraced the blessings of the Millennium. These were they who had asked to be taught how to live in peace, but wanted nothing to do with our religion or our God. They simply did not believe in Jesus Christ. They did not believe that it was actually Jesus Christ who had returned, even though they had seen Him. These were those people who had not been consumed by His coming, but who could not abandon their cultural beliefs and traditions. They did not believe that Zion dwellers lived as long as was rumored, or that we did not experience disease and death. They thought this millennial state was the result of changes in the earth, vast technologies, and the fulfillment of prophecies inherent to their traditional religion.

Because of their agency, they were free to believe anything they wished. They were honorable people. They were also deceived. When they requested help or knowledge, we gave them as much as they could absorb because most of our technology was spiritual, not technical. Their millennial experience was hampered by their lack of faith.

They had never been our enemies, and still were not, but they lived separately from us, in a society that depended upon primitive manufacturing and an economy-driven social order. Had their society been established prior to the Millennium, all the world would have viewed it as Utopia. To us of Zion, it looked harsh and primitive. We sent missionaries among them, but their hearts were fixed. At the point of this vision they still existed apart from Zion.

I must have still been working in Zion, or perhaps I had come back to witness this event. I'm not sure.

I found myself standing with a sizeable group upon a hill just outside of the Holy City. We were watching a planet pass close by the earth. The sky grew dark as this planet came into view.

We were able to see how the few people outside of Zion were reacting via the seer stones we all possessed. We didn't need to pull them from our pockets and look into them, the knowledge was transferred to our awareness merely by our wondering or wanting to know. There was great terror among them and a doomsday mentality. They ran about with reckless abandon and resignation, preparing for mass extinction. What remained of pre-millennial society crumbled and was never restored.

I saw many people die of fear, but I also saw many of them fall upon their knees and cry out to Christ. Of course, He comforted them. Citizens of Zion gathered these last few and took them to safety at last.

We upon the hill were at peace. There was no fear, only deep interest. The planet was close, red-orange in color, with impact craters across its face. As it passed, it was close enough that we could see mountains and valleys, former rivers, and fine details upon its surface. This planet was at rest and had no life upon it.

It filled about a third of the whole sky. We commented among ourselves how different the new sky was. The constellations were entirely different, and the old moon was gone. The sky was crystal clear, and because of our translated state, we saw it perfectly. We understood this planet, where it had been, how it had served God, where it now rested, and why we were passing it, but that knowledge has not remained with me.

It did no damage to the earth and had no effect upon us. We understood, of course, that it was the earth that was moving, not this big, old, faithful planet in our sky. It moved beyond us slowly until it was no longer visible.

A New Heaven and a New Earth

The next little vision I saw took me to a time after the Millennium. I was viewing the earth from out in space, as we call it now. The earth had been moved to a new location far beyond the galaxy we call the Milky Way. This had been accomplished by the same "folding" process that had placed the earth in its mortal rotation around our sun.

There was a new heaven here. All of the stars were different. They were brighter and glorified. There was a massive sun in the sky, which I understood to be the greatest of all the creations of God, and where Father and our Savior dwelt. I was looking at the new earth beneath me. It was glowing nearly as brightly as the sun. The earth had been celestialized, and presently there were no people upon the earth, and nothing remained of man's long tenure there. Everything man had built was gone, as well as trees, grass, and flowers. The earth was perfectly smooth and as clear as glass. It was itself a giant Urim and Thummim. The earth had died at the end of the Millennium and had now been "resurrected" by God. It was at long last prepared to host those who had once lived as mortals upon her face, and who were finally qualified to dwell in her fiery glory.

The judgment day had just occurred, and every former inhabitant of earth was now dwelling in their new kingdoms, except the

Celestial Kingdom. The earth was now ready to become that Celestial abode but for one finishing detail.

I was with a large group of people who were returning to the earth with a large city. We were not in or on the city, but beside it, bringing it with us. We were moving through space at a rapid pace, bringing the first of many cities to the earth. We were a vast company of those who had run the good race, who had fought the good fight, and finished the course. Any one of us could have brought this city by ourselves, but we were there to share in this eternally historic event because this was "our" celestial home now for the remainder of eternity.

The city beside me was the most beautiful structure ever created. God Himself had designed it, and we had been sent to construct it. Not only was it incomparably beautiful, but it was glorious beyond any mortal ability to describe it. I thought then, and now as I am attempting to describe it, that such beauty could only have come from the mind of God. It was a single, glorious building, but it was the size of a city, glowing white with sparkling accents of color. We brought it from the presence of Father, to be the first and greatest structure on the earth. It was well over a square mile, a mile high, and with its many spires, arches, and architectural wonders, it was approximately pyramidal in shape. This would be the residence of our Savior, who was now to dwell with us forever.

As we slowed to place the city at the exact northern pole of the new earth, I knew that we could reshape the earth to anything we desired. We could call forth gardens, rivers, or mountains in endless variety and wonder—but the era of green grass was past because those things belonged to the telestial and terrestrial orders, and the earth was now celestial. Those things which had been wondrous and beautiful to us before would eventually not even come to mind any more, for the wonder and glory before us far exceeded all other possible orders of living.

I recall feeling total, absolute joy. It was not only joy for ourselves, but also for the earth, which had waited so long and faithfully for evil to be wiped from her face. She was now glorified and perfected—and finally at rest—and we, we were finally home. The journey was finally over. A million years of preparation, mortal life, trials and suffering, a thousand years of work in the Millennium and the judgment were now done, and our lives were about to begin.

I suddenly found myself back in my spirit body standing at the foot of my bed, looking at my dead body. My guide was standing beside me, looking at me. I glanced at the digital clock on my bed stand and the third hour had passed.

This is the end of the vision, but as I felt myself returning to my cold and diseased body, I also realized with great solemnity that it was only the beginning of my journey.

AFTERWORD

Having penned nearly 100,000 words in Spencer's voice, from his vast experiences, I feel it worthwhile to say a few things on my own.

It has been a thoroughly amazing experience to write *Visions of Glory.* I have come to view it as an authorized biography of Spencer's visionary journey to Zion.

If you were to ask me if I believe that his visions are "true," I would reply that I have felt the Holy Spirit working upon me as I transcribed it from his words to mine. Every experience you have just read, and all major details, came from Spencer's lips.

I will also confess that I have been intrigued by the fact that nothing Spencer told me conflicted with my own view of the latter days. What he described to me was congruent with both my spiritual and intellectual understanding of those times. For me, it was like reading a book and loving it, then going and seeing the movie. His experiences added the visual depth that my prior "reading" lacked.

I do believe that Spencer saw what he saw. But I don't believe it should always be interpreted as literal, or even prophetic, for anyone but Spencer himself. Anyone else who reads must interpret how or even if it applies to them. I think it should be prayerfully studied and compared to scripture, your own understanding, and your faith, and then left to Jesus Christ Himself to reveal to you your own journey to Zion.

Anyone who has studied the latter days, the Second Coming, or the building of Zion in scripture will quickly admit that it is hard to interpret, and most of it is given as a metaphor or type of things to come, rather than as specific and actual events to watch for. I wouldn't expect Spencer's visions to be any different.

My answer will also be that I don't know what it should mean to you, or to anyone else who reads it. Spencer will readily admit that he doesn't know what every part of it means to even him still. Some things that for years he has interpreted as being literal, have recently revealed themselves to be metaphorical, and the other way around. All he really knows is that for whatever reason, he saw what he saw, and the Lord has given him permission after all these years to share it with us.

If you look at the overall theme of his experiences, you will see elements of every person's journey to Zion, whether it is to the Zion we will build in Missouri, or the spiritual Zion we must each build in our hearts. Ultimately, both viewpoints may be accurate in the sense that when one makes the spiritual journey, the physical journey may also unveil itself before us.

—John M. Pontius

APPENDIX

The following apocryphal dreams and visions are included as an illustration that many others have seen and recorded similar visions of the latter days as did Spencer. It is also interesting to observe that some of these were not LDS, and yet they saw parallel views of these times. In addition to these few examples, I am sure others exist in hearts that are too timid to reveal them. Such was the case with Spencer until recently.

After Spencer had dictated this book, I remembered a few of these and pointed them out to Spencer. He was surprised they existed and read them with interest.

I should also point out that some of these descriptions are rather graphic and should be read to children and tender souls with some discretion.

John Taylor's Dream (1877)

I went to bed as usual at about 7:30 PM. I had been reading a revelation in the French language. My mind was calm, more so than usual if possible, so I composed myself for sleep, but could not. I felt a strange feeling come over me and apparently became partially unconscious. Still I was not asleep, nor exactly awake, with dreary feeling. The first thing that I recognized was that I was in the tabernacle of Ogden, Utah. I was sitting in the back part of the building for fear they would call on me to preach, which however they did, for after singing the second time they called me to the stand. I arose to speak and said that I didn't know that I had anything especially to say, except to bear my testimony of the Latter-day work, when all at once it seemed as if I was lifted out of myself and I said, "Yes, I have something to say and that is this: Some of my brethren have been asking, "What is becoming of us? What is the wind blowing?" I will answer you right here what is coming very shortly."

I was then in a dream, immediately in the city of Salt Lake, and wandering around in the streets and in all parts of the city, and on the doors of the houses I found badges of mourning and I could not find a house but was in mourning. I passed my own house and found the same sign there, and I asked the question, "Is that me that is dead?" Someone gave me the answer, "No, you will get through it all."

It seemed strange to me that I saw no person in the streets in all my wandering around the country. I seemed to be in their houses with the sick, but saw no funeral procession, nor anything of the kind, but the city looking still and as though the people were praying. And it seemed that they had controlled the disease, but what the disease was I did not learn; it was not made known to me. I then looked over the country, north, east, south, and west, and the same mourning was in every land and in every place.

The next thing I knew I was just this side of Omaha. It seemed as though I was above the earth, and looking down upon it. As I passed along upon my way east I saw the road full of people, mostly women, with just what they could carry in bundles on their backs, traveling to the mountains on foot. I wondered how they would get through with such a small pack on their backs. It was remarkable to us[?] that there were so few men among them. It didn't seem to me as though the cars were running, the rails looked rusty and the roads abandoned; and I have no conception of how I traveled as I looked down upon the people.

I continued east by the way of Omaha and Council Bluffs, which were full of disease. There were women everywhere. The state of Illinois and Missouri were in a tumult, men killing one another, women joining the fighting, family against family in the most horrid manner.

I imagined next that I was in Washington and I found desolation there. The White House was empty and the Halls of Congress the same, and everything in ruins. The people seemed to have left the city and left it to take care of itself.

I was in Baltimore. In the square where the Monument of 1812 stands in front of the Charles Hotel. I saw dead piled up so as to fill the street square. I saw mothers cutting the throats of their own children for their blood. I saw them suck it from their throats to quench their own thirst and then lie down and die. The water of Chesapeake Bay was stagnant, and the stench arising from it on account of their throwing their bodies into it so terrible, that the very smell carried death with it. I saw no man except they were dead or dying in the streets and very few women. Those I saw were crazy and in an ugly condition. Everywhere I went I beheld the same sights all over the city; it was terrible beyond description to look upon.

I thought this must be the end; but no, I was seemingly in an instant in the city of Philadelphia. There everything was still. No living soul was there to greet me. It seemed the whole city was without any inhabitants. In the south of Chestnut Street and in fact everywhere I went, the putrefaction of the dead caused such a stench that it was impossible for any living thing to breathe, nor did I see any living thing in the city.

Next I found myself in Broadway, in the city of New York, and there it seemed the people had done the best they could to overcome the disease, but in wandering down Broadway I saw the bodies of beautiful women lying, some dead and others in a dying condition, on the sidewalks. I saw men come out of cellars and ravish the persons of some that were yet alive and then kill them and rob their bodies of all the valuables they had upon them. Then before they could get back to the cellar they would roll over a time or two and die in agony. In some of the back streets I saw them kill some of their own offspring and eat their raw flesh, and in a few minutes die themselves. Everywhere I went I saw the same scene of horror and destruction and death and rapine.

No carriages, buggies, or cars were running; but death and destruction were everywhere. Then I saw fire start and just at that moment a mighty East wind sprang up and carried the flames over the city and it burned until there was not a single building left standing there, even down to the waters edge. Wharves and shipping all seemed to burn and follow in common destruction where the "great city" was a short time ago. The stench from the bodies that were burning was so great that it was carried a long distance cross the Hudson Bay and carried death and destruction wherever it penetrated. I cannot paint in words the horror that seemed to compass me about; it was beyond description of man.

I supposed this was the end; but it was not. I was given to understand the same horror was being enacted all over the country, east, west, north, and south. Few were left alive, still there were some.

Immediately after I seemed to be standing on the left bank of the Missouri River, opposite the City of Independence, but there was no city. I saw the whole state of Missouri and Illinois and all of Iowa, a complete desert with no living being there. A short distance from the river however, I saw twelve men dressed in temple robes, standing in a square or nearly so (and I understood it represented the Twelve Gates of the New Jerusalem.) Their hands were uplifted in consecration of the ground and laying the corner stone of the temple. I saw myriads of angels hovering over them, and saw also an immense pillar of clouds over them and heard the angels singing the most heavenly music. The words were "Now is established the Kingdom of God and his Christ, which shall never more be thrown down."

I saw people coming from the river and from the desert places a long way off to help build the temple and it seemed that hosts of angels all helped to get material to build with and I saw some of them who wore temple clothes come and build the temple and the city, and all the time I saw the great pillar of clouds hovering over the place.

Instantly, however, I found myself again in the tabernacle at Ogden. And yet, I could still see the building go on and I got quite animated in calling on the people in the tabernacle to listen to the beautiful music, for the angels were singing the same music I had heard before. "Now is established the Kingdom of God and his Christ, which shall never more be thrown down."

At this I seemed to stagger back from the pulpit and Brother Francis D. Richards and some others caught my arm and prevented me from falling. Then I finished so abruptly. Still even then I had not fainted, but was simply exhausted. Then I rolled over in bed and awoke just as the city clock was striking twelve.

(Wilford Woodruff Journals, June 15, 1878, Church Historian's Office; also manuscript copy of the same copied by Joseph F. Smith; Unpublished Revelations 78, p. 119–123; see also *Visions of the Latter Days*, p. 103–106.)

The Cardston Prophecy (1923)
by Sols Caurdisto

The Cardston Prophecy, which I have reproduced here, is found in the "Family File of Edward
J. Wood," and was included in the book "The Life of Edward J. Wood" by Melvin Tagg, Pages 148–153. The following is a letter from Edward. J. Wood, then president of the Cardston Alberta Stake, regarding the author of this vision.

Cardston, Alberta Canada
December 14, 1933
Robert W. Smith, Esq. Salt Lake City, Utah

Dear Brother Smith:

I am pleased to answer your letter of December 1st first as to the letter of a non-member who wrote of "impressions" received while going through the temple before it was dedicated, the truth of which letter you ask me to verify and which I am pleased to do. It was a Quaker lady who was a magazine writer from eastern Canada. She has some relatives in Lethbridge, about 60 miles from Cardston; and being so deeply impressed on her first visit, she had them bring her a second time - this time I was acting as guide. She would sit in each room and never said a word to any in the company, but seemed to be in deep meditation all the time.

When she reached her own home several weeks after, she wrote this letter which has caused so much comment all over the Church. We have never been able to understand how she seemed to know so much about our faith and our belief in our future life and works after death. I never learned her real name. She visited us along in 1921. I have never heard from her since that time, but the letter is genuine, and of her own "impressions!" received while in the temple while on the two visits she mentions.

Sincerely you're Brother,

O/S Elder J. Wood, Pres. Alberta Stake

This is her letter and vision in her own words:

We have been to the temple erected by your church wherein are to be performed the sacred rites in accordance with your faith. The first time I was strongly impelled to describe to you my impressions. I did so but before the completion of the letter, I received some news that so affected me that acting upon the spur of the moment, I destroyed the document in its entirety.

The continued feeling within me of dissatisfaction as to something left undone, coupled with the desire upon the part of the members of my household who had not visited the temple, led to our second visit to Cardston, in which you so kindly consented to accompany us, notwithstanding the inclement weather and personal inconvenience to yourself which the journey entailed. It was because of this and many other evidences of your friendship that has given me the privilege to presume to bother you with what after all may be foolish fantasies of a too impressionable mentality. To me it does seem so, for never before in my life have such powerful impressions been infringed upon my inner consciousness as during my visit thru the temple. Especially was this true at our second visit. The impressions of our first visit were repeated with such overwhelming intensity and variety of detail that I must positively inform you of my experience.

It seems to me it were a sacred duty upon my part to do this, and knowing as I do that your friends will lightly ridicule what to me is a personal matter, I am going to give you in detail my experience in the hope, that if it is well, maybe it is something more than imagination, that you and others of your faith may wisely analyze and correctly use whatever may be gleaned from this letter.

A fortress in time of storm, was the first thought that shaped itself in my mind with my first view of this ancient, yet modern temple; mellowed with the spiritual usage of ancient civilization and customs, yet alert, virile, and watchful.

A grand, solemn, strong, beautiful, useful house of spiritual progression which seemed to be the embodiment of architectural expression of ancient civilization and glories suddenly reincarnated and for a future and higher civilization than our own. Strength and beauty exaggerated the more flimsy houses and buildings of the town and gave a painfully obvious example of how the soul within is expressed thru the material body, either in the individual or nation, or a race, either in the man or his architecture. Try how I would I could not get away from the feeling that the town itself was inferior to the latest building, so new and yet so old. Even the electric lights failed to change this thought, that the temple and the town represented two different epochs of humanity's spiritual development expressed in architecture. The town embodied the present epoch, science, art, invention harnessed purely for trade or commerce, irrespective of past or future development. The temple embodies the accumulated knowledge of the ancient world combined with the modern inventions of science and inspiration as the road to a higher future development so near at hand. Let me put it down even another way.

There is a place called Cardston. A temple linking the past with the present has been built at Cardston and the town has become a collection of flimsy huts nestling at the foot of the temple which will continue to function for the spiritual purposes for which it is raised.

Just as the exterior impressions compared with the present and future epochs so did the interior also reflect comparison. Of the beautiful and artistic effects I need not dwell; abler pens can describe the interior from this viewpoint. Sufficient for me to say that the shape of the temple is a cross, that each apartment is symbolical in artistic and structural effects of some stage of humanity's progress thru the ages. In fact, everything physical is a stepping stone to spiritual progress as such is typified in these ceremonies. All this was kindly and intelligently explained to us by Mr. Duce on one occasion and by Mr. Wood on the second visit; but I am afraid I was very indifferent and inattentive upon both occasions, for which I tender them my sincere apologies. I had no intentions of being rude or discourteous, but from the moment of entering the temple until leaving, I was placed in the position of having, as it were, to listen to and grasp a dual narrative all the time, with the result that so engrossed was I at times that I am afraid I was so absent-minded as to appear inattentive if not positively stupid.

I have stated that my impression of the exterior of the building was that of a place of waiting for a higher civilization than our present one. This would suggest a condition of emptiness, but that is not what I mean. An ordinary newly erected building has no atmosphere at all until it has been inhabited some time; after which, it has, as it were, a living atmosphere. What kind of an atmosphere this is, is largely determined by the spiritual development and thought of the persons using and inhabiting the building. This applies especially to places of worship or consecration, and is very noticeable to a sensitive person. Sometimes such an atmosphere is agreeable, exalting, and so on; sometimes very much the reverse, depending upon the spiritual harmony or otherwise of the persons under this atmospheric rule; but was not so as far as it was concerned while outside the temple.

I could not understand the overwhelming scene of ancient atmosphere which the building actually possessed in its very granite blocks in spite of the fact that I know a few months previous these stones had been laid, yet the feeling of age predominated. I dismissed the feeling as well as I could by thinking that the place of the structure was responsible for the suggestion of age, but when I entered the temple, how quickly I found there was nothing to suggest to me that present atmosphere of which I have spoken, but was it empty? Emphatically no! Time and again as I listened to the speaker explaining some phase of the building or its meaning, I would be seeing beyond him some illustration of kaleidoscopic nature, depicting what he was describing, only more completely and vividly. The characters were so plain to me that I required all my self control to keep silent from room to room. This continued and only ceased when we were out in the frost and snow once more.

There was no set plan for presenting these pictures to me. It seemed as if when I thought something mental, a picture instantly presented itself in explanation of some word of the conductor, which would have the same effect. I was not afraid, only awed by the wonder of it all and the fearful impressive feeling that I received which seemed to imbed every little detailed scene into my brain, from which it will ever remember and record; and vivid as all of it was, these incidents herein related are the ones upon which I received instructions.

The scenes which I observed of an historical character seemed chiefly to verify and amplify the speaker's outline of past history, and so I do not feel impressed to record such, except to state that the same patriarchal characters whom I observed directing and influencing the early movements of the Church, were the same down through every age and epoch, and as the scenes advanced to more modern times, I saw among these spiritual characters and counselors, persons whose features I had previously observed as being in the material body on other historical occasions. It seemed as though the temple was filled with the actual spiritual bodies of these previous leaders of your church, each seeming to have the work that person was engaged in whilst in the flesh. In that temple I saw persons who were leaders of your church, during its march across the American desert now engaged in helping these higher patriarchs under whose orders they seemed to be working. It was these latter spiritual leaders, if I may use that term, who seemed to be instructed to show me the scenes here recorded.

I can give no time as to the happening, except that the impressions I received were of actual present or immediate future. I saw first a brief but comprehensive sketch of the present state of the world, or as you would term it, the Gentile Kingdoms. Each country in turn was shown, its anarchy, hunger, ambitions, distrusts and warlike activities, and so on, and in my mind was formed from some source the words, "As it is today with the Gentiles."

I saw international war again break out with its center upon the Pacific Ocean, but sweeping and encircling the whole globe. I saw that the opposing forces were roughly divided by so-called Christianity on the one side, and by the so-called followers of Mohammed and Buddha on the other. I saw that the great driving power within these so-called Christian nations, was the Great Apostasy of Rome, in all its political, social and religious aspects. I saw the worldwide dislocation and devastation of production and slaughter of people occur more swiftly and upon a larger scale than ever before. I saw an antagonism begin to express itself from those so-called Christian nations against your people. I saw those with a similar faith to yours in the far east begin to look toward Palestine for safety.

I saw the international world war automatically break down, and national revolution occur in every country, and complete the work of chaos and desolation. I saw geological disturbances occur, which helped in this work as if it were intended to do so. I saw the Cardston Temple preserved from all of this geological upheaval. I saw the international boundary line disappear as these two governments broke up and dissolved into chaos. I saw race rioting upon the American continent on a vast scale.

I saw hunger and starvation in this world; I saw disease produced by hunger, strife and chaos complete the end of this present order or epoch. How long these events were in reaching this consummation I do not know, but my impression was from the outbreak of the international war these things developed into a continuous procession, and almost ran concurrently, as it is with a sickness, the various symptoms are all in evidence at one and the same time, but in different stages of development. My intensified thought was "What of the Church, if such is to become of the Kingdoms of the earth? [My question] was immediately answered by a subconscious statement. "As it is in the church today," and I saw these higher spiritual beings throughout the length and breadth of the air, marshaling their spiritual forces, and concentrating them upon the high officials of your church upon earth.

I saw the spiritual forces working upon those officers, impressing and moving them, influencing and warning them. I saw the spiritual forces begin to unfold these things into the minds of your elders and other high officials, especially during their spiritual devotions and official duties, and those activities which exalt the mind of the individual or groups. I saw the impressions take hold and inspire the more receptive and spiritual men, until it was all clearly revealed to them in the way the spiritual patriarch desired.

Again I seemed to hear the words, "As it will be." I saw the high officials in council, and under inspired guidance issue instructions to your people to re-consecrate their lives and energies to their faith, to voluntarily discipline themselves, by abstaining from all those forms of indulgence which weaken the body, sap the mentality and deaden the spirit, or waste the income.

I saw further on, instructions given whereby places of refuge were prepared quietly but efficiently by inspired elders. I saw Cardston and the surrounding foothills, especially north and west, for miles, being prepared as a refuge for your people quietly but quickly.

I saw elders still under divine guidance, counseling and encouraging the planting of every available acre of soil in this district, so that large supplies would be near the refuge. I saw the church property under cultivation of an intensified character, not for sale or profit, but for the use of the people. I saw artesian wells and other wells dug all over that territory so that when the open waters were polluted and poisoned that the people of the church and their cattle should be provided for.

I saw the fuel resources of the district develop in many places and vast piles of coal and timber stored for future use and building. I saw the territory carefully surveyed and mapped out, for the camping of a great body of the people of the church. I saw provision also made for a big influx of people who will not at first belong to the church, but who will gather in their tribulation.

I saw vast quantities of surgical appliances, medicines, disinfectants, and so on, stored in the temple basement. I saw inspiration given the elders whereby the quantity, quality and kind of things to be stored were judged, which might not be attainable in this territory in time of chaos.

I saw defensive preparations working out the organizations of the camps on maps. I saw the mining corridors used as places of storage underground: I saw the hills surveyed and corrals built in sequestered places for cattle, sheep, and so on, quietly and quickly. I saw the plans for the organization of the single men and their duties, the scouts, the guards, the nurses, the cooks, the messengers, the children, the herders, the temple guards, and so on. I saw these things going on practically unknown to the Gentile world, except the Great Apostasy, whose knowledge and hatred is far reaching, in this day of its temporary power. This was going on piece by piece as the Elders were instructed so to do.

I saw the other officials obeying the inspired instructions, carrying their message and exhorting the people to carry out, from time to time the revelation given them, whilst all around throughout the Gentile world the chaos developed in its varying stages, faction against faction, nation against nation, but all in open or secret hostility to your people and their faith. I saw your people draw closer and closer together, as this became more tense and as the spiritual forces warned them through the mouth of your elders and your other officers. I saw the spiritual forces influencing those members who had drifted away, to re-enter the fold. I saw a greater tithing than ever before. I saw vast quantities of necessaries supplied by members whose spiritual eyes had been opened. I saw a liquidation of properties and effects disposed of quietly but quickly by members of the church, as the spiritual influences directed them.

I saw the inspired call sent forth to all the church, to gather to the refuges of Zion. I saw the stream of your people quietly moving in the direction of their refuge. I saw your people moving more quickly and in larger numbers until all the stragglers were housed. I saw the wireless message flashed from Zion's refuge to Zion's refuge in their several places that all was well with them, and then the darkness of chaos closed around the boundaries of your people, and the last days of tribulation had begun.

—Sols Caurdisto

Warning to America (1880) by President Wilford Woodruff

I warn future historians to give credence to my history; for my testimony is true, and the truth of its record will be manifest in the world to come. All the words of the Lord will be fulfilled upon the nations, which are written in this book. The American nation will be broken in pieces like a potter's vessel, and will be cast down to hell if it does not repent—and this, because of murders, whoredoms, wickedness and all manner of abominations, for the Lord has spoken it.

(M. Cowley, Wilford Woodruff, *History of His Life and Labors*, Bookcraft, p. 500.)

Destroying Angels are Active (1931) by President Wilford Woodruff

I refer to these things because I know not how long I may have the privilege of bearing my testimony of the Gospel of Christ on the earth. The revelations that are in the Bible, the predictions of the patriarchs and prophets who saw by vision and revelation the last dispensation and fulness of times plainly tell us what is to come to pass. The 49th chapter of Isaiah is having its fulfillment. I have often said in my teachings, if the world wants to know what is coming to pass, let them read the revelations of St. John. Read of the judgments of God that are going to overthrow the world in the last dispensation. Read the papers and see what is taking place in our own nation and in the nations of the earth, and what does it all mean? It means the commencement of the fulfillment of what the prophets of God have predicted. In the Doctrine and Covenants there are many revelations given through the mouth of the prophet of God; these revelations will all have the fulfillment, as the Lord lives, and no power can hinder it. In one of the revelations the Lord told Joseph Smith: "Behold, Verily I say unto you, the angels are crying unto the Lord day and night, who are ready and waiting to be sent forth to reap down the fields."

I want to bear testimony to this congregation, and to the heavens and the earth, that the day is come when those angels are privileged to go forth and commence their work. They are laboring in the United States of America ; they are laboring among the nations [43] of the earth; and they will continue. We need not marvel or wonder at anything that is transpiring in the earth. The world does not comprehend the revelations of God. They did not in the days of the Jews; yet all that the prophets had spoken concerning them came to pass. So in our day these things will come to pass. I heard the Prophet Joseph bear his testimony to these events that would transpire in the earth.

We cannot draw a veil over the events that await this generation. No man that is inspired by the Spirit and power of God can close his ears, his eyes or his lips to these things.

(Wilfred Woodruff, *Millennial Star* 58:738–9.)

A Great Test Coming (1930)
by Heber C. Kimball

The western boundaries of the state of Missouri will be swept so clean of its inhabitants that as President Young tells us, when we return to that place there will not be so much as a yellow dog to wag his tail. Before that day comes, however, the Saints will be put to the test that will try the best of them. The pressure will be so great that the righteous among us will cry unto the Lord day and night until deliverance comes. Then is the time to look out for the great sieve for there will be a great sifting time and many will fall. This Church has before it many close places through which it will have to pass before the work of God is crowned with glory. You can not endure on borrowed light. Each will have to be guided by the light within themselves. If you do not have a knowledge that Jesus is the Christ, how can you stand? Do you believe it?

(General Conference Report, October 3–5, 1930, page 59.)

An Army of Elders (1931)
by Heber C. Kimball

An army of Elders will be sent to the four quarters of the earth to search out the righteous and warn the wicked of what is coming. All kinds of religions will be started and miracles performed that will deceive the very elect if such were possible. Our sons and daughters must live pure lives so as to be prepared for what is coming.

After a while the gentiles will gather to this place by the thousands, and Salt Lake City will be classed among the wicked cities of the world. A spirit of speculation and extravagance will take possession of the Saints, and the result will be financial bondage.

Persecution comes next and all true Latter-Day Saints will be tested to the limit. Many will apostatize and others will stand still, not knowing what to do. Darkness will cover the earth and gross darkness the minds of the people. The judgments of God will be poured out upon the wicked to the extent that our Elders from far and near will be called home, or in other words the gospel will be taken from the Gentiles and later on be carried to the Jews.

The western boundary of the State of Missouri will be swept so clean of its inhabitants that as President Young tells us, 'When you return to that place, there will not be left so much as a yellow dog to wag his tail.'

Before that day comes, however, the Saints will be put to tests that will try the integrity of the best of them. The pressure will become so great that the more righteous among them will cry unto the Lord day and night until deliverance comes.

Then the Prophet Joseph and others will make their appearance and those who have remained faithful will be selected to return to Jackson County, Missouri and take part in the building of that beautiful city, the New Jerusalem.

(Heber C. Kimball, *Deseret News*, May 23, 1931.)

A Dream (1894)
Charles D. Evans

In August, 1894, an article appeared in The Contributor, (Vol. 15, No 20, p. 638–647). The Contributor was the forerunner of The Improvement Era. The article was entitled "A Dream." In the article an account was given of a vision or dream of Charles D. Evans, a Patriarch then living in Springville, Utah, of the last days, which is reproduced below:

While I lay pondering, in deep solitude, on the events of my present, my mind was drawn into a reverie such as I had never felt before. A strong solicitude for my imperiled country utterly excluded every other thought and raised my feelings to a point of intensity I did not think it possible to endure. While in this solemn, profound and painful reverie of mind, to my infinite surprise, a light appeared in my room which seemed to be soft and silvery as that diffused from a northern star. At the moment of its appearance the acute feeling I had experienced instantly yielded to one of calm tranquility.

Although it may have been at the hour of midnight and the side of the globe whereon I was situated was excluded from the sunlight, yet all was light and bright and warm as an Italian landscape at noon; but the heat was softer and more subdued. As I gazed upward, I saw descending through my bedroom roof, with a gently gliding movement, a personage clothed in white apparel, whose countenance was smoothly serene, his features regular, and the flashes of his eye seemed to shoot forth scintillations, to use an earthly comparison, strongly resembling those reflected from a diamond under an intensely illuminated electric light, which dazzled but did not bewilder. Those large, deep, inscrutable eyes were presently fixed upon mine, when instantly placing his hands upon my forehead his touch produced an indescribable serenity and calmness, a calmness not born of earth, but at once peaceful, delightful and heavenly. My whole being was imbued with a joy unspeakable. All feelings of sorrow instantly vanished. Those lines and shadows which care and sorrow impress upon us were dispelled as a deep fog before a blazing sun. In the eyes of my heavenly visitor, for such he appeared to me, there was a sort of lofty pity and tenderness infinitely stronger than any such feeling I ever saw manifested in ordinary mortals. His very calm appeared like a vast ocean stillness, at once overpowering to every agitated emotion.

By some intuition, or instinct, I felt he had something to communicate to soothe my sorrows and allay my apprehensions. Whereon, addressing me, he said:

"Son, I perceive thou hast grave anxieties over the perilous state of thy country, that thy soul has felt deep sorrow for its future. I have therefore come to thy relief and to tell thee of the causes that have led to this peril. Hear me attentively. Seventy-one years ago, after an awful apostasy of centuries, in which all nations were shrouded in spiritual darkness, when the angels had withdrawn themselves, the voice of prophets hushed and the light of Urim and Thummim shone not, and the vision of the seers was closed, while heaven itself shed not a ray of gladness to lighten a dark world, when Babel ruled and Satan laughed, and church and priesthood had taken their upward flight, and the voice of nations, possessing the books of the Jewish prophets [the Bible] had ruled against vision and against Urim, against the further visits of angels, and against the doctrine of a church of apostles and prophets, thou knowest that then appeared a mighty angel with the solemn announcement of the hour of judgment, the burden of whose instructions pointed to dire calamities upon the present generation. This, therefore, is the cause of what thou seest and the end of the wicked hasteneth."

My vision now became extended in a marvelous manner, and the import of the past labors of the Elders was made plain to me. I saw multitudes fleeing to the place of safety in our mountain heights. The church was established in the wilderness. Simultaneously the nation had reached an unparalleled prosperity, wealth abounded, new territory was acquired, commerce extended, finance strengthened, confidence was maintained, and peoples abroad pointed to her as a model nation, the ideal of the past realized and perfected, the embodiment of the liberty sung by poets, and sought for by sages.

"But," continued the messenger, "thou beholdest a change. Confidence is lost. Wealth is arrayed against labor, labor against wealth, yet the land abounds with plenty for food and raiment, and silver and gold are in abundance. Thou seest also that letters written by a Jew have wrought great confusion in the finances of the nation which, together with the policy of many wealthy ones, has produced distress and do presage further sorrow."

Factions now sprang up as if by magic. Capital had entrenched itself against labor throughout the land; labor was organized against capital. The voice of the wise sought to tranquilize those two powerful factors in vain. Excited multitudes ran wildly about; strikes increased; lawlessness sought the face of regular government. At this juncture I saw a banner floating in air whereon was written the words, "Bankruptcy, Famine, Floods, Fire, Cyclones, Blood, Plague."

Mad with rage men and women rushed upon each other. Blood flowed down the streets of cities like water. The demon of bloody hate had enthroned itself on the citadel of reason; the thirst for blood was intenser than that of the parched tongue for water. Thousands of bodies lay entombed in the streets. Men and women fell dead from the terror inspired by fear. Rest was but the precursor of the blood work of the morrow. All around lay the mournfulness of a past in ruins. Monuments erected to perpetuate the names of the noble and brave were ruthlessly destroyed by combustibles. A voice now sounded aloud these words: "Yet once again I shake not the earth only, but also heaven. And this word yet once again signifies the removing of things that are shaken as of things that are made; that those things that cannot be shaken may remain."

Earthquakes rent the earth in vast chasms, which engulfed multitudes; terrible groanings and wailings filled the air; the shrieks of the suffering were indescribable awful. Water wildly rushed in from the tumultuous ocean whose very roaring under the mad rage of the fierce cyclone, was unendurable to hear. Cities were swept away in an instant, missiles were hurled through the atmosphere at a terrible velocity and people were carried upward only to descend an unrecognized mass. Islands appeared where ocean waves once tossed the gigantic steamer. In other parts voluminous flames, emanating from vast fires, rolled with fearful velocity destroying life and property in their destructive course. The seal of the dread menace of despair was stamped on every human visage; men fell exhausted, appalled and trembling. Every element of nature was a demon of wrathful fury. Dense clouds, blacker than midnight darkness, whose thunders reverberated with intonations which shook the earth, obscured the sunlight. Darkness reigned, unrivalled and supreme.

Again the light shone, revealing an atmosphere tinged with a leaden hue which was the precursor of an unparalleled plague whose first symptoms were recognized by a purple spot which appeared on the cheek, or on the back of the hand, and which, invariably enlarged until it spread over the entire surface of the body, producing certain death. Mothers on sight of it, cast away their children as if they were poisonous reptiles. The plague, in grown persons, rotted the eyes in their sockets and consumed the tongue as would a powerful acid or an intense heat. Wicked men, suffering under its writhing agonies, cursed God and died, as they stood on their feet, and the birds of prey fastened on their carcasses.

I saw in my dream the messenger again appear with a vial in his right hand, who addressing me, said: "Thou knowest somewhat of the chemistry taught in the schools of human learning, behold now a chemistry sufficiently powerful to change the waters of the sea."

He then poured out his vial upon the sea, and it became putrid as the blood of a dead man, and every living soul therein died. Other plagues followed I forebear to record.

A foreign power had invaded the nation which, from every human indication, it appeared would seize the government and supplant it with monarchy. I stood trembling at the aspect, when, lo, a power arose in the west which declared itself in favor of the Constitution in its original form; to this suddenly rising power every lover of constitutional rights and liberties throughout the nation gave hearty support. The struggle was fiercely contested, but the Stars and Stripes floated in the breeze, and bidding defiance to all opposition, waved proudly over the land. Among the many banners I saw, was one inscribed thus: "The government based on the Constitution, now and forever;" on another "Liberty of Conscience, social and religious and political."

The light of the gospel which had but dimly shone because of abomination, now burst forth with a luster that filled the earth. Cities appeared in every direction, one of which, in the center of the continent, was an embodiment of architectural science after the pattern of eternal perfections, whose towers glittered with a radiance emanating from the sparkling of emeralds, rubies, diamonds and other precious stones set in a canopy of gold and so elaborately and skillfully arranged as to shed forth a brilliancy which dazzled and enchanted the eye, excited admiration and developed a taste for the beauty beyond anything man had ever conceived.

Fountains of crystal water shot upward their transparent jets which in the brilliant sunshine, formed ten thousand rainbow tints at once delightful to the eye. Gardens, the perfections of whose arrangement confounded all our present attempts or genius, were bedecked with flowers of varied hue to develop and refine the taste, and strengthen a love for these nature's chastest adornments.

Schools and universities were erected to which all had access; in the latter, Urims were placed for the study of the past, present and future, and for obtaining knowledge of the heavenly bodies and of the construction of worlds and universes. The inherent properties of matter, its arrangements, laws, [and] mutual relations were revealed and taught and made plain as the primer lesson of a child. The conflicting theories of geologists regarding the formation and age of the earth were settled forever. All learning was based on eternal certainty. Angels brought forth the treasures of heaven which had lain hid in the womb of the dumb and distant past.

The appliances for making learning easy surpassed all conjecture. Chemistry was rendered extremely simple by the power which the Urims conferred on man of looking into and through the elements of every kind; a stone furnished no more obstruction to human vision than the air itself. Not only were the elements and all their changes and transformations plainly understood but the construction, operations and laws of mind were thus rendered equally plain as those which governed the coarser elements.

While looking though the Urim and Thummim I was amazed at a transformation which even now is to me marvelous beyond description, clearly showing the manner in which particles composing the inorganic kingdom of nature are conducted upward to become a part of organic forms; another astounding revelation was a very clearly shown me of the entire circulation of the blood both in man and animals. After seeing these things and gazing once more upon the beautiful city, the following passage of scripture sounded in my ears: "Out of Zion the perfection of beauty, God shineth."

On this I awoke to find all a dream.

(As recorded in: Larson, *The Moon Shall Turn to Blood*, Crown Summit Books, p. 147–153.)

The Dream of the Plagues (1884)

The present times seem to be more than usually prolific of prophetic dreams among the Latter-day Saints. In nearly every settlement the people have been warned of events soon to occur; and visions of the future glory of the Kingdom of God upon this earth have passed like a panorama before many of those who love God and obey His commandments. Some two or three years ago, I had retired for the night, when suddenly a glorious messenger appeared at my bedside and awoke me from my slumber. The light of his presence filled the room, so that objects were discerned as clearly as at noonday.

He handed me a book, saying, "Look, and see what is coming to pass." I took the book in my hands and, sitting up in bed, examined it carefully and read its contents. In size this book was about seven by ten inches, opening like a copybook and bound in beautiful covers, on the front of which was stamped in gold letters its title, which was The Book of the Plagues. The leaves were printed only on the front side of each, and were composed of the very finest quality of pure white linen, instead of paper. The typography throughout was in the finest style of the printer's art. Each page was composed of a picture printed in colors as natural as art can copy nature, which occupied the upper half of the space, below which was the printed description of the scene represented.

On the first page was a picture of a feast in progress, with the long table set upon a beautiful lawn, over which were interspersed clumps of fine shrubs and towering trees. In the background through the foliage, could be discerned a stately suburban villa, adorned with all the ornaments of modern architecture. The landscape presented the appearance of midsummer. The sky, and indeed the whole atmosphere, appeared of a peculiar sickly brassy hue, similar to that which may be observed when the sun is wholly eclipsed, and the disc is just beginning again to give its light. Throughout the atmosphere small white specks were represented, similar to a scattering fall of minute snowflakes in winter.

About the table a party of richly dressed ladies and gentlemen were seated in the act of partaking of the rich repast with which the table was laden. The minute specks falling from above were dropping into the food apparently unheeded by all, for a sudden destruction had come upon them. Many were falling backward in the agonies of a fearful death; others drooping upon the table, and others pausing with their hands still holding the untasted food, their countenances betraying a fearful astonishment at the peculiar and unlooked for condition of their companions. Death was in the atmosphere; the judgments of God had come upon them as silently and swiftly as upon the proud Sennaeharib and his host of Assyrians.

In one corner of this picture was a small circular vignette, showing the front of the store of a dealer in pork. The wide sidewalk was covered by an awning supported on posts at the outer edge, and on this walk were shown barrels of pork, long strings of sausages, fresh slaughtered hogs, piles of smoked bacon and headcheese; and along the edge of the walk, next to the store, beneath the front windows, leaned a number of large hams and pieces of side meat, reaching across the whole front, except a small space at the doorway. There were twelve of these pieces, and on each piece was painted a large letter, in order to make as a whole the word abominations.

Below this scene was the description: "A Feast among the Gentiles, commencement of the Plague." And in smaller type below, a note saying that the particles of poison, though represented in the picture, are so small as to be invisible to the naked eye.

On the next page was another picture. It was a street scene in a large city. In the foreground were the residences of wealthy city merchants. The character of the buildings gradually changed; along the view and in the distance were shown the great buildings of trade and commerce in the heart of a large metropolis. On the sidewalks throughout the long vista, the busy, throbbing, rushing crowd had been cut down like grass before the mower.

Again it was a midsummer scene. The same atoms of poison were falling through the air, but their work was done; the same sickly brazen atmosphere that seemed thick with foul odors laid upon the earth, in which no breeze stirred a leaf of the foliage. Upon the balconies of the richly decorated residences, across the thresholds of the opened doorways, along the walks and upon the crossings, lay the men, women and children, who a few days before were enjoying all the pleasures of life. Further on, the dead were everywhere. Houses of business that had been thronged with customers stood with open doorways, frowning upon streets covered with the dead. Across the thresholds of the banks lay the guardians of wealth, but no thieves were there to take the unlocked treasures within. The costly merchandise of a thousand owners laid untouched upon the counters and shelves. In the noonday glare of the sickly sun, not a soul was shown alive; not one had been left to bury the dead—all had been stricken or had fled from the death-dealing plague and the doomed city. Along midway upon the street, a hungry drove of those horrible ugly slaughterhouse hogs, (which may be seen in the pens attached to the filthy slaughtering places in the outskirts of many cities), was tearing and devouring the dead and feasting upon the bodies of rich and poor alike with none to molest them.

Below this picture was the description: "Progress of the Plague among the Gentiles. A street scene in a large city." Nearly fifty of these pictures I carefully observed, wherein the fearful effects of this and other plagues were almost as vividly portrayed as if I had actually seen them.

The last scene in the book was descriptive of the same plague as the first. A beautiful park-like, grassy prairie was surrounded by elm and cottonwood trees, the area embraced being about eighty rods across. In the centre of this enclosure was a large cone-shaped tent of a bright purple color, about thirty feet in height by twenty in diameter at the base. Midway in height in this tent was a floor dividing the inside into two stories. Near this tent was another, a round wall tent, about thirty feet in diameter, and nearly as high as the first. This was clean and white. Leaving a space of about a hundred yards from these central tents were hundreds of small rectangular wall tents in rows, reaching as far as the surrounding trees, each tent clean and white, and appearing to be of a size suited to the wants of an ordinary family. Not a human being, animal, bird or vehicle was in sight. Not a breath of air appeared to be stirring. The same atmosphere as in the previous pictures, with the atoms of poison, was represented, and the same time and season of the year.

Below this picture was the description: "A camp of the Saints who have gathered together and are living under the daily revelations of God, and are thus preserved from the plague." I understood from this that each family was in its tent during the hours of the day that the poison falls, and thus were preserved from breathing the deathly particles.

Handing the book to the messenger, who all this time had remained by my side, he vanished from my view as suddenly as he had appeared. I awoke my wife, who was soundly sleeping, and commenced to relate to her what I had just beheld. After telling her the description of the two pictures at the beginning of the book, and commencing on the third, this third picture and all up to the last was suddenly taken from my memory, so that I have never been able to recall them; but still I remember that they were scenes about the plagues and judgments.

In the revelations given to the Prophet Joseph, among the many plagues and judgments portrayed, that given in the Doctrine and Covenants, Sec. 29:17–20, has always seemed to me to fully coincide with what has been related in the account of that dream. But whether that plague or another is meant, it does not matter. Plagues will come and the wicked must suffer; but the Saints will be preserved by the very principle for which the wicked persecute them, which is present revelation from the Almighty.

(Author Unknown, Published in *Contributor* Volume 5, 1884 No. 112.[2])

---

2   The *Contributor* was published by the Church as a monthly periodical from 1879 to 1896.

Orson Pratt Prophecy (1866)

If it be asked, why is America thus to suffer? The answer is, because they have rejected the kingdom of God, and one of the greatest divine messages ever sent to man; because they have sanctioned the killing of the Saints, and the martyrdom of the Lord's prophets, and have suffered his people to be driven from their midst, and have robbed them of their houses, and homes, and land, and millions of property, and have refused to redress their wrongs. For these great evils, they must suffer; the decrees of Jehovah have gone forth against them; the sword of the Lord has been unsheathed, and will fall with pain upon their devoted heads. Their great and magnificent cities are to be cut off. New York, Boston, Albany, and numerous other cities will be left desolate. Party will be arrayed in deadly strife against party; State against State; and the whole nation will be broken up; the sanguinary weapons of the dreadful revolution will devour the land. Then shall there be a fleeing from one city to another, from one State to another, from one part of the continent to another, seeking refuge, from the devastations of bandits and armies; then shall their dead be left unburied, and the fowls of heaven shall summer upon them, and the beasts of the earth shall winter upon them. Moreover, the Lord will visit them with the deadly pestilence which shall sweep away many millions by its ravages; for their eyes shall fall from their sockets, and their flesh from their bones, and their tongues shall be stayed in their mouths, that they shall not be able to blaspheme against their Maker. And it will come to pass, that the heavens will withhold their rains and their fruitful fields be turned into barrenness, and the waters of their rivers will be dried up, and left in standing pools, and the fish therein will die; and the Lord will send forth a grievous plague to destroy the horses and cattle from the land. Thus by the sword and by pestilence, and by famine, and by the strong arm of the Almighty, shall the inhabitants of that wicked nation be destroyed.

(Orson Pratt, *Millennial Star*, Vol. 28, p. 633–634 October 6, 1866.)

ABOUT JOHN PONTIUS

For me, the hardest part of writing a book is the "About the Author." It has never been my intent to write LDS books, or a doctrinal blog or website, so explaining why I do is not easy. Perhaps the best way to explain what I do is, long ago, I decided to obey any time I could discern the Lord's will in my life. The hazards of learning to hearken to the voice of the Lord seems to be that you might end up on a more difficult journey to somewhere far better than you intended. What I do and why I do it is one of those far better things.

After living thirty-three years in Alaska, raising a family there and building several careers, the Lord sent us to Utah rather suddenly a few years ago. Terri and I were both raised in Utah, but we have spent the majority of our lives in "the mission field." Returning to Utah has been like coming home and has brought us nearer to additional family, children, and grandchildren.

Since coming to Utah, I have met many people who have blessed my life and taught me many things. One of those was Spencer, whose words you have read in this book, and whom I now count as a dear friend.

Moving to Utah has also given me the opportunity to speak at many firesides, write several additional books, begin and maintain my blog, "UnBlogmySoul," and accomplish many unexpectedly blessed things only the hand of the Lord could have brought to pass.

I could not have written this book or any other eternally weighty thing without the Lord's hand. His hand has lead me places I did not want to go, but when I actually got there, I recognized it as my "far better land of promise."

Terri is the love of my life, my best friend, and the kindest mortal I have ever met. Together we have eight children and twenty-one grandchildren.